DEVELOPMENT DISCOURSES

Prasenjit Maiti

ATLANTIC®
PUBLISHERS & DISTRIBUTORS

Published by
ATLANTIC®
PUBLISHERS & DISTRIBUTORS
B-2, Vishal Enclave, Opp. Rajouri Garden,
New Delhi-110027
Phones : 25413460, 25429987, 25466842

Sales Office
7/22, Ansari Road, Darya Ganj,
New Delhi-110002
Phones : 23273880, 23275880, 23280451
Fax : 91-11-23285873
web : www.atlanticbooks.com
e-mail : info@atlanticbooks.com

ISBN 81-269-0533-6

Printed in India
at Nice Printing Press, Delhi

". . . in a society such as ours . . . there are manifold relations of power that permeate, characterize and constitute the social body, and these relations of power cannot themselves be established, consolidated nor implemented without the production, accumulation, circulation and functioning of a discourse."

—Michel Foucault, *Power/Knowledge*

FOREWORD

I have had major problems with my understanding of "beneficiaries" ever since I joined the development sector as a grass-roots activist. I habitually express this discomfort of mine at all seminars/symposia that propose to deliberate on issues and concerns of development. It is rather disquieting to notice that participants from NGOs/Universities/Research Institutes who attend such workshops are more often than not programmed to grapple with the concept of beneficiaries from the "authorized" point of view of the concerned funding agencies that belong to the First World.

Development worldwide is being increasingly dichotomized into mutually exclusive [?] stakeholder *versus* beneficiary categories, regardless of the ongoing debate between the rights-based social work and the resource-driven structural adjustment worldviews. My professional peers apparently regard me as an anachronism of sorts whenever I happen to raise such disturbing issues [as a member of the Indian Association of Women's Studies or otherwise] before academics and/or activists.

Our higher educational institutions may create effective spaces for public policy research and discourse in order to address changes in the manner in which we ought to negotiate with the constantly moving targets of development. Action research may build on theory by taking recourse to community-level praxes and the dynamics of change management.

The author has made an effort to reconcile theory and praxes in this collection of essays underpinned by insights gained from his academic-turned-practitioner career. The different negations and negotiations analyzed in the present Volume require a critical gaze on the part of different institutions that interface with the actors as well as agencies of meaningful [sustainable] change. I welcome his endeavour to focus on ideas that are relevant in our era of NGOisation [!] when empowerment is generally appropriated by piecemeal notions of development.

CHANDA ASANI
Centre for Rural Development
SNDT Women's University
Juhu Campus, Mumbai-400049

PREFACE

This collection of essays seeks to explore common lessons from political sociology and development studies and, in this process, tries to resolve the tension between my academic and practitioner worldviews. I have tried, with limited success, to highlight one principal concern in this Volume that development is more often than not a multicultural construct of everyday politics that is context-bound and predicated by statements of informed choices on the part of the stakeholders and/or beneficiaries involved.

So development is more about who gets what, when, how, where and why in terms of an authoritative allocation of values that is underpinned by definitions of stakeholders or beneficiaries or affected persons. Such definitions are power statements that are scripted by agencies that generally tend to view development as an unevenness that may be restructured in terms of human and physical engineering as a level playing ground where players are equipped with uniform access to resources and similar opportunities. This is, however, a contentious issue without any simple answers. Such an interventionist approach may not always be sponsored by the mode of production or the marketplace of politics that, by definition, thrives on discrepancies and discriminations among unequally affected persons.

I have sought to analyze the issues and concerns of development from a politico-sociological point of view by stepping beyond established concepts and preconceived notions. I occasionally developed insights while working with the community at the field-level and incorporated such empirical lessons during strategy implementation exercises that served to reconcile theory with praxes.

I thank the contributors to *Urban Development Debates* [New Delhi: Atlantic, 2004] from whom I have learnt considerably while engaged in publication-related liaison of this insightful book series. Dr K.R. Gupta, Chairman of Atlantic Publishers & Distributors, is a constant source of inspiration.

My family stood by me as always when I was working on this book while my daughter Srabana Nandana ensured impossible hours that I never knew existed before spending quality time in her delectable presence.

PRASENJIT MAITI

CONTENTS

INTRODUCTION

> As far as the deconstructive position . . . goes, however, I think assessment has fallen short . . . . Or it may just be that something else new comes along that goes better with cappuccino.[1]

Discourses on development may not necessarily always exposit specifics related to the entire arrangement of ideas we more often than not tend to address as progress or uplift or even well-being.

Such discursive analyses may rather prefer to engage with capacities of stakeholders involved in the polyphony of development in order to gaze in a panoptican manner at their statements of power and the microphysics of their realities as obtained during the days and works of collective hands to raise and drop uncomfortable questions at the inception and withdrawal phases of our projects focused on development.

We may be more interested in the politics of development while examining the discourses related to the negations of and negotiations with development. Such politics may not always emanate from the engagements we ordinarily associate with the social costs of and human prices for development.

For is it not a fact that development may not always come across as a construct that is conveniently described and defined in terms of displacement and democracy and priority and choices and majoritarianism?

Why exactly do ethnic populations get involuntarily dispossessed while statements of development and material progress happen to redefine their body politic? When should development reorient itself as a strategy rather than as a discourse that may be read differently by variously impacted groups of stakeholders?

These are disturbing questions with no customized answers as yet. Our attempt to review established models and debates in the manner of dialogues may at times appear to be somewhat heuristic.

But the chapters that constitute this work are ontologic exercises that make an attempt to examine the meanings and perceptions of hegemony as a dialectic of nothingness beleaguered in terms of the tension between the signifiers and their signifieds.[2]

What we prefer to address as development may not always be ensured by following a predetermined approach. Such development generally emerges out of chaos and leads to cohesion of priorities and utilities.

From negations to negotiations is an arduous process of inquiry and further critiques that may leave us with more intellectual discomfort that we may possibly afford.[3] But the questions still need to be raised. The answers—if any—will follow in due course.

NOTES

1. See Todd May, *Reconsidering Difference: Nancy, Derrida, Levinas, and Deleuze* [University Park, Pennsylvania: The Pennsylvania State University Press, 1997], Ch 2, p. 77.
2. See Prasenjit Maiti, "History and Counterhistory", *Economic and Political Weekly* [1 July, 2000]: While we are not quite convinced of the treatment of history as a mere collection of certain so-called grand narratives, we are also not entirely in consonance with the politics-from-below point of view that tends to examine history as an absolute discourse in terms of black and white. What we mean is we cannot possibly afford to discuss our categories of analysis in straitjacketed terms like either the subaltern or the elite. We do not feel very comfortable with such drastic units and would rather prefer to interrogate these in order to explore other in-between areas of research as a more viable probability . . . . But we are finally presented with a readerly text in a postmodern context where it is fashionable to assume that the 'author is dead', and what is available is only the reader's interface with the text. So we have to necessarily analyse the inner narratives from within the text if we are to catch up anywhere near with reality that, however, has its own flux and logic.
3. See "The Public Communications Policy of the Asian Development Bank: Disclosure and Exchange of Information" [25 October, 2004]: It is now widely accepted that information sharing is essential to give real meaning to the goal of participatory development. Consultations with communities in which projects are undertaken cannot be effective without the provision of timely, relevant information. Furthermore, transparency is an important element in promoting economic growth and financial stability, facilitates effective governance, and strengthens public confidence in major institutions.

SECTION I
NEGATIONS

1

DEMOCRACY VERSUS DEVELOPMENT

"Democracy is no guarantee against the abuse of human rights."[1]

Key Words. Choice, Community, Consensus, Democracy, Development, Displacement, Entitlement, Evaluation, Freedom, Intervention, Monitoring, Participation, Politics, Semiotics, Stakeholders.

Introduction

This introductory chapter briefly discusses certain issues and concerns that are habitually raised during developmental interventions with regard to relocation of affected persons and their livelihoods as a part of rehabilitation and resettlement exercises of projects generally sponsored by international donor and/or bilateral funding agencies.[2]

Such agencies usually wish to conform to the best practices of involuntary displacement by factoring in a comprehensive R&R programme in the developmental projects concerned so that their global images are not undermined *vis-a-vis* civil societies.

This brings us to certain conceptual categories that we may happen to take recourse while building up our arguments and counter-arguments in this chapter. Choice, for instance, is all about preferences informed by systems of values and an effective demand supported by purchasing capacities at the marketplace of both politics as well as commodities. Choice, however, is not a deciding factor in programming resettlement induced by involuntary displacement.[3]

Community refers in this chapter to project affected persons who are without any entitlements to land whatsoever at their present locations *i.e.,* they are without the extended protection of and/or recognition by the state apparatuses. They may happen to possess a few benchmarks of legal identity such as electricity and telephone bills, voter identity cards and educational certificates but for all practical purposes they are men and women without any defined politico-legal site in the power arrangement of state affairs:

> A few state governments in India have of late waged a war of attrition with the Union Government over the contentious issue of providing cooked mid-day meals to underprivileged primary school children.
>
> This is primarily a central government-funded public welfare scheme where the center provides uncooked cereals [and transportation of foodgrains] free of cost.
>
> However, "cash-strapped" state governments plead inability to provide cooked meals to children in the below poverty level category, and seek to provide uncooked cereals instead [that too on an irregular basis], although it costs about INR 1 per child per day to provide cooked meals for the stipulated 200 days a year.
>
> The Supreme Court of India, the country's apex federal court, in an interim judgment, has recently ordered these state governments to immediately comply with the Union Government's regulations or else the center's aid to the states will be diverted to sponsor the mid-day meals project in primary schools.
>
> NGOs like the Right to Food and Work Network, Campaign against Child Labour, West Bengal Education Network and the Kolkata NGO Forum of Street and Working Children organised demonstrations by underprivileged children on 14 November, 2002—Children's Day—in Kolkata and across West Bengal to protest against the state government's inability to provide mid-day meals to primary school students.[4]

Project affected persons illegally settled along canal banks on the fringes of a large metropolitan city like Kolkata but will be doubly made illegal if they happen to be not in possession of identity cards that make them entitled to relocation-related benefits.

Such are the critical paradoxes of development induced by welfarist worldviews and rigid sets of culture root paradigms that do not always take into consideration the best material conditions of well-being possible given the ground realities and field-level basket of choices available to development agencies.

Consensus is a product of creative group dynamics geared to achieve certain practical ends with regard to certain immediate concerns. There may not be any democracy possible without any consensual monitoring and evaluation of project objectives, planned benefits and perceived interventions. But consensus is also about manipulations that may distort the ethos of community participation and democratic empowerment of primary stakeholders.

So this chapter would appear to be predicated upon a back to basics approach to democracy and its different shades of meanings as understood by its practitioners *i.e.*, ordinary unknown and faceless citizens to whom democracy may occasionally assume the physical construct of the manifestation of power trappings as understood by daily interfaces with the police, judiciary, bureaucracy, taxes, laws, elections and selections.

This conception of democracy may appeal to many as a hardheaded approach to understand the archaeology and/or microphysics of power discourses that tend to escape the initiated academic who has limited contextual access to the architecture of ontology-driven statist narratives.

We are interested in this chapter to establish correlations between democracy, development and displacement in a manner that may be conceived in terms as shown in Model 1.

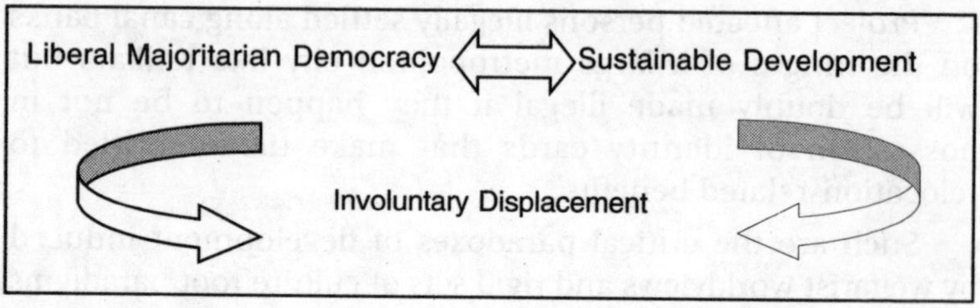

Model 1: Democracy Development Displacement

This model demonstrates that liberal democracy more often than not has in-built compulsions to adopt as well as adapt the rhetoric of development as understood from the above while the praxes of development instinctively draw upon the metaphors of participatory democracy in order to become more broad-based and plural in a multicultural sense.

But development in terms of constructions and conglomerates may often lead to large scale involuntary displacement of indigenous peoples and project affected persons. This also implies that displacement is a logical corollary of a certain school of development that cannot organically evolve from the grass-roots and small narratives of everyday life.

This posits the most critical question of this chapter: if displacement habitually takes place in liberal democracies, then what exactly is expected from the institutions and watchdogs of democracy? It was recently reported in the print media that Narmada Bachao Andolan activists were nowhere to be found when a certain affected village within the project area was about to be submerged by the river waters although they had pledged united resistance and a show of strength with the villagers concerned.

Are our state apparatuses powerful enough to appropriate the institutions of democracy so that popular resistance is minimized in the process? The different case studies referred to in this chapter tend to confirm our apprehensions in this regard.

Entitlement of the beneficiaries involved is an important concern of this chapter as well. We have started building our discourse from a point where it is a laid down fact that affected persons are generally without any legal entitlements if they happen to be illegal encroachers on privately owned land or public property. State apparatuses may ultimately have to legalize squatters' colonies as happened in the case of refugee settlements in West Bengal.

But what about cases where certain sections of affected persons are left without any relocation benefits whatsoever while others gain access to such resettlement programmes? This somewhat negates the idea of distributive justice, as similarly placed populations are unequally affected by developmental interventions.[5]

SPECIFIC PRINCIPLES OF DISTRIBUTIVE JUSTICE[6]

1.0 Egalitarian

Every person should receive equal benefits and burdens. People should be rewarded with positions of responsibility according to their intelligence, capacity for devotion to the public good and education. Persons should be rewarded financially according to the number of years they have held a job.

2.0 Socialist

People should be assigned burdens according to abilities, benefits according to need, according to their work effort and according to the quantity and quality of their work.

3.0 Libertarian

Burdens should be assigned as they are voluntarily accepted, benefits as others voluntarily give them and as one creates them for oneself through labour on materials of which one is rightful owner.

Monitoring and evaluation of project-related interventions are required in order to make available the benefits of the project to affected persons in an equitable manner. But even external and internal monitoring may not be able to ensure that justice, as predicated by development, will be carried out.

This is due to the fact that possible eviction of affected persons without identity cards issued by the relevant authorities will defeat the cause justice as fairness [following John Rawls].[7]

KEIP: Case Study[8]

One of the major components of the Kolkata Environmental Improvement Project [2002-07] funded by the Asian Development Bank and jointly implemented by the Kolkata Municipal Corporation and the Irrigation & Waterways Department, Government of West Bengal in Rehabilitation of canals/water bodies and Resettlement of informal canal bank dwellers who will be ousted from their present unauthorized settlements during implementation of KEIP's Canal Improvement Component:

> Kolkata Environmental Improvement Project [KEIP] is a major project cofunded by the Asian Development Bank [ADB], Department for International Development [DFID], the West Bengal Government and the Kolkata Municipal Corporation.
>
> The project involves several agencies such as KMC, the Irrigation Department of Government of West Bengal and the West Bengal Pollution Control Board. KMC as the prime executing agency has started work in March, 2002 and is expected to continue till December, 2007.
>
> The project's objective is to improve the welfare and well being of the people of Kolkata, especially the poor, through an improved urban environment, equitable access to municipal services, and more effective municipal management.[9]

KEIP's R&R Component is "unique" in the sense that it deals with encroachers who are without any legal entitlements pertaining to their land holdings that are used either for residential or commercial purposes. KEIP in fact proposes to accord a quasi-legal status to informal canal bank dwellers in possession of valid identity cards by providing them with a lifetime tenurial security at the relocation sites.[10]

Face to Façade

Discourses on the politics of development may include subtexts of choice as underpinned by community consensus [or the lack of it] against the larger backdrop of liberal democracy as we tend to understand the arrangements of power intricacies factored into the multiplicity of concepts that are more often than not reflections of complicity rather than that of manufactured consent [following Noam Chomsky]:

> Villagers opposed to the construction of a large dam across the river Beda, in the state of Madhya Pradesh, are on indefinite hunger strike to protest their illegal confinement by police after a peaceful demonstration last week. They were obstructing the building of the dam and the absence of land-based rehabilitation.[11]

What practitioners at the field-level today understand by development and what academics handling high theory understand by progress are perhaps two quite different interpretations at the construction stage of semiotics *i.e.* progress can [and often does] construe images of long duree sustenance ranging across generations whereas development may indicate any short-term/tactical manoeuvre spanning decades that in most cases is informed by the contingencies of crises management. Progress is much more intellectual in its general appeal than development that is definitely less patrician so far as the edifices of culture and civilization are concerned:

> Around 200 tribal families from nine villages in Nandurbar district on the banks of the Narmada river have launched the 'Bhoomi Hakk Satyagraha' [land rights movement] in response to a decision by the Narmada Control Authorities [NCA] to raise the height of the Sardar Sarovar dam to 110 m.[12]

So development is more down to earth and tangible by its end-users. This is essentially what makes it a veritable bone of contention across political systems and arrangements of power irrespective of local contours or global dynamics. Development emerges as a tool to be yielded for more power and further political mileage at the cost of undermining progress in real terms:

> It's been a minor victory for the Bhil tribals of Dhorpada village. After three long decades of struggle the government

finally conceded to a broad compromise: tribals who can prove they have been tilling a piece of land as early as 1978 will be allowed to keep the land.[13]

Progress can really be studied as a counterpoint to development as the sense of history is often missing in developmental interventions. Development tends to be piecemeal as its very logic at times stems from the rationale of the compulsions of power. This is not to suggest—however—that development is all politics and naught else:

> Survival International, a global tribal rights body, and several Indian non-governmental organisations [NGOs] have alleged that a meeting organised by the government to decide the fate of the Jarawa in the Andaman & Nicobar Islands violated a judicial order protecting this threatened indigenous community.[14]

Development is definitely larger than the scope of the politics of everyday life but it also has a panoptican role to play [following Michel Foucault] *vis-a-vis* all vestiges of civil society that requires its critical and immediate attention. In this sense it has emerged as a millennial avatar to whom political actors turn instinctively with an underlying agenda of oneupmanship in order to outmanoeuvre dissent and all forms and statements of protest:

> While the state's criminal law provides for the 'setting off' of a sentence, according to the time already spent in jail by an under-trial, this was not earlier applicable to tribal areas. As a result, many tribals spend more than their fair share of time in jail.[15]

Secessionism that often leads to militant terrorism is nurtured by the sense of relative deprivation and marginalization from the so-called mainstream [a vague term that is defined to mean a set of culturally pliable mechanisms that offset the grass-roots]:

> Unpaid labour may be illegal but it's a stark reality for the Gond tribals living in forest villages in Madhya Pradesh. Tribal communities are often treated as labour colonies by local forest departments.[16]

This is a conducive scenario where the politics of development may have a field day if the apparatuses of the state are not adequately responsive to popular needs and aspirations.

Canal Evictions

Asian Development Bank is funding the Kolkata Environmental Improvement Project to the tune of 16.5 billion rupees to renovate the canals of Kolkata. This will mean the removal of some 5000 poor families living along the canals. The city and state governments had few plans of rehabilitating the families, according to Rabial Mallick, secretary of the Kolkata NGO Forum.

According to Malay Dewanji of Kolkata Basthuhara Samity [Association of Shelterless People in Kolkata], around 1000 families have already been evicted without rehabilitation. In the last quarter of 2000 Mallick and Dewanji contacted Denis Murphy and Ted Anana, coordinator of Eviction Watch, who got in touch with ADB officials.

In a letter to Arjun Thapan, ADB official in charge of the Kolkata project, KBS listed their demands as follows: resettlement should not be more than two kilometers from their present houses; compensation to be given to the people for the construction of their houses; NGOs to monitor the project; project-affected poor people to be employed as workers in the project; and NGO/CBO representation in Project Committees.

In December last year an ADB official informed Denis Murphy that the ADB had told the Kolkata government resettlement should be not more than two kilometers from the affected families present houses.[17]

Price of Development

The Asian Development Bank, which is funding the Kolkata Environment Improvement Project, is all for rehabilitation of squatters who have to be evicted for the city's facelift. But the citizens must take note: Whatever has to be done will require money, which the ADB can lend, provided they return it with 13 per cent interest.

This is the crux of what Alex K. Jorgensen, principal project implementation officer and head, Urban Development, ADB India Resident Mission, told a delegation of anti-eviction activists in Kolkata on Tuesday evening: "ADB is lending money. It is not cheap money. The taxpayers should be aware that the more money they spend, the more they pay in taxes. There is no free money," he said. The bankman added candidly that whoever gives the money has the keys. "KMC doesn't control the money. Even the state government doesn't control the money. The money is with me."

At the onset of discussion, Kolkata Municipal Corporation director general [projects] Raghabendra Das made it clear that the Tolly's Nullah, Beliaghata and Bagjola canals—where evictions have already taken place—were outside the ADB project areas. When it was pointed out that State Urban Development Minister Asok Bhattacharya and Mayor Subrata Mukherjee had both said eviction in these areas was a precondition for the Rs. 1,100 crore ADB loan, Jorgensen said, "ADB has no involvement in any political statement issued by anybody." Even in ADB project areas, the evictees could not expect to "get rich;" they would be only assisted to "move to a new place" and given the "right to live there".

For how long? Neither Jorgensen nor Das had an answer. He, however, conceded that settlers—"We now prefer to call them encroachers"—in other places evicted without rehabilitation may create "social tension" which would not be helpful for a smooth run of any development plans.

The ADB favoured a "logical" rehabilitation policy. "We are trying to keep pushing the Central Government to make a comprehensive rehabilitation Act which will be applicable in all states and all municipalities," he said. Lastly, Jorgensen had a note of advice for the activists. "I think your job is also to keep pushing—and keep agitating—hopefully through democratic channels."[18]

KEIP: Objectives

Several existing canals will be improved under KEIP's R&R component.[19] These will be dredged and desilted to restore their original design cross-sections. Linings will be constructed to improve hydraulic efficiency, and culverts and bridges will be replaced/upgraded, as appropriate, to eliminate drainage constrictions . . . . Improvement of the canals may require the resettlement of up to 12,000 canal bank dwellers.[20] The benefits of the canals and waterways programme would be in two main categories. First, there would be health and amenity benefits which impact on the beneficiary population in Kolkata as a result of the improvements. In addition, there would be cost savings arising from reduction in the time lost due to flooding and reduced flood damage to dwellings and other properties.[21]

Issues and Concerns

Freedom and intervention are two related yet opposite concepts that need to be studied in a diligent manner while developing our arguments for and against evictions and/or relocation of affected persons.

Freedom implies that primary stakeholders have considerable flexibility of socio-economic choices while deciding upon the pros and cons of development. Freedom of choice also implies that affected persons have access to the right to information, as knowledge at this stage serves as a power discourse [following Michel Foucault].

Intervention, however, suggests that secondary stakeholders are in a best position to judge what will be beneficial for primary stakeholders. This involves a certain pedagogy of politics and power arrangements imposed from the above that instinctively serves to displace the affected persons from the central concerns of development.

So we tend to derive at circles within circles: from democracy to development to displacement and next from freedom to choice to intervention to relocation and/or eviction. This is a series of Chinese boxes that tends to lead us to zero at the end of our critical engagements with the puzzles of human entitlement matrices:

> Globalization meant welcoming foreign investors usually to modern, well-developed urban centers where two cities co-exist: the area of the rich and middle class people

[exclusive subdivisions, high rise buildings, well-lighted parks, offices and malls equipped with the latest information technology gadgets, etc.], and the congested slums that do not have the most basic services such as clean drinking water, electricity, sanitation, schools and clinics.

Massive forced evictions are also occurring in Asia due to big projects like the Narmada, Three Gorges, and Bakun Dams, and the Mekong River development programmes whose objectives are irrigation, flood control and the generation of hydro-electric power for the ever-increasing demands of the cities. Many peasant farmers migrate to the cities as a result.

In South Asia many urban evictions are due to infrastructure projects, such as the construction of new roads and expressways, road widening, canal improvement, flood control projects and beautification clean-ups to make the city attractive to tourists. Thousands of poor families are evicted without sufficient notice, consultation, compensation, and provision of alternative housing.

Massive infrastructure projects and beautification clean-ups in the urban centers restarted in Southeast Asia with the recovery of their economies. This in turn resumed demolition of slums.

Some of the big projects that will evict thousands of people are the following: Kolkata Canal Improvement Project, Lyari River Expressway, Dhaka Slum Clearance, Surabaya Normalization Project, Jakarta Bay Reclamation Project, Manila North and South Rails, Pasig River Rehabilitation, Laguna Lake Ring Road, and Camanava Flood Control Project, The Asian Development Bank, the World Bank, and the Japan Bank for International Cooperation fund many of these projects.[22]

R&R constitutes major exercises in human engineering in the larger context of development *per se*. It is true that canal bank dwellers have no legal status *vis-a-vis* their present settlements but it is equally imperative to maintain a workable balance between the compulsions of development and the realities of displacement.

Generally, displacement as a result of acquisition is legally sanctioned while there is no legal framework that governs the process of displacement itself: the land acquisition law protects the sanctity of what causes displacement [*i.e.*, the dam] but not the displaced. In the absence of legal safeguards to ensure accountability on the part of the State, resettlement and rehabilitation entitlements promised often by executive order have rarely been implemented in its entirety covering all affected people.[23]

The concept of programming resettlement as development programme mode is gaining currency though practice is limited. "Good practices" in this respect are those that: [a] focus on means of livelihood rather than on assets; [b] assume an inclusive relationship between people and assets; and [c] admit of a negotiated definition of "just" compensation. The record indicates that in those cases in which compensation packages were negotiated with PAPs and other stakeholders, the process has resulted in better outcomes for the resettlement process as a whole. Even when, for whatever reason, the negotiated form of compensation proves not to be the most appropriate or effective option, PAPs tend to feel more satisfied, as a result of the negotiation process . . . . There is an inverse relationship between scale of displacement and extent of achieving successful resettlement outcomes even in countries with best policy, institutional capacity and political commitment to do proper resettlement.[24]

No development project can result in complete alienation of the rights, customary and legal, of people through payment of a one-time compensation or facilitated relocation. On the contrary, the process must result in the creation of new rights that will render people direct beneficiaries of the development project. Just as displacement is not an inevitable consequence of infrastructure development, resettlement need not necessarily result in impoverishment. Central to positive resettlement and rehabilitation will be the empowering of people particularly the economically and socially marginalised as a result of both the process and outcomes of resettlement with development.[25]

R&R assumes critical significance when implemented in democratic political systems that are yet to resolve the tension between the logic of liberal open market economies and the rhetoric of state welfarism predicated by non-merit expenditures incurred on non-performing assets.

Politics of Development

India is such an example of a political system where logic and rhetoric are yet to reconcile skewed issues of human development, as the level playing field required for such diverse exercises [plus their implications] is not readily available:

> The West Bengal Government, in response to a Supreme Court ruling that states should not compromise with children's food, had earlier petitioned that it was unable to implement the central government-funded mid-day meals project due to severe funds crunch. But the apex court rejected the petition and cautioned on 3 September, 2002 that central aid to the states would be diverted for the meals project if cooked meals were not duly provided in schools.
>
> The People's Union for Civil Liberties [Rajasthan] filed a petition in May, 2001 in connection with the "right to food" in the Supreme Court, demanding that the country's food stock should be used without delay to prevent hunger.
>
> The Supreme Court, in its "interim order" passed on 28 November, 2001, converted the benefits of eight nutrition-related federal schemes into legal entitlements and directed the state governments to provide cooked mid-day meals for all children in government and government-assisted schools.[26]

While there is no national resettlement policy, land acquisition in India is covered by a national law, the 1894 Land Acquisition Act and its subsequent amendments. The LAA allows for land acquisition in the national interest for water reservoirs, canals, plants, fly ash ponds, transmission lines and highways to be carried out by the respective States, in accordance with its provisions.[27]

West Bengal, on the other hand, has a protracted history of radical political mobilization [the so-called "tradition of unorthodoxy"[28]] more often than not impacted by refugee movements since Independence and Partition [1947]:

> The West Bengal Government and the Kolkata Municipal Corporation have made a name for themselves in international civil society circles as a gross violator of the housing rights of its poor citizens. On 22 September, 2001 it evicted some 20,000 people from Tolly Nullah; 10th December, 2002 another 40,000 people; 2 February, 2003 some 7,000 Dalits; and on 15 December, 2003, 75,000 people along the canal side settlements at Bagbazar and Cossipore area.
>
> In the latest evictions, the West Bengal Government and the Kolkata Municipal Corporation did not notify the residents about the eviction, neither were they provided with rehabilitation. As in the past, both governments employed heavily armed policemen and paramilitary forces. The operations were conducted while the men were out of the community working and only the women and children were left to face the brunt of the violent evictions.
>
> As if to show its low regard for the Universal Declaration of Human Rights and the United Nations, the West Bengal Government conducted the evictions on 15 December, 2003 a few days from Human Rights Day while last year it did this during Human Rights Day itself.
>
> Consequently, as a state party to such treaties, the Government of India has the responsibility of calling to account the West Bengal Government and the Kolkata Municipal Corporation for their violations of the human rights of Indian citizens. Their record of violating human rights, namely, forced evictions, with impunity has become a source of international embarrassment for the Government of India.[29]

So the stakeholder versus beneficiary debate assumes new meanings so far as KEIP's priorities and objectives are concerned. For instance, the priority of urban good governance has as one of its important objectives streamlining the existing bureaucracy and available manpower to make service delivery mechanisms more efficacious. But compulsions of the politics of everyday life may dictate otherwise.

Stakeholder versus Beneficiary

R&R is no exception. This component in fact provides an opportunity to examine the stakeholder versus beneficiary debate in the context of the development versus displacement debate. Whether prospective canal bank oustees *i.e.,* affected persons can be described as stakeholders or beneficiaries will determine the outcome of KEIP's development versus displacement debate. This discourse may be better understood by carrying out an in-depth social impact assessment of R&R in the context of concerned ADB involuntary resettlement policy guidelines.[30]

Social impact assessment variables point to measurable change in human population, communities, and social relationships resulting from a development project or policy change as follows:

1. Population characteristics mean present population and expected change, ethnic and racial diversity and influxes & outflows of temporary residents as well as the arrival of seasonal or leisure residents.
2. Community & Institutional structures mean the size, structure and level of organization of local government including linkages to the larger political systems. They also include historical and present patterns of employment and industrial diversification, the size and level of activity of voluntary associations, religious organizations and interests groups and finally how these institutions relate to each other.
3. Political and social resources refer to the distribution of power authority, the interested and affected publics, and the leadership capability and capacity within the community or region.
4. Individual and family changes refer to factors, which influence the daily life of the individuals and families, including attitudes, perceptions, family characteristics

and friendship networks. These changes range from attitudes toward the policy to an alteration in family and friendship networks to perceptions of risk, health and safety.

5. Community Resources include patterns of natural resource and land use, the availability of housing and community services to include health, police and fire protection and sanitation facilities. A key to the continuity and survival of human communities are their historical and cultural resources. Under this collection of variables we also consider possible changes for indigenous people and religious sub-cultures.[31]

PRINCIPLES FOR SOCIAL IMPACT ASSESSMENT[32]

1. Involve the potentially affected publics [identify and involve all potentially affected groups and individuals].
2. Analyze impact equity [identify who will win and who will lose and emphasize vulnerability of under-represented groups].
3. Focus the assessment [deal with issues and public concerns that really count, not those that are just easy to count].
4. Identify methods and assumptions and define significance [describe how the SIA is conducted, what assumptions are used and how significance is determined].
5. Provide feedback on social impacts to project planners [identify problems that could be solved with changes to the proposed action or alternatives].
6. Use SIA practitioners [trained social scientist employing social science methods will provide the best results].
7. Establish monitoring and mitigation programmes [manage uncertainty by monitoring and mitigating adverse impacts].
8. Identify data sources [use published scientific literature, secondary data and primary data from the affected area].

9. Plan for gaps in data [evaluate the missing information and develop a strategy for proceeding].

An initial social assessment is required for every development project in order to identify the people who may be beneficially and adversely affected by the project. It should assess the stage of development of various subgroups and their needs, demands and absorptive capacity. It should also identify the institutions to be involved in the project and assess their capacities. The ISA should identify the key social dimensions aspects [such as involuntary resettlement, indigenous peoples, poverty reduction and women in development] that need to be addressed under the project. The ISA should be undertaken as early as possible in the project cycle and preferably by the time of fact-finding for a project preparation technical assistance. If the ISA identifies that resettlement is likely to be involved in the project, a resettlement plan should be prepared, preferably in conjunction with preparation of the project feasibility study.

OBJECTIVES AND PRINCIPLES OF ADB'S INVOLUNTARY RESETTLEMENT POLICY[33]

1. Involuntary resettlement should be avoided where feasible.
2. Where population displacement is unavoidable, it should be minimized by exploring all viable project options.
3. People unavoidably displaced should be compensated and assisted, so that their economic and social future would be generally as favourable as it would have been in the absence of the project.
4. People affected should be informed fully and consulted on resettlement and compensation options.
5. Existing social and cultural institutions of resettlers and their hosts should be supported and used to the greatest extent possible, and resettlers should be integrated economically and socially into host communities.

6. The absence of a formal legal title to land by some affected groups should not be a bar to compensation; particular attention should be paid to households headed by women and other vulnerable groups, such as indigenous peoples and ethnic minorities, and appropriate assistance provided to help them improve their status.
7. As far as possible, involuntary resettlement should be conceived and executed as a part of the project.
8. The full costs of resettlement and compensation should be included in the presentation of project costs and benefits.
9. Costs of resettlement and compensation may be considered for inclusion in Bank loan financing for the project.

Benefit versus Benefit

"That people should be at the center of development is increasingly recognized. However, there may be instances where a development intervention such as a road or a power generation project should proceed for the greater benefit of society, in spite of its potential adverse effects on some people.

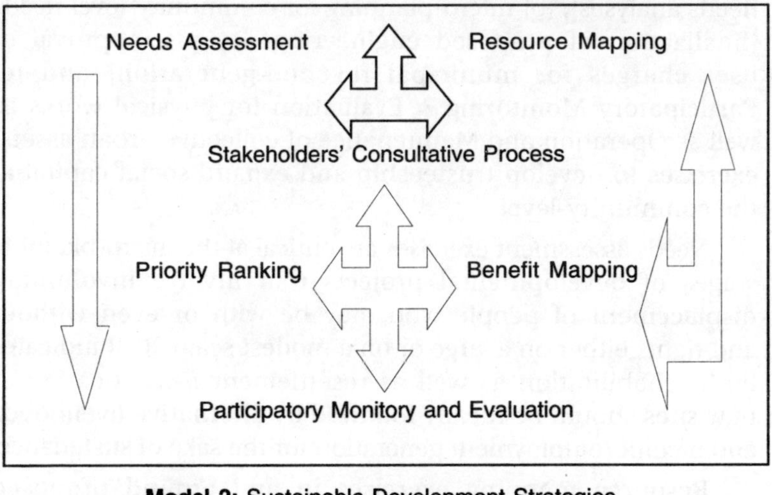

Model 2: Sustainable Development Strategies

"In such cases, the people who may be adversely affected by the development intervention should be consulted; compensated for their losses; and assisted to rebuild their homes and communities, reestablish their enterprises, and develop their potentials as productive members of society at a level generally at least equivalent to that which was likely to have prevailed in the absence of the development intervention. Attention to such matters is especially important when the people who may be adversely affected are poor and vulnerable, do not have the capacity to absorb such adverse impacts, and cannot remain productive without significant help."[34]

Stakeholders' Consultative Process

SCP will promote stakeholder involvement in the Project, and contribute to the effective implementation of the Project investments. SCP is designed to cover stakeholder awareness, participation and education with respect to the implementation and management of the Project facilities.

SCP involves primary stakeholders [prospective/potential project beneficiaries] in [a] needs assessment exercises [related to physical works, awareness-generation campaigns and training needs analyses], [b] micro-planning for community-level needs [finalization of proposed engineering designs, approval of user charges for municipal revenue-generation] and [c] Participatory Monitoring & Evaluation [of physical works as well as Operation and Maintenance of collective urban assets] exercises to develop trusteeship and expand social capital at the community-level.[35]

Needs assessment exercises are critical at the micro-planning stages of developmental projects that involve involuntary displacement of people who may be with or even without and rights either on a large or on a modest scale. R&R indicates both rehabilitation as well as resettlement *i.e.* relocation at new sites should be ideally followed by alternative livelihoods and income/employment generation for the sake of sustenance.

Resource mapping exercises in and around proposed relocation sites may be carried out during the pre-relocation stage so that affected persons may be given a working idea of new sources of living at the resettlement sites. Local institutional and support mechanisms should also be worked out by secondary stakeholders so that primary stakeholders may either continue to or begin to receive all sorts of humanitarian aid.

This is especially crucial for the vulnerable sections of the affected persons population who would be unequally impacted by the processes of relocation such as the aged, the estranged, the sick, the disabled and the poor without any community or family-level support.

Micro-level plans should always be methodologically informed by priority ranking and matrix scoring applications so that community-level choices, perceptions and felt needs are effectively highlighted in such studies.

Gender issues should also be mainstreamed and factored in the relocation-related action plans so that women-headed households and women-specific problems may be accorded topmost priority.

SCP underpins crises management [tactical] and sustainable development [strategic] approaches by utilizing different time frames and priorities for the purpose of resource and benefit mapping informed by "an authoritative allocation of values" *i.e.,* who gets what, when, how, where and why [following David Easton].

PM&E utilizes SCP in order to reorient conventional top-down approaches to M&E [that more often than not fail to mobilize and motivate primary stakeholders so that they become proactive in terms of development]. PM&E considers persons affected by project-related interventions as the agency [rather than the target] of sustainable development.

So the politics of community participation is imperative in order to make SCP-related developmental endeavours successful. Primary stakeholders have to be schooled as well as deschooled so that their dystopic worldviews may be adequately reoriented to participate in the carnival of development-related polyphonies that would be ordained by the telos and logos of everyday material conditions of life at the grass-roots.

We realize at this juncture that semiotics plays a critical role in developmental discourses. To signify is to choose between alternatives while choice in itself is conditioned by orientations of and inclinations to different value-specific schools of development.

So PM&E underpinned by SCP happens to be a dialogue between primary and secondary stakeholders [implementing/funding agencies and professional consultants] that is initiated at the inception phase of any urban development project and continues till the post-project phase to sustain benefits, examine [environmental] impacts and draw lessons *vis-a-vis* project interventions.

Infrastructural impact assessment ensures that development strategies, instead of being implemented from the above, are conjoined by participatory exercises between primary & secondary stakeholders and sustained by dialogues at the field & project management levels in order to institutionalize good practices of learning from one another.

Lessons Learnt

R&R-related exercises are in fact points of coincidence between human/social and physical engineering. Development consultants, urban planners, executing agencies and funding bodies *i.e.*, the secondary stakeholders should be sensitized enough while undertaking projects that involve rehabilitation and resettlement of affected persons impacted by the compulsions of involuntary displacement.

There are inevitable traumas and human disruptions related to relocation. We are planning movement of reluctant persons who will be compelled to leave behind their home and hearth in search of new habitats. But let us not also lose sight of the fact that primary stakeholders would also be made to pursue their memories in a collective manner during this process of resettlement while their collective psyche will continuously refer back to the communal baggages of relative deprivation informed both by material constructs such as artifacts and ideational tools such as cost-benefit analyses.

We have to be prepared for narratives within narratives that may toggle big stories with little stories: the failure of Operation Barga in West Bengal and the resultant series of migrations on the part of landless agricultural labourers from their villages typecast by severely fragmented and commercially unviable land holdings to metropolitan centres such as Kolkata in order to survive on the marginalities of the urban sensibility.

We also have to balance between betterment of best practices and establishment of practices *per se* that are neither good nor bad nor ugly *i.e.*, value-free milestones of development that may appear to be paradoxical in the manner of functional anarchies. But we have to reconcile with such compulsions of reality in order to conform to the developmentalist worldview of the executing agencies concerned.

Pedagogics of Displacement

Different sets of stakeholders involved in development projects concerned with R&R may approach the problem of relocation in ways more than one. While this may indicate distributive justice for a certain group of stakeholders, this may also suggest retributive justice for yet another group of stakeholders.

The messages to be disseminated to the affected persons may assume monologic overtones due to the fact that developmental dialogues between primary and secondary stakeholders may not always be feasible during rehabilitation and resettlement exercises.

Perceptions, developmentalist or not, depend upon the kind of stakes one has in the project as well as on one's quality and brand of political socialization. These will always differ from one individual to another. Senses and sensibilities, therefore, will also tend to vary across a cross-section of stakeholders impacted in an uneven manner by project-related physical interventions.

Conclusion

Resettlement planning provides the means to mitigate displacement's adverse impacts and to create development opportunities for project-affected people:

> While adequate resettlement planning may increase the initial investment costs of a project, long-term benefits include fewer delays and cost escalations during project implementation, an increased benefit stream from economically productive resettlers, and reduced welfare costs to society at large.[36]

Performance of R&R-related exercises will critically impact on project-related interventions *per se* as such activities at the field-level will determine the future progress of canal improvement works that is a major project component designed to upgrade the existing physical environmental conditions of Kolkata by efficacious outflow of storm water and waste water. Water-clogging adversely affects mandays while reduced mandays lead to non-sustainable livelihoods on the part of project affected people ["affected persons"]/primary stakeholders who stand to win or lose impacted by development interventions.

R&R may be approached at a perspective level to offset the inevitable dislocations at the inception phase. Urban development strategies more often than not emerge from deterministic chaos *i.e.*, there is generally a method that underpins dislocations and conflicts that attend the inception phases of developmental projects in metropolitan cities. This is to be ordinarily expected, however, as cities generally share complex histories, cultural baggages and collective memories that are multiple and not always amenable to unilinear project interventions:

> After the no-harm agenda and the post-Rio boom, the World Bank claims to have reached a "third generation" of environmental reforms. According to the director of its Environment Department, the present reforms are marked by a "major effort [...] to incorporate the environment into sectoral and national strategies." One prominent example is the Bank's new Global Overlays Initiative. This has "as its overriding objective the internalization of global externalities into national environmental planning and the Bank's sector work, operations and dialogue with governments and partners." The World Bank has also

identified some strategic priorities, which should incorporate lessons from the 1994 bankwide resettlement review.[37]

Development is not extrinsic like politics imposed from the above to impact on end-users of limited resources. Actors who will interface with their own ground-level institutional arrangements/mechanisms during the project cycle/ interventions should be catalyzed to facilitate social capital that coheres organic ethos of community existence.

Deriving lessons from project interventions is imperative. Urban development is often made complicated by political overtones and culture root paradigms that may not work in tandem with the project's rationale and objectives/outputs. This necessitates reassessing community-level needs and perceptions in order to minimize dislocations with regard to implementation of physical work, poverty alleviation programmes and awareness-generation activities.

Urban development strategies should always focus on the perspective approach *i.e.,* master plans should identify the mandate and scope of proposed interventions but should also extend perspective visions beyond the project cycle to facilitate sustainable development.[38]

Primary stakeholders/affected persons should be empowered to sustain developmental impacts of the project *i.e.,* their entitlements should be converted into capacities [in the context of project limitations]. This will ensure that project interventions and their benefits sustain over a considerable period of time and motivate future development and further popular initiatives at the grass-roots level where communities have been made capable to make critical decisions affecting the quality of their everyday life.

SOCIAL IMPACT ASSESSMENT VARIABLES[39]

Axes of civic participation/preparedness should be identified in order to plan developmental interventions in consultation with both primary as well as secondary stakeholders. This is despite the fact that development generally emerges out of chaos and can seldom be planned in a rigid

Project/Policy Stage				
Project/ Policy Setting (type)	Planning/ Policy Development	Construction/ Implementation	Operation & Maintenance	Equity of minority groups
Potentially affected publics [PAPs]	Perceptions of risk, health and safety	Influx of temporary workers	Trust in political and social institutions	Alteration in size of local government
Distribution of power/ authority	Formation of attitudes towards the project	Change in community infrastructure	Change in income characteristics	Change in employment

manner. Field-level lessons, therefore, should be utilized to coordinate between theory and praxes.[40]

APPENDIX I

INVOLUNTARY RESETTLEMENT [WORLD BANK GROUP]: KEY CONCEPTS[41]

Replacement Cost

The World Bank's policies require that all affected assets [land and structures] are compensated at their replacement cost. Replacement cost of an affected asset is equivalent to the amount required to replace the asset in its existing condition. Since in most of the Borrower countries, and especially at the project sites, there may not be markets in old housing that function well, the replacement cost of structures should be equal to the cost of constructing/purchasing a new structure, without making any deductions for depreciation. The legal frameworks of many countries do not provide compensation at replacement cost. The Bank accepts a combination of compensation permissible under the local legal regimes with other allowances [with variable terminology] so that the total is equal to the replacement cost of affected assets.

Income Restoration

Restoration of the incomes of all affected persons is one of the key objectives of the Bank's resettlement policy. It requires that after resettlement, all of the affected persons should have incomes, which are at least equivalent to their pre-project income levels. Restoration of incomes, the standards of living and the productivity levels of the affected persons constitute the core of the Bank's resettlement policy. Though resettlement programmes should be designed to help improve the standards of living and income levels of the affected population, they must minimally be restored. Resettlement planning is one of the main mechanisms through which the Bank and the Borrower work towards ensuring that the incomes of all categories of affected persons are restored after resettlement.

Squatters and Encroachers

Squatters and encroachers are persons without legal titles to the land and structures occupied/used by them. The term "squatters" is typically used for those occupying structures for residential/commercial purposes, while "encroachers" are those occupying land for agriculture. The Bank's resettlement policy explicitly states that the affected persons cannot be denied compensation/resettlement assistance based on the lack of legal title. Bank projects, therefore, need to make provisions for helping squatters/encroachers achieve the objectives of the Bank's resettlement policy.

Displacement

Displacement is the impact that necessitates resettlement of affected persons. Displacement could be physical, *i.e.*, where the affected persons are required to relocate, or economic, where the impact of loss of incomes forces the affected persons to move or to initiate alternative strategies of income restoration.

Project Affected Persons

Persons affected by land acquisition, relocation, or loss of incomes associated with change in land use due to the project are defined as project-affected persons [PAPs]. Though project-affected persons may form the unit of impact for the purpose of baseline surveys, some of the resettlement entitlements could actually be provided to the households as units of entitlement.

Linear Resettlement

Linear resettlement is usually involved in projects producing linear patterns of land acquisition [highways, railways, canals, power transmission lines, etc.]. It is differentiated from site-specific resettlement because of the problems that arise when resettlement actions have to be coordinated across multiple jurisdictions and different cultural and linguistic areas.

Urban Resettlement

Resettlement in urban or peri-urban settings is usually referred to as urban resettlement. It is differentiated from rural resettlement since the types of problems involved and the strategies proposed to address them are substantially different from those in rural resettlement.

Indigenous Peoples

Project where resettlement of indigenous peoples is required need to be prepared and implemented with extreme sensitivity to the socio-cultural requirements of indigenous groups. The Bank's Operational Directive 4.20 deals with issues in development projects with indigenous peoples. Where IPs need to be resettled in a project, the requirements of OD 4.30 and OD 4.20 need to be complied with. The entitlement policies, costs and budgets, institutional arrangements for implementation, etc. can only be worked out once the baseline surveys are completed.[42]

NOTES

1. See Anita Roddick, "Infinite Justice", *Resurgence* [Issue 217]. http://resurgence.gn.apc.org/issues/roddick217.htm
2. The author wishes to thank Resettlement Plan Implementation Working Group members of the Asian Development Bank-funded Kolkata Environmental Improvement Project [2002-07] in connection with the lessons learnt and insights developed during interactive dialogue sessions. Website links [URLs] cited in this chapter—apart from textual notes—also [on certain occasions] serve to cross-reference issues and concerns for researchers.

3. According to the Indian National Institute of Urban Affairs, nearly 30 million Indians were expected to be living in urban slums in 2001. More than five million people live in slums in Mumbai, nearly the same number in the eastern city of Kolkata, while the national capital, New Delhi, is home to an estimated 6,00,000 slum families. As democracies, the Indian State Governments might be expected to be wary of relocating slum dwellers for fear of losing the political support of people who make up a sizable chunk of the population of India's metropolises. Yet in Maharashtra State, for example, many forced evictions of slums dwellers do occur, and resistance is strong because of the lack of relocation schemes or policies for resettling slum residents. This is despite the Maharashtra Project Affected Persons Rehabilitation Act [1986], which, while allowing the State to acquire land for the purpose of public interest through purchase and exchange or by compulsory acquisition, requires the State Government to arrange to provide civic amenities in the area where it re-locates affected persons. In 1999, the Bharatiya Janata Party [BJP] drafted a national slum policy that advocated removal of all "untenable" slums. The definition of what constituted an untenable slum was left out, leaving the forced eviction of slum dwellers open to political expediency. The situation is aggravated by the fact that neither central nor state planning functions have a focused strategy towards tackling the housing or land-related issues in cities. http://users.iafrica.com/i/if/ifasrech/fr/pimple.htm. Also see *Global Survey on Forced Evictions: Violations of Human Rights*, No. 9 [p. 44] Centre on Housing Rights and Evictions [April 2003] in this connection. http://www.cohre.org/downloads/survey9.pdf
4. See Prasenjit Maiti, "When Hunger Asks a Question: Food and Federal Politics in India." http://www.freeindiamedia.com/agriculture/3_feb_agri.htm
5. See Jan Garrett, "Justice: A Word with Many Meanings". The fundamental principle of distributive justice: In assignment of benefits and burdens, those who are equal in relevant ways should be treated equally, those who are unequal in relevant ways should be treated unequally in proportion to their inequality. http://www.wku.edu/~jan.garrett/ethics/justice.htm
6. *Ibid.*
7. See Garrett, "Rawls' Mature Theory of Social Justice". John Rawls is widely regarded as one of the most important political philosophers of the second half of the twentieth century. He is primarily known for his theory of justice as fairness, which develops principles of justice to govern a modern social order. Rawls' theory provides a framework that explains the significance, in a society assumed to consist of free and equal persons, of political and personal liberties, of equal opportunity, and cooperative arrangements that benefit the more and the less

advantaged members of society. Darrel Moellendorf writes that Rawls' conception of justice, like any conception of justice whatsoever, is an associational conception. It is about relationships between members of an association. Rawls' is chiefly concerned with the political association known as the modern nation-state. Moellendorf and other defenders of "cosmopolitan justice" apply the approach Rawls developed for the nation-state to the global community, which may be understood as an economic association even if there is no effective international political association. More may be said later about cosmopolitan justice. Here the important point is that Rawls' initial concern with justice is related to relationships between persons within an association. Rawls' theory urges us to conceive of society "as a fair system of cooperation over time, from one generation to the next." He says that "the . . . relationship of citizenship . . . [is] a relation of citizens within the basic structure of society, a structure we enter only by birth and exit only by death". http://www.wku.edu/~jan.garrett/ethics/matrawls.htm

8. See KEIP Background Information.
9. http://www.kolkatamunicipalcorporation.com/keip.html
10. Resettlement issues are also reviewed during environmental impact assessment [EIA], which is now required for selected Bank-financed projects. One of the criteria for a project to be classified under the Bank's environmental Category A, which includes projects with potentially significant adverse environmental impacts, is displacement of a large number of people. http://www.adb.org/Documents/Policies/Involuntary_Resettlement/default.asp
11. http://www.infochangeindia.org/HumanItop.jsp?section_idv=13
12. *Ibid.* The Omkareshwar dam project, one of a series of large dams on the River Narmada in the state of Madhya Pradesh, will flood 30 villages and 93 sq. miles of forest and farmland. According to papers seen by the *Guardian*, no impact study has been done and no resettlement plans have been finalized. The World Bank... [has] refused to finance Omkareshwar and other large dams on the river because of environmental and social concerns.... According to documents seen by the *Guardian*, the Indian government had asked Unit Trust of India and Barclays to help arrange the finance for the dam, to run over 14 years. http://www.innercitypress.org/icglobal.html
13. *Ibid.*
14. *Ibid.*
15. *Ibid.*
16. *Ibid.* One of the great humanitarian challenges is responding to the needs of internally displaced peoples [IDPs]. Worldwide, internally displaced people outnumber refugees two to one. As *Internally Displaced*

People: A Global Survey details in five regional profiles covering 48 countries, more than 25 million people have been displaced by conflict—but remain within the boundaries of their birth nation. http://www.culturalsurvival.org/publications/csq/csq_article.cfm?id=F2D75FCD-FF29-4C9C-AD08-20720C5E6425&region_id=10&subregion_id=0&issue_id=14

17. See *The Organizer* [LOCOA (Leaders and Organizers of Community Organization in Asia) Newsletter, Malaya Quezon City, Philippines]. http://www.locoa.net/news/Co-news-in-asis-1.htm
18. See "Taxpayers must foot rehabilitation bill: ADB". *Times News Network* [22 January, 2003]. http://timesofindia.indiatimes.com/articleshow/35054972.cms
19. http://www.keiponline.com/canal_improvement.htm
20. See KEIP Background Information.
21. See Kolkata Environmental Improvement Project [Rehabilitation of Lakes and Canals] Final Report [Egis Consulting Australia (January 2000)], Ch. 8 [Economic Analysis], p. 8.1.
22. See Ted Anana, "Struggling for Housing Rights in Asian Cities". http://www.hurights.or.jp/asia-pacific/no_34/02.htm Asian cities, rapidly growing, urbanizing and attracting more migrants from the rural areas, will continue to be the arena of the poor's struggle to assert their rights, including the right to adequate housing and the right to live in the city. The odds seem stacked against them. Organizing of communities, using whatever useful and effective methodologies and strategies, has to be pursued in order to create a massive force that governments cannot refuse to heed. This is supported by links with sympathetic people in the media, academe, and government, and support from other social movements. Spread out in most Asian cities, such a force can create a regional impact that can oblige governments, intergovernmental institutions and donors to heed the urban poor. *Ibid.* The author is the Coordinator of *Eviction Watch* [Quezon City, Philippines], a regional programme of the *Asian Coalition for Housing Rights.*
23. See "Displacement, Resettlement, Rehabilitation, Reparation and Development [as a result of dams]." http://www.eldis.org/static/DOC7649.htm
24. *Ibid.*
25. *Ibid.*
26. Maiti, "When Hunger Asks a Question", *op. cit.*
27. See "Resettlement Policy in India". http://www.his.com/~mesas/resindia.htm

28. See Marcus F. Franda, 'West Bengal', in Myron Weiner (ed), *State Politics in India*, Princeton University Press, Princeton, 1968, p. 249.
29. See Rajeev John George, "Kolkata Evictions". http://www.achr.net/impacts.htm The author is Convener of the Indore-based National Forum on Housing Rights—India. "Aftershocks is about the transformation of the Welfare State into an instrument of Corporate Governance. It examines the acquisition/displacement of two quake-affected villages for lignite mining and generation of electricity. It probes the microcosm in the nature of a study "from below" of Globalisation of Economy and Corporatisation of Democracy." http://southasia.net/talk/messages/1/1193.html?1029789423
30. http://www.adb.org/Documents/Policies/Involuntary Resettlement/reset400.asp
31. See Guidelines and Principles for Social Impact Assessment prepared by the Interorganizational Committee [United States Department of Commerce, National Oceanic and Atmospheric Administration & National Marine Fisheries Service] May 1994. http://www.nmfs.noaa.gov/sfa/social impact guide.htm
32. *Ibid.*
33. Source: *Involuntary Resettlement* [Manila: Asian Development Bank, November 1995].
34. In particular, the World Bank's approaches and operational directive on involuntary resettlement are generously drawn upon because of (i) the similarities between Bank and World Bank operations in Asia; and (ii) the World Bank's much longer experience, dating back to atleast 1980, with adopting and implementing involuntary resettlement policies that are particularly relevant to Asia . . . . Involuntary resettlement is a sensitive area involving competing economic, social and political interests that may be difficult to balance in the best of circumstances. Because the Asian Development Bank has limited knowledge of resettlement, lessons drawn from the experiences of Developing Member Countries and other agencies need to be considered when addressing the issues. Any proposed policy and planning principles should be introduced and implemented with sensitivity to the particular political, legal, economic, social and cultural contexts of a DMC. Such policies and principles should be revised and refined based on lessons learned. http://www.adb.org/Documents/Policies/Involuntary Resettlement/reset100.asp
35, See Maiti, "Silenced Rivers". Trust indicates a system of values; a system of values implies social mores; and social mores are themselves an important institution. So trust can, and often does, lead to the sustenance of institutions. http://www.india-seminar.com/2001/498/498%20comment.htm
36. See Introduction [Guidelines for Aid Agencies on Involuntary

Displacement and Resettlement in Development Projects] to Background Papers on Relocation [DFID Workshop, 26 May, 1998], p. 5.

37. See "Mainstreaming Sustainability? The World Bank and the Rehabilitation of the Indian Coal Sector" [Berne Declaration position paper (13 May, 1996)]. http://www.hartford-hwp.com/archives/52a/035.html
38. Almost every aspect of sustainable development will be affected by the quality of civil society, political participation and decision-making, and responsible and reliable governance. http://usembassy.state.gov/tokyo/wwwhgl0469.html
39. http://www.nmfs.noaa.gov/sfa/social_impact_guide.htm
40. The American Anthropological Association [AAA] Committee for Human Rights [CfHR] recently released a report on possible International Finance Corporation [IFC, a member of the World Bank Group] involvement in human rights abuses associated with hydroelectric dam development on the Biobío River in Chile [Johnston and Turner]. This report responded to a complaint filed with the CfHR by anthropologist. Theodore Downing, who charged that the IFC contributed to the ongoing violation of Pehuenche human rights. Many members of the Pehuenche, an indigenous group in Chile, are being forcibly resettled as a result of the recent construction of a dam on the Biobío River at Pangue, and efforts to build a second dam at Ralco, both located in Pehuenche territory. Downing's complaint denounced actions by the IFC [which financed the dam project]; ENDESA [Empresa Nacional de Electricidad S.A.], a Chilean-based transnational corporation; Empresa Electrica Pangue S.A. [Pangue S.A.], a limited liability subsidiary of ENDESA and the recipient of an IFC loan for the construction of the dams; and the Pehuen Foundation, set up by ENDESA in consultation with the IFC. The Chilean environmental and indigenous non-governmental organizations [NGOs] charged that ENDESA and the Pehuen Foundation had committed abuses against the indigenous Pehuenche Indians. Downing, who served IFC as an independent external consultant to investigate and report on these charges, alleged that ENDESA violated Pehuenche human rights with the knowledge, acquiescence and, in some cases, active collaboration of IFC personnel. He documented these violations in his report. IFC refused to release the report, and subsequently threatened to sue Downing if he made the report or any of his research findings available to the Pehuenche or to the public. In response, Downing charged that the IFC's actions constituted a violation of his rights and professional obligations as an anthropologist, whose participatory research methods required him to share his findings with the population he had studied. Downing's report contained documentation of extensive, unmitigated

damage resulting from deforestation of Pehuenche community lands, multiple confirmed threats of involuntary relocation, practices by the Pehuen Foundation that constitute a dramatic assault on the customs and cultural traditions of the Pehuenches, and actions to cover up vital information that would permit the discussion of alternatives to lessen the present and predictable cultural, economic and environmental damage. The Foundation itself was established as a result of secret negotiations between IFC and ENDESA on ways to mitigate the social impacts of the Pangue dam; it was restructured in further closed-door negotiations in April, 1997, so that it became an instrument facilitating Pehuenche resettlement to make way for the Ralco Dam. The absence of informed participation and lack of structural opportunity for such participation contributed crucially to the Foundation's subsequent failures to meet mandated goals. To investigate Downing's complaints, the CfHR consulted independent sources of information about the case, including World Bank staff, members from both the IFC and the IBRD [International Bank of Reconstruction and Development, the main member of the World Bank Group]. The CfHR held an open forum at the Association's Annual Meeting in November, 1997 where representatives of the IFC, the IBRD, Chilean sociologist Claudio Gonzalez Parra, and Downing spoke and responded to questions from members of the Committee and the Association at large. Committee members also met and spoke extensively with these and other people connected to the case. http://www.aaas.org/spp/sfrl/per/per13.htm

41. http://lnweb18.worldbank.org/ESSD/sdvext.nsf/65ByDocName/KeyConcepts
42. http://wbln0018.worldbank.org/Institutional/Manuals/OpManual.nsf/toc20F7D6F3F04DD70398525672C007D08ED? OpenDocument

2

DEVELOPMENT VERSUS DISPLACEMENT

> The World Commission on Dams report vindicates much of what dam critics have long argued. If the builders and funders of dams follow the recommendations of the WCD, the era of destructive dams should come to an end . . . . Had the planning process proposed by the WCD been followed in the past, many dams would not have been built.
>
> —Patrick McCully, Campaigns Director of the Berkeley, California-Based *International Rivers Network*, United States of America.

Key Words. Displacement, grand narratives, grass-roots activism, hegemony, high culture, indigenous, knowledge, majoritarianism, popular resistance, power, values.

Prologue

Development is more often than not a paradigm of choices and policy alternatives that is informed by the critical and tense relationship between the differences in perception among primary and secondary stakeholders.[1] Development is also an authoritative allocation of values [following David Easton] but in this case such values indicate statements of power that are underpinned by so-called "superior" knowledge discourses:

> The process of politics helps to identify people or institutions who make decisions that are binding on the society . . . [Government is]. A permanent Structure [institution] composed of decision makers who make society's rules about conflict resolution and the allocation of resources and who possess the power to enforce

> them . . . . Authority is the feature of a leader or an institution that compels obedience, usually because of ascribed legitimacy. For most societies government is the ultimate authority in the allocation of values . . . [Legitimacy is]. Status conferred by the people on the government officials, acts, and institutions through the belief that the government's actions are an appropriate use of power by a legally constituted governmental authority following correct decision-making policies. These actions are regarded as rightful and entitled to compliance and obedience on the part of the citizen.[2]

Simply put: the State and its planners are supposed to know best where and why and how and when and by whom dams should be built, highways constructed and bridges as well as railway tracks designed and similar developmental interventions planned as actors identified with the high culture of dominant politics:

> The proponents of the dam claim that this plan would provide large amounts of water and electricity, which are desperately required for the purposes of development. Opponents of the dam question the basic assumptions of the Narmada Valley Development Plan[3] and believe that its planning is unjust and iniquitous and the cost-benefit analysis is grossly inflated in favour of building the dams. It is well established that the plans rest on untrue and unfounded assumptions of hydrology and seismicity of the area and the construction is causing large-scale abuse of human rights and displacement of many poor and underprivileged communities. They also believe that water and energy can be provided to the people of the Narmada Valley, Gujarat and other regions through alternative technologies and planning processes, which can be socially just and economically and environmentally sustainable.[4]

These are only a few demonstrative cases but they all have one common feature: the utility of hegemonic [majoritarian?] decisions under no circumstances may be questioned, especially by the stakeholders [project-affected persons] who are doubly marginalized at the levels of politics and the economy.

Sardar Sarovar Project

The Government of India claims that the multi-purpose Sardar Sarovar Project would be able to irrigate more than 1.8 million hectares [mostly in Gujarat and some in Rajasthan in West India] and solve drinking water problems in drought-prone areas like Kutch and Saurashtra in Gujarat. The Sardar Sarovar Dam is the largest among the 30 large dams planned to be constructed on the Narmada River in Central and Western India.[5] This dam, with a proposed height of 136.5 meters [455 feet], has emerged in the not-so-recent past as the focal point of the Narmada Bachao Andolan's concerted activism, opposition and resistance.[6]

The NBA has steadfastly maintained that tall claims on the part of the government are exaggerated and untenable.[7] [The SSP would instead displace more than 3,20,000 persons and adversely affect the livelihood of innumerable others.] NBA activists have even estimated that a population of at least 1 million would be dislocated if the SSP were to be completed [as a result of displacements caused by the canal system and other allied projects]. Although CVJ Varma's conclusions on the basis of the actual performance [*karma*] of large dams in India can be questioned, the most eloquently describes the growing need for water and power in India, and concludes that it is the duty [*dharma*] of dams to meet these growing needs:

> In a recent report written by some of us for the World Commission on Dams ["Large Dams: India's Experience"], an exhaustive look at the facts and figures available establishes that until 1978 most dams were not assessed for their environmental and social impacts. Even when they began to be assessed, alternatives to the dam were never assessed and mostly not even considered. Also that the current system of granting environmental clearances is subject to all sorts of political and administrative pressures, resulting in clearances being granted to projects without assessing their impacts or even when they are

> non-viable. What is worse, the concerned ministry has little ability to ensure that the parameters and conditions of clearance are adhered to. In fact, they are disregarded and flouted as a rule. Perhaps the best indicator of how lightly the nation has taken the environmental and social damage that large dams cause is the absence of data on these aspects. We do not know what the environmental impacts of most dams were. In most cases we do not know whether any of the safeguards prescribed actually worked. We do not even know the total number of people displaced or the area of forests submerged by large dams.[8]

The NBA has been opposing this project for a decade now, and its activists sought to highlight demerits of the SSP during 1990-91 by employing statements of protest such as *dharnas* [sit-ins] and *satyagraha* [non-violent non-cooperation]. The World Bank [that was about to finance the dam for $450 million] was subsequently compelled to set up an independent review committee—the Morse Commission—the first of its kind. The Morse Report indicted the World Bank on many counts, and [tacitly] supported the major human ecological concerns raised by the NBA. Adverse international reaction that had followed the Morse Report finally decided the World Bank against financing the SSP.

The Supreme Court of India, the country's apex court, had suspended further construction of the dam in 1995, at a height of 80.3 meters, following a writ petition by the NBA demanding a comprehensive review of the SSP. However, the Supreme Court, in an interim order [February, 1999], had given the go-ahead for the dam's height to be raised to a height of 88 meters [85m + 3m of "humps"]. But this can lead to floods during the monsoon season, displacing 2000 tribal households in about 50 villages.

The Judgment

The Supreme Court finally delivered judgment on the SSP on 18 October, 2000: it permitted immediate construction of the dam up to a height of 90 meters [in a 2 to 1 majority judgment]. The judgment further authorized construction up to the originally planned height of 138 meters in 5 meter increments, subject to approval by the Relief and Rehabilitation Subgroup of the Narmada Control Authority.

The Supreme Court's judgment has not fundamentally altered the Narmada Water Disputes Tribunal Award that had earlier decided that land should be made available to the dispossessed at least a year in advance before submergence [Clause IX, Subclauses IV[2][iv] and IV[6][i]. The Supreme Court's clearance of the SSP, moreover, has not been able to resolve critical issues involved, such as cost-benefit analyses of development-induced displacement [especially in the context of India's postcolonial democracy[9]], rehabilitation of project-affected persons and assertion of their idiom of social justice, grass-roots [dis]empowerment and the rhetoric of environmental and human ecological problems:[10]

> Postcolonial theory promotes ways of seeing and thinking that could make for a world of greater environmental and social justice. Exposing the colonization of people and nature as being reciprocally supportive processes identifies a base camp for further study and possibilities for resistance. As well, postcolonialist ideas can be a source of empowerment for colonized, marginalized, and oppressed peoples.
>
> These perspectives show us that today's 'environmental discourses', although "radical" to the mainstream, are not radical enough. Discourses are not fixed; they shape us as we simultaneously affect them. Critical thinking about and deconstruction of these is liberating. Recognizing and contesting our own individual and collective complicities is a radical, constructive act.[11]

The Supreme Court judgment 2000 stands violated as the governments are all out to commit contempt of the court order for full resettlement before any increase in the height of the Sardar Sarovar dam. It was the electoral gimmick of Narmada which Modi used and Uma Bharti supported that resulted in the Narmada Control Authority, more an engineer's body than a multi-disciplinary monitoring body, permitting the raise in the height of Sardar Sarovar dam to 110.64 meters. With about 1,500 families in Maharashtra and 10,000 families in M.P. still living in the Sardar Sarovar Project-100 meters affected region, such a decision was an inhuman conspiracy against the people of the Valley. Narmada Sagar too was pushed to its attained height of 245 meters, without following a single legal process leave aside rehabilitation, by the Narmada Hydropower Corporation and the State Corporate Powers.

In the case of the giant plan of "harnessing Narmada waters", it is now obvious the projects are flawed with distorted economics and without caring and compensating for environmental destruction, despite fake reports on compensatory afforestation. Moreover, even at the present height, both the dams will not bring any water benefit to Madhya Pradesh or Maharashtra. Sardar Sarovar, at the cost of human disaster will produce not more than 30 MW of power in seasons with water stock available.

The Debate

This chapter makes an attempt to study the NBA as an important social movement in present-day India. We prefer to argue that big river dams are informed by a certain definition of development that is intellectually hegemonized by the compulsions of globalization in the absence of indigenous negotiations and critical engagements with the dynamics of market forces that—by definition—foster inequality and thrive on the unevenness of international development that is [arguably] a skewed construct. Such a definition may not only reorient our notion[s] with regard to what constitutes sustainable development[12] but may also reorient our developmentalist worldviews:

> More and more attention is being paid to sustainable districts in recent years, the question being how sustainable development and management can be achieved, not only with regard to buildings but also in relation to complete neighbourhoods. The aim is to combine satisfactory environmental performance with high levels of liveability in neighbourhoods where people live, work and recreate with pleasure.[13]

This is—therefore—an exercise in the politics of subversion of knowledge that ought to be first challenged and next resisted by alternative vision[s] of public action and development underpinned by civil societal initiatives in the context of unequal exchanges and an as-yet-unjust North-South dialogue [as is evident in the USA's ever-expanding anti-Business Process Outsourcing lobby *vis-a-vis* India's call centres and medical transcription sector just before the American Presidential Elections of 2004]:[14]

> In view of the very fact that there is hardly any voluntary organisation in Madhya Pradesh which is active or even prepared to work effectively in the area of Rehabilitation & Resettlement of the Project-Affected Families, the State Government has formulated a four-tier system so as to ensure participation of NGOs for the work of rehabilitation & resettlement. They are [i] village-level consisting of 5 members from the oustees of each village coming under submergence, [ii] each such village has a Punarwas Sathi amongst the oustees, [iii] one Punarwas Sahayak has also been appointed on an honorarium basis of Rs. 750 per month for a group of 5 to 8 villages and [iv] similarly, there is also a provision to appoint, if necessary, a social worker from the specific area who may or may not be from amongst the oustees on an honorarium of Rs. 2,000 per month for each of the Rehabilitation Officer Zones. At the same time, the State Government has constituted the District and Tehsil level Advisory Committee to advise the administration on matters of rehabilitation of oustees. These committees include local MLAs and MPs and other elected members of Panchayats.[15]

According to the World Commission on Dams [22 March, 2000], India is second only to China in terms of population [1 billion] and dam building, with 4291 dams. Irrigation is the primary or only function of 96 per cent of the dams; only 4.2 per cent were built for hydropower generation. Estimates of the number of people displaced by large dams in India range from 21 to 40 million.

Ensuring food security is one of the main objectives of India's development policy. Its irrigation potential increased from 22.6 million hectares in 1951 to 89.6 million hectares by

1997 and food production grew fourfold to 200 million tonnes, two-thirds of the increase coming from irrigated land. However, analysis of the costs and benefits of dams in India is hampered by a lack of post-construction assessment:[16]

> The internationalization of the Narmada Bachao Andolan, or Save Narmada Movement, has had a great impact on India's state sovereignty. <http://www.geocities.com/CapitolHill/6027/State.html> International environmental NGOs, such as Oxfam, the Environmental Defense Fund and the International Rivers Network, took advantage of the porous nature of the state's territorial and national borders. International actors intervened in the domestic affairs of the Indian state and built up the fire of the Save the Narmada Movement. The NGOs took part in enormous amounts of information exchange, proving that the state is unable to maintain "absolute control over territorial borders." Also, these interactions caused new, transnational identities to be formed, eroding the state identity. Thus state sovereignty was compromised as a result of the internationalization of the Narmada Bachao Andolan.[17]

"Damn the Dams"

The global debate about large dams is at once complex and simple. It is complex because the issues are not confined to the design, construction and operation of dams themselves but embrace the range of social, environmental and political choices on which primary stakeholders' aspirations to development and enhanced well-being depend. Dams fundamentally alter the character of rivers and the use of natural resources and more often than not entail a redistribution of benefits from local-level users to new groups of beneficiaries at a regional or national-level. At the heart of the dams-specific debate are issues of equity, good governance, justice and power—issues that underlie the many intractable problems faced by humanity.

We also argue in this paper that the very logic of globalization cannot be always reconciled with the institutions and imperatives of democratic politics. However, globalization can, and actually does, facilitate a certain kind of development that is more often than not biased in favour of the North rather than the South. Globalization, therefore, entails a paradox of sorts: its dynamics require an enabling exercise of good governance characterized by democratic freedom, rule of law, civil liberties and human rights while the Structural Adjustment Programmes[18] of globalization may erode the popular bases of government.

We would also try to identify and highlight certain angularities[19] of the movement, and develop a few insights that may be located beyond the texts of conventional subaltern critiquing and Strengths, Weaknesses, Opportunities, Threats analyses. Let us first recount the facts and figures, and subsequently develop and substantiate our argument[s] during the course of this exercise:

> The March 6 judgment punished Arundhati Roy for having criticised the judgment given by Justices Pattanaik and Ruma Pal on August 28, 2001 on another contempt case against her. A petition filed by five lawyers had alleged that Arundhati Roy, senior lawyer Prashant Bhushan and Narmada Bachao Andolan [NBA] leader Medha Patkar shouted abusive slogans against the Court during a protest demonstration by the NBA outside the Court premises on December 13, 2000. Justices Pattanaik and Ruma Pal dismissed the charges against the three but found Arundhati Roy *prima facie* guilty of contempt of court for having made certain "derogatory" averments in her affidavit.
>
> In her affidavit, Arundhati Roy had criticised the Court for displaying "a disturbing willingness to issue notice," on the basis of "an absurd, despicable, and entirely unsubstantiated petition," to her, Medha Patkar and Prashant Bhushan, who "happen to be people who have publicly . . . questioned the policies of the government and severely criticised a recent judgment of the Supreme Court" in the Sardar Sarovar Case. Arundhati Roy had inferred in her affidavit that the notice indicated "a disquieting inclination on the part of the Court to silence criticism and muzzle dissent, to harass and intimidate those who disagree with it." The affidavit drew this

conclusion: "By entertaining a petition based on an FIR that even a local police station does not see fit to act upon, the Supreme Court is doing its own reputation and credibility considerable harm."

The Court issued a *suo motu* notice to Arundhati Roy in this connection. In response, Arundhati Roy filed an affidavit denying that she had attributed any improper motive to any particular Judge and refuting the allegation that she had "scandalised" the authority of the judiciary. The notice was issued on the basis of a misreading of her first affidavit, she said. She had also stated that she could not be persuaded to change her impressions about the Court because the Court had neither ordered an inquiry into the functioning of the Registry to find out how a grossly defective petition against her was admitted, nor taken action against the petitioners for filing a false case.

In their judgment, Justices Pattanaik and Sethi said that they had no option but to convict her because she had committed the offence of criminal contempt of the Court by "scandalising its authority with *mala fide* intentions" and, further, had not shown "any repentance or remorse." Instead, they said, she had persistently and consistently tried to justify her action which, *prima facie*, was contemptuous of the Court. The Judges did not address her grievance about the Court's failure to order an inquiry into the role of the Registry and to take action against the petitioners. Many informed observers said that the judgment only vindicated Arundhati Roy's observation in her affidavit: "a disquieting inclination on the part of the Court to silence criticism and muzzle dissent, to harass and intimidate those who disagree with it."

In explaining why they had no option but to convict Arundhati Roy, the Judges expansively cited two factors on top of the lack of remorse on her part that explained why she had "landed herself in the dock of the court." The first factor was that she "drifted away from the path on which she was traversing by contributing to the Art and Literature." The second factor was that she had

> "resorted to all legal tactics and pretences" [*sic*] to frustrate the present proceedings against her. Even a critic of Arundhati Roy would find it difficult to believe how these factors had any bearing on her conviction for criminal contempt of court.[20]

Construction of large dams on the River Narmada in Central and Western India, and its disastrous impact on millions of people inhabiting this river valley have emerged as one of the most controversial socio-ecological issues in contemporary India.

NGOs and other activist groups such as the Friends of River Narmada, an international coalition of volunteer individuals and organizations [primarily of Indian descent], provide a support and solidarity network for the Narmada Bachao Andolan. They communicate grass-roots viewpoints to the global community through dedicated websites in order to generate debates on whether the SSP [and such similar projects] should be allowed to continue or not in the larger interests of human ecology and sustainable development.

The Indian State, however, has never really been able to reciprocate any similar grass-roots level dialogue, and has even treated the SSP as an exercise in pragmatic politics [realpolitik?] that would focus on cost-benefit analyses in terms of an authoritative definition of development.[21] The State's intransigent attitude is yet to be entirely overhauled despite the President of India's [implicit] criticism of his own government on 6 December, 2000 during presentation of the Ambedkar International Award for Social Change to environmental activist Baba Amte.

Whither Indian Democracy?

Political participation in India has been transformed in many ways since the 1960s. New social groups have entered the political arena and begun to use their political resources to reshape the political process. Scheduled Castes and Scheduled Tribes, earlier excluded from politics because of their position at the bottom of India's social hierarchy, have begun to take advantage of the opportunities presented by

India's democracy. Women and environmentalists constitute new political categories while the spread of social movements and voluntary organizations has shown that despite the difficulties of India's political parties and state institutions, the country's federal democracy continues to prosper.

The issue of distribution of responsibilities and powers in federal political systems is generally contentious. India, for instance, is a quasi-federal democracy where the federal dialogue with the states is more often than not predicated by the Union Government's administrative/policy-level decisions *i.e.* the Centre decides on a particular course and only thereafter seeks input from the states. In today's coalition politics, regional powerbrokers are able to chip away at this imbalance. As a result, Centre-State relations are often marked by confrontation, and efforts to create a more cooperative process are needed.

Recently, state governments reached a consensus with the Government of India with regard to imposition of President's Rule in the states vide Article 356 of the Constitution of India related to emergency provisions. During a meeting of the Inter-State Council at Srinagar in Jammu & Kashmir it was decided that checks and balances would be exercised *vis-a-vis* Article 356, made infamous during Prime Minister Indira Gandhi's one-party rule, as follows:

1. The Union Government will henceforth impose Article 356 as a weapon of last resort to dislodge the elected government in a state following breakdown of constitutional machinery therein when all the possible avenues of federal dynamics have been explored and resources of federal solutions to set up an alternative administration exhausted.
2. Article 356 will not be imposed in an indiscriminate manner. Its use shall be rule-bound and guided by constitutional conventions in order to safeguard India's federal democratic ethos.
3. The concerned state government will have to be duly notified/alerted well in advance that such a contingent situation may arise in the near future so that corrective steps may be taken and remedial measures adopted.

4. The notification of President's Rule will be subject to prior approval/ratification by the Lok Sabha and Rajya Sabha of the Union Parliament. This was earlier suggested by the Supreme Court of India in one of its judgments.
5. The Government of India will explain the rationale of President's Rule in its notification issued in this connection by the President of India.
6. The reasons behind imposition of President's Rule will also be explained in detail in the concerned Governor's recommendation report submitted to the Union Government.[22]

An important aspect of this rise of civil society is the expansion of non-governmental organizations. To an extent, this has been sponsored by the Indian State. For instance, Central Government's Seventh Five-Year Plan [1985-89] recognized the contribution of NGOs in facilitating development and consequently substantially raised their funding. The 1987 survey of 1273 NGOs found that 47 per cent received funding from the Central Government. NGOs have also received overseas donations. Certain NGOs even cooperate with the Central Government to implement public policies, such as poverty alleviation in a decentralized manner. Other NGOs like the Association for Protection of Democratic Rights or the People's Union for Civil Liberties act as watchdogs of India's civil society. NGOs also try to enhance the political awareness of different social groups, encouraging them to demand their rights and resist social injustice.

Beginning in the 1970s, activists began to form broad-based social movements that championed social interests so long neglected by the state and political parties. A case in point: the farmers' movement that organized hundreds of thousands of demonstrators in the National Capital Territory of New Delhi, demanding higher prices on agricultural commodities and more investment in rural areas. Members of Scheduled Castes led by the Dalit Panthers have reasserted the identity of former Untouchables. Women now interact and exchange ideas in order to define and promote women's issues. Environmental activism such as the Narmada Bachao Andolan has also emerged, compelling the government to be more responsive to environmental issues and redefining the problematics of development, displacement and democracy through the accommodation of indigenous cultures and sustainable development.

With its competitive elections, relatively independent judiciary, media watch and civil society, India continues as a democratic federal system. Still, India's democracy is under stress. Political power within the Indian state has become centralized at a time when India's civil society has become mobilized along the country's multicultural axes. India's political parties are also in crisis. The Indian National Congress has been in a state of decline. The Bharatiya Janata Party, although it has a stronger party organization, is yet to transcend the limits of its Hindu nationalist agenda and formulate a programme that would appeal to India's plural society. The Janata Dal continues to suffer from lack of leadership and factional warfare.

Thus the expansion of India's civil society has made Indians less certain of the federal state's powers of transformation and more confident of the power of the individual and local community. This development has shifted a larger share of the initiative for resolving India's social problems from the state to the civil society. Fashioning party and state institutions that would accommodate the multiple interests that are now being mobilized in Indian society is the major challenge confronting Indian federal polity in the new millennium.[23]

Symbolic Interactionism

Observations of Keshav Bhai, an *adivasi* [tribal] NBA activist from Nimgavan village in the state of Maharashtra in Western India, in conversation with fellow activists, are rather significant. We come to realize that indigenous ways of tackling problems are occasionally better suited for sustainable development rather than solutions imposed from the above by what we generally prefer to address as "rational" modernity:

Savita: How were things in the village before the dam?

Keshav Bhai: We didn't have much interaction with the city. We used to farm for a living, we had Mother Narmada for water, the forests used to provide us with wood and various kinds of fruits. We used to grow grain on the farm that would last the whole year. Most of the farming was on the Narmada flood plains [after the rains and after the waters had receded]. It was easy to farm here since the land was flat and there was not much clearing to be done. We did some farming near the huts, too.

Savita: Were all these mountains covered by forests?

Keshav Bhai: Yes, 30 years back this place was covered with dense forests. The forests were destroyed about 10-15 years back. I will explain why that happened. Before the forests were destroyed we used to cut small portions for farming. But the jungle was not our enemy; after all, we are forest people. We used to cut very few trees.

Aravinda: Were the forests there in 1980?

Keshav Bhai: Yes, they were there. The forests started disappearing around 1988-90.

Aravinda: When the surveyors came what was the reaction of the villagers?

Keshav Bhai: The surveyors told us that when the dam is built we would be compensated land for land, house for house. We would be provided with education and other amenities. The dam was being built in Jalsindhi. I used to work for that project. After three years, Morarji Desai, who was the then Prime Minister, came and told us that there were a lot of dams being planned on Narmada. I didn't know that. The one in Jalsindhi was by the governments of Maharashtra and Madhya Pradesh, and would be submerged by the SSP project in Gujarat. So they halted the construction of the dam in Jalsindhi after sinking crores [ten million] of rupees [USD 1 = INR 45 approximately]. He told us that the SSP was for the future generations, for the nation. Gujarat needs a lot of water and electricity. He promised to compensate us with flat land, nice houses and a lot of money. We were happy at that time.

Aravinda: You believed the government then?

Keshav Bhai: Yes, we did. Around 1985, the Bagul committee was here to survey the land and determine how much loss each person would incur in terms of land and other property. We have been in possession of this land for generations. And we wanted this land to be registered by the officials. The officials were using this to exploit us. The government had sent about 50 officers. This turned out to be very expensive for us because we had to host these people. These people demanded that we provide them with chicken and alcohol. The village had to provide them with about 10-12 chickens and 4-5 pots of alcohol everyday. They also extorted money from us. If anyone in the village had to get their land or house registered they would have to pay Rs. 50. They would also force us to sell our goats and cattle. They would make us sell a goat for Rs. 50 when the market value of the goat was Rs. 800. Medha Patkar and Vasudha Digambar arrived on the scene around this time. We placed our issues before them. Medhatai and others took photographs of these officials when they were drunk. This scared the officials enough to pack their bags and leave. We started getting organized. We decided not to feed these people with chicken and alcohol, even if they didn't do the survey. We also stopped paying forest officers. Villagers from different villages started to get organized. Maharashtra has about 33 villages that would be submerged by the dam. We figured that if we approached the government as a group then they would listen to us. The government was afraid now. We asked the government to show us the land for compensating 33 villages in Maharashtra. We organized district level meetings with government officials every three months. There were about eight representatives from each village. But nothing happened even after three years of negotiations.

Aravinda: A lot of people still believe that if you are compensated adequately then you can make progress. What do you say?

Keshav Bhai: We do not believe that development for us is possible through displacement and compensation. People have been leaving their land since 1992. The government has been sending the displaced people to faraway places like Sholapur and Gujarat. One of our demands was that we be relocated close to our villages. We do not want to lose our roots. The government tried to compensate us with land close by, but there were a lot of problems. The provided land was often fragmented. If a person were to receive five acres, he would get three acres in one village and two acres in another. We do not want that. In the Fatehpur Amda village, the compensation officer pleaded with us to look at the land. So we went with him. The land looked good, but I noticed that there were some banana and sugarcane planted already. We went to the people living in nearby huts [who were also *adivasis*], and asked about these plants. They told us the bananas belonged to them and the sugarcanes belonged to a neighbour. We explained to them about the Sardar Sarovar Project and told them the government was going to be using this land [their land] for compensation. They told us there would be a big fight if that happened. The compensation officer was not happy with what we did. He did not want us to talk to these people. The story was the same wherever the government tried to find land for compensation. We told the government we would not go to Guajrat because we do not speak the language there. We are from Maharashtra and we wanted to be compensated here. Once the Andolan started we refused all government officials from entering our village for 2-3 years, excepting the doctor [who came to the village only once a year, anyway]. The government wanted to break the Andolan badly, and sent the police [on the pretext of surveying the land] to harass the people. The cops killed a 15-year-old lad on 19 November, 1993.

Savita: By *lathi* [baton] charge?

Keshav Bhai: No, he was killed by a bullet. We organized a march along with thousands of people on 22 November to protest against the killing. The police attacked us with *lathis,* and injured about 300-400 persons who had to be admitted to the hospital. Some persons had their arms broken while some had their legs broken. People were scared and were considering compensation again. Earlier we had made demands for some forestland. This caught the attention of Sharad Pawar who was the then Chief Minister of Maharashtra. He got approval of 2,700 hectares of forestland. Pawar came to the district meeting and told us: "We are satisfying all your demands. You wanted forestland. And here we are approving 2,700 acres of forest land for you." We had agreed, but how many people would be accommodated on only 2,700 hectares of land? The government's response was that everyone would have to be accommodated on this land. And was this land meant for agriculture or housing? It was not clear. We earlier claimed that at least 10,000 hectares would be required to compensate the 33 villages in Maharashtra. The government returned with another 1,500 hectares next year, but the villages would now be split with only 4,200 acres. Moreover, we wanted 10,000 hectares of forestland [without the forests having to be destroyed]. We wanted all these questions to be answered before the dam was built. We started protesting at this point in different places like Mumbai and Delhi. There was a big protest in Harsukh against the SSP.

Aravinda: How many people were there?

Keshav Bhai: There were lakhs [one hundred thousand] of people. We announced that the SSP represents *vinash* [destruction] and not *vikas* [progress]. It had to be stopped. In Pherkua we protested for 36 days. There were 10,000 policemen; we were 10,000 ourselves and there were 10,000 people hired by the Gujarat government [who were paid daily by the government]. Nothing happened even after 36 days. . . . We took a resolution that we would not be allowing any government officials into our village. We carried out several such protests. The government started using new tactics during this time. The collector in this district at the time, a man called Gill, was quite ruthless. He came to the villages and started tempting persons one by one. The government officials were now telling the villagers that "*adivasis* would go to heaven" if they accepted compensation. They were now tempting people with stories of *adivasis* who have made it rich after compensation. Gill tried to buy me with Rs. 1 lakh, a big house and a fat salary. But I did not budge. I was in Manivilli for the *satyagraha*. He followed me there and tried hard to break me. I started telling everyone that Gill is a thief looting the *adivasis*. This was embarrassing for Gill since there was a World Bank official in the area at that time. Gill is himself with the World Bank, drawing a salary of Rs. 50,000 per month because of his work in the Narmada Valley! We were always afraid that once *adivasis* are relocated close to cities they would be destroyed. This was evident from the story of the *adivasis* displaced by the dams on the Tapti. Our fears turned out to be true. Money was never important for *adivasis*. But once people were relocated close to cities with five acres of land, they could not survive. They would sell their lands for money and then blow their money away. Let me give you an example from this village: I used to know this family. They used to live here together, they used to spend a lot of time with me. They accepted compensation from the government and were relocated to Amli village. But they could not survive there. Their money was spent in a year. Then they sold some of the wood they had. They finally sold their land. What would they do now? A lot of people who accepted compensation are selling their lands now. We have been thinking for the last 2-3 years. The dam will make our lives difficult here and accepting compensation is also difficult. We have approached the government asking for solutions. The people from Gujarat started making attempts to destroy our villages when we started opposing the dam in 1987. *Dalals* [middlemen] started coming from Gujarat telling the villagers they would buy the Sagwan wood from our forests. People sold their trees for a few hundred rupees and the *dalals* made crores from the wood.

Savita: Was all of this area covered with Sagwan forests back then?

Keshav Bhai: Yes, the forests stretched till Manivilli about 80-100 kilometers away. And everything got destroyed. We tried hard to protect them. We didn't have a chance. These people from Gujarat were threatening us: "Why are you opposing the dam? Why don't you let us cut the trees? We will beat you up if you oppose us." After the Andolan gained strength, we started protecting whatever that has remained. We have stopped the destruction of the forests.

Savita: Are you planting trees? Are you regenerating the forests?

Keshav Bhai: No, there is no need to plant trees. All you need to do is protect the land. The government is planting a lot of trees, but all the trees in the plantation are dying. The government is wasting crores of rupees. If you protect the land, the forests will come back. For example, a couple of years back the villagers from Seldah accepted their compensation and left their village. There is dense forest full of wild animals in Seldah now. The land is very fertile here; the forest will grow back.[24]

While we are not convinced with the treatment of present-day narratives as a collection of so-called grand narratives, we are also not always in consonance with the politics-from-below point of view that tends to examine contemporary social activism and public action as an absolute discourse in terms of black and white.

We cannot, therefore, afford to discuss our categories of analysis in straitjacketed terms such as either the subaltern or the élite. We are not quite comfortable with such categories, and would rather interrogate these in order to explore other in-between areas of our research.

This is why we do not want to examine the marginalized subaltern as someone who is bereft of any further paraphernalia of identity. There are intra-subaltern strife and tension, problems of sustaining a workable stock of social capital[25] within the subaltern ranks and file. Moreover, can we at all afford to look at the subaltern as a class or should we rather focus on a neoinstitutional [actor-oriented] argument that has to be located within the framework of postcolonial India's politics of State repression and displacement?

It is thus clear by now that the judgment on Sardar Sarovar Project by the court of law permits further construction [of the dam] that which will lead to forcible eviction and destitution through flooding of houses and lands, without rehabilitation of a few thousand families. The judgment thus has paved the way for violation of right to life and livelihood of innocent toiling masses and integrated natural resource-based communities. Will it not be a violation of the Constitution itself?

The judgment on the dam is then symbolic of both: the court's supporting violation of the Constitution against the common people from disadvantaged sections of society and judgments [such as the ones in Bhopal Gas tragedy, Enron and Niyogi murder] based on misinformation due to outdated, inadequate processes and procedures to appraise the complex reality. While the judiciary is one of the four pillars of democracy, the time has come to recognize that peoples' movements constituted by civil society organizations cohere an additional fifth one that may even assume the role of influencing the judiciary, its value framework, its anti-people biases and bringing in not just judicial reforms but a virtual revolution.[26]

Social Semiotics

When added to the English intellectual's need to explain the ideological aspect of the class experience they had drawn upon, the work of Louis Althusser provided a different and effective way of characterising the mechanisms which validated institutional *inaction* in the face of political conditions which demanded some kind of mass response. In brief outline, and without doing his work the justice it deserves, what Althusser set out to do was to make some sense of the way in which a formally revolutionary organization like the French Communist Party could have so radically misread the conditions leading up to and accompanying the Paris revolt of 1968.

Drawing on notions first elaborated in the 1930s by Antonio Gramsci [1971], Althusser adapted structuralism to account for the evolution of the apathetic mindset displayed by the working class in relation to the stand taken by the students. This also served to explain the failure of the formal Left to recognise the revolutionary potential in the situation. What emerged was a highly abstract theory of ideological organization that drew on aspects of Gramsci's notion of *hegemony* and on the linguistically founded psychoanalysis of Jacques Lacan.

In Althusser's account, the individual is "interpellated" or *named* into a specific ideological niche through the agency of *Ideological State Apparatuses* [ISAs]. These would include the Church, School, family, bureaucracy and other social institutions. The individual's relationships with these are such that she or he acts in society as if these are the natural way of doing things, and it is relative to these that a person "imagines" a place in the world. Thus, given a set of relations to the institutional ISAs in one's life, as enumerated above, so one will develop this imaginary relationship with all the other institutions and persons of society. In ideological terms, this is said to come about without a person ever necessarily becoming conscious of the mode of production reproduced through the concrete economic character of these institutions.[27]

Subalternism: Development from Below?

Battles of everyday life are sometimes best resolved with the help of organic resources. But subaltern actors are often without the *permission to* narrate[28] and are, as a result, almost inevitably relegated to the margins of an élitist grand narrative that is empowered by superior [?] knowledge of the material conditions of existence.[29] This contention of ours is corroborated by the *International Rivers Network* which has listed 30 "unsafe dams" in India on their website.[30]

Activist Shripad Dharmadhikary has itemized the movement's *alternative* agenda so that civil societal engagements can effectively resist implementation of the State's *developmentalist* agenda:

1. The NBA would try to involve all aspects of the civil society;
2. The NBA envisions the issue [in hand] as much larger than fights over a specific project . . . the NBA is a coalition that challenges development philosophy, supports 'right to life', and challenges power/energy policy;
3. The coalition works to mobilize locally affected people;
4. The coalition demands local rights to fisheries;
5. The NBA would take steps toward decommissioning/removal of dams;
6. The coalition advocates re-operation/partial decommissioning to free land for people who have not been resettled;
7. Dam decommissioning is the next logical step as part of a spectrum from re-operation to decommissioning;
8. Experiences with decommissioning would help change mindsets;
9. It is important to share information and debate issues.[31]

The Narmada Bachao Andolan has been non-violent, but certainly assertive. It has sought to innovate, sharpen and widen the means of non-violent *satyagraha*, which otherwise had become a routine affair, often ineffective *vis-a-vis* India's postcolonial political arrangements.

Like every movement, the Narmada Bachao Andolan has developed its own means, idioms and worldview for the purpose of spreading and sharpening the issues at stake. According to Seetaram Kaka of Kadmal village in Nimad, who has been a key activist:

> The movement has changed our lives. Now we cannot see anyone being exploited, anyone [unfairly] amassing wealth. We immediately question him, take his extra *rotis*

[bread] and give to one who has nothing! Now, even suppose we were displaced, this new vision will be with us and we can devise our own ways. We can speak what others cannot. Women in *adivasi* areas and in the conservative society of Nimad have been in the forefront of the struggle against the dam. They question and argue with the officials and police; and they lead the rallies and meetings. Assertive tribal women like Jadikaki, Dedlibai, Khiali, Pinjaribai, Pervibai and Geeta; and from Nimad: Rukmini kaki and Kamala didi along with numerous young girls and women, have all been in the forefront of the movement. They mobilize villages, speak in urban and semi-urban places, and have gone to jails and faced police beatings. Though caste differences do not arise in the tribal regions, this has traditionally created social tensions and a wide gap among the [non-tribal] village communities of Nimad. However, through involvement in the Andolan, and the churning of joint struggle, the caste system of discrimination has been steadily weakening. The Andolan has been a stimulus, too, for the hidden, creative capacities of the people. The *bhajan mandali* of Jalkheda, the puppet troops of Pipri youths, the *gayanas* [songs] and the dances of the tribal regions, have all been parts of the movement, strengthening one another. A wonderful chemistry is at work here, with the young people, both boys and girls, the activists and supporters of various castes and backgrounds collaborating and generating new comradeship.[32]

So when do people at the grass-roots finally begin to identify themselves with their *own* institutions? This can only happen when they are compelled to de-identify themselves with the state's agencies [of coercion] that have been *mai baap* [parents][33] to them, as in India, since time immemorial.

Institutions: Politics from Above?

Popular institutions serve as indices to assess the quality of grass-roots activism. Such institutions, moreover, have a proclivity to become somewhat indispensable as their networks expand and become increasingly detailed in terms of organization; their levels of encompassment and embeddedness in the everyday politics at the grass-roots rise accordingly.

The role of social trust and networks of cooperation in the context of such decentralized governance is rather vital. As Confucius had once remarked that trust is the single most important factor in the political lives of men.[34] Trust leads to social bonds and intra- as well as inter-institutional connectedness, and this actually coheres institutions, so to say.

Trust indicates a system of values; a system of values implies social mores; and social mores are themselves an important institution. So trust can, and often does, lead to the sustenance of institutions. Neoinstitutionalism as a dominant frame of reference in present-day political sociology serves to explain the reality of governance or even the lack of it. It introduces a fresh way of looking at and handling institutions.

For what are institutions but formal agencies and domains of human interaction? And is not the problem of governance really a problem of interaction in its primary sense, a problem of interface involving both the state and its civil society/societies?[35]

If rules are the accepted [and expected modes] of behaviour, then institutions are the facilitating channels that help socialize such behaviour. Theorists such as Douglass C. North, Robert D. Putnam and Subrata K. Mitra have developed this neoinstitutionalist paradigm.[36]

Neoinstitutionalism—in order to understand this baffling phenomenon of good governance[37]—deals with actors *and* institutions as well as actors *in* institutions. Governance derives from an able handling of institutions. Actors who function through institutions tend to make a lot of difference as to how such institutions perform.

The kind of legitimacy and politics of ecology that we have in mind here would ideally emerge from real life, indigenous knowledge and intimate culture root paradigms of everyday life. We cannot deny the fact that institutions are necessary. But what are social institutions other than interactive arrangements of power that are best evolved indigenously?[38] Institutions are:

1. A collective mode of behaviour,
2. A matrix that sustains popular action and imagination,
3. An integrating dynamic, and
4. A procedural and regulatory imperative within a political system.

But this is not encouraged so far as environmentalist values of the establishment in India are concerned. We have to also remind ourselves that democratic political systems are required to grapple with adaptation, goal attainment, integration and latent pattern maintenance. Mitra has cautioned that "if the wielders of power concede the point to those who challenge established values and norms, they risk losing their legitimacy. On the other hand, the failure to give satisfaction to the discontented might deepen their sense of outrage and alienation which can further reduce their legitimacy."[39]

> We need to protect nature for our very survival. To do this we first need to know the ways of nature, both in general and in the given climatic condition of one's habitat, in particular. The grasp of nature's technology gives the conviction that working in harmony with nature yields far greater dividends than application of force or violating her laws. It also provides clues to processes promoting less expensive, sustainable development and universally shared prosperity.
>
> Unfortunately what dominates is the opposite approach—of managing and *controlling* nature before even trying to know her ways of working. Virtually all "developmental" activities organised by the state and elite lead to destruction of natural systems—the energy use pattern, choice of technologies for generating the predominant forms of energy, 'modernist' farming technologies, high-entropy-energy-based industrial and transport systems, and resource-depleting architectural patterns. Yet, for each of

these there are eco-friendly and sustainable though less glamorous alternatives.[40]

Our neoinstitutional argument is also supported by rational choice analysis that suggests that any democratic regime[41] would legitimately prefer entrenchments of its own power and authority rather than problems of governance. This, however, prompts an essential cost-benefit analysis, namely what amount of political investment to establish pro-people, responsive institutions at the grass-roots would yield good governance?

Users and Actors of Development	Identification with Pro-Poor Actors	Institutions of Public Action	Arrangement of Social Realities	Social Capital as the Rhetoric of Development
Resource-Driven Development	Sustainability in terms of Pro-People Growth	Empowerment as Growth and Human Capital Development	Environment-Savvy Tools & Indigenous Techniques	Communitarianism in order to sustain the real gains of development
Participatory Clientele	Livelihoods of Beneficiaries	Rights and Values	Human Ecology	Embeddedness of Human Capacities
Politics of Development	Well-being of Stakeholders	Material Conditions of Life	Civil Society Networks	Entrenchment of Institutions and Values and Norms

Model 1: Ponderables of Development

It is often difficult to measure the impact of social and economic well-being of the recipients of development *i.e.*, those who are located at the receiving end of the critical and multifaceted processes of development.

The above model demonstrates the tension between different ponderables of development *i.e.*, how best can primary stakeholders resolve the dilemma of development versus displacement in the context of democracy that in itself is ostensibly a political commitment to cater to majoritarian agenda and informed choices and enlightened priorities.

A liberal democratic regime like India's can be politically *successful* and thereby continue in power if it is able to properly read its ground realities and problems thereof. These problems are more or less popular in nature, and have a propensity to develop into discontent of the ruled actors against their ruling institutions. So the actors in power have to redress these grievances of the actors at the grass-roots in a political manner by effectively establishing and handling pro-people institutions.[42] Only then organic identification would bind actors with institutions; only then the incipient involvement noticed at the level of "actors and institutions" would, arguably, transcend itself to the level of "actors in institutions", consolidating both the level and the quality of environmental/ ecological governance in this process.

Epilogue

We may revisit the ideas raised in this chapter in the light of major environmental developments and disasters that took place in India since then such as super cyclones, earthquakes, forest fires, flash floods, deforestation and siltation of rivers, leading to adverse impacts *vis-a-vis* the environment at large: extreme summers and winters and lack of rainfall during the onset of the official monsoon season.

Sustainable urban development concentrates on ways of developing and managing in a sustainable way. Different accents are placed—in one project, one specific sustainability aspect is analysed and advice given on improvements in *e.g.*, energy performance, greenery in the neighbourhood or use of materials. In another project, the total performance package regarding the environment and quality of living of a neighbourhood is subjected to a complete analysis.

Let us consider former Prime Minister Atal Behari Vajpayee's grandiose plan to join the length and breadth of India by road and river networks: all the major rivers of the country should be joined so that resources may be equitably shared by all. This happens to be an environmentalist's nightmare for obvious reasons.

India's General Elections 2004 has raised certain fundamental inquiries with regard to the country's future planned and projected agenda of development: the electorate has voted both the National Democratic Alliance at New Delhi as well as Chief Minister Chandrababu Naidu at Hyderabad out of power on the ground [according to media analyses] that development in terms of the services and financial sectors does not always augur well for the average unknown citizen at large.

So was the so-called feel good factor a product of media overkill and hype triggered by an over-ambitious political propaganda machinery? We have to understand such a problematic issue while posited in the larger context of development as an antipode of democracy. For instance in South East Asia where even after the stock exchange crisis a policy framework sustained by Asian Values has established the fact that development may very well be achieved in real terms without the vestiges of representative and decentralized/delegated democracy as we understand the notion in India.

Many of India's environmental problems arise from attempts to meet the basic needs of its enormous population for food and energy . . . India is faced with the following environmental problem areas. [1] Water resources are in short supply in regions such as the Deccan Plateau due to dry seasons and the lack of adequate storage facilities. In addition, poor surface water irrigation has resulted in waterlogging and water loss, while some areas experience annual flooding periods. Domestic waste and runoff containing pesticides and fertilizers have contributed to water pollution. Ground water problems include overpumping, salinity, and pollution due to seepage from fertilizers and pesticides. [2] Soil damage has occurred in 20% of India's soils through the presence of salinity and alkalinity, acidity, waterlogging, cracking, and erosion. [3] During the past 20 years, 4.0 million hectares have been deforested—in a country that had 74.9 million hectares of forest area in 1978. Continued recession of India's forests is due to clearing, fuel needs, fires, and grazing. [4] Great loss of wildlife has occurred due to urban and rural encroachment; there exist 25 endangered species. [5] Fisheries have been overexploited. [6] Coastal zones have experienced sea erosion and marine pollution. [7] Air pollution is most pronounced in urban centers, although rural regions have been subjected to similar problems as a result of the burning of wood and dung.[43]

Conclusion

So we are brought back to square one: is the development versus displacement debate in the context of liberal democracies in reality situated at the site of another critical debate between the stakeholders of development versus the beneficiaries of development?[44]

We may conclude that development is necessarily an open-ended process that emerges from chaos and polemics while delegation and decentralization of the effects of such development may not always be entirely unplanned.

What we now increasingly recognize as the participatory mode of development is nothing but a dialogue between primary and secondary stakeholders facilitated by consultative processes of distribution, dissemination, devolution and exchange of ideas with regard to the maximum benefits that may accrue to the project-affected people at large.

But such deliberations informed by the larger perspective of displacement require to be located in the context of a democratic culture in order to exert their impact so as to be efficacious in a utilitarian manner.

Development entails planning ahead so as to capture fleeting realities and moving targets: it also predicates field-level extrapolations that may coordinate fluid politics and erratic priorities of the material conditions of everyday life.

NOTES

1. This chapter is an updated version of Prasenjit Maiti, "'Till the Rivers All Run Dry': A Human Ecological Analysis of the Narmada Bachao Andolan," *Electronic Green Journal*, Issue 14 [Spring 2001 (Earthday)], University of Idaho Library. http://egj.lib.uidaho.edu/egj14/maiti1.html A brief version of this paper is also available as "Silenced Rivers" [*Seminar* 498 (2001), New Delhi]. http://www.india-seminar.com/2001/498/498%20comment.htm
2. http://vms.cc.wmich.edu/~rogers/psci200/out2Society.html
3. http://www.narmada.org/nvdp.dams/index.html

4. See "A Brief Introduction to the Narmada Issue". http://www.narmada.org/introduction.html
5. Sources include dedicated websites on the Narmada Bachao Andolan. The author is grateful to Susanne Wong of the *International Rivers Network* and Subramanya Sastry of the Baroda, Gujarat-based *Narmada Bachao Andolan* among other activists and academics for their kind cooperation helped facilitate his research. Narmada literally means Endower of Bliss. See Sanjay Sangvai, *The River and Life: Story of the Narmada Bachao Andolan* [Mumbai: Earthcare Books, 2000], p. 9 in this regard. Also see Kuntala Lahiri-Dutt, "Imagining Rivers", *Economic and Political Weekly* [1-7 July, 2000].
6. Save the Narmada Movement. The NBA, established in 1989, is a coalition of environmental and human rights activists, scientists, academics and project-affected persons working to resist the Narmada Valley Development Project. The NBA is also trying to compel the government to empty the partially filled reservoir of the Sardar Sarovar Dam. See the NBA Press Release by Medha Patkar ["Increasing Narmada Waters Submerges Maharashtra Villages: Tribals Forcibly Displaced Without Resettlement"]: As the increasing submergence waters of the Narmada entered the Maharashtra villages affected by the Sardar Sarovar Project, the state government sent police to displace the people forcibly and demolished their houses, without resettling them according to the law. The people in the Chimalkhedi have been resisting attempts by the police to break their backs and the struggle. The floodwaters have been increasing since Saturday [26 July, 2003], due to the increased dam height of 100 meters, at alarming proportions, and there are indications that the submergence level will increase further due to the release of 1,05,000 cusecs water from the upstream Tawa dam. Water level at dam site on 26th midnight was 100.29 mts. On Saturday afternoon at 15:00 hours 13 gates of Tawa dams were opened at 5 feet level, which means roughly after 30 hours the increased water flow will be reached at Sardar Sarovar Dam site. On 27 July, morning, the discharge from Tawa was 1,50,000 cusecs. The water has submerged, and the first villages of Maharashtra have been marooned and the people have been forcibly displaced. Village Chimalkhedi got marooned, becoming an island. In the morning of 27 July, the police along with hired labourers from Kevadiya Colony demolished the houses in the village. They tried to bribe Noorji, a young activist of the Andolan, promising him Project-Affected Family status and asking him to make people bow down to the pressures and shift. Noorji refused it strongly and said that until the land for land based rehabilitation is extended to all the affected, he will keep fighting tirelessly. By noon, the police demolished Dharamsingh's home. While this action was going on, people resisted this brutal attack, staying

non-violent. The police also let their cattle loose on their fields. Subsequently they arrested all the people from the village, who resisted and thwarted attempts of the police to take them away in a barge. Their belongings were seized and removed from their homes and taken to the tinsheds, the silver coloured "relief" camps. In the evening, all were released with a threat that they would have to move as the waters are going to rise dangerously within the next few hours. It is yet another instance and evidence, if that was needed, to show that the governments have conspired to force submergence and thereby the displacement on the people without any proper and lawful resettlement. As the floodwater is going to increase there will be more submergence and destitution. We consider that Maharashtra and Madhya Pradesh governments, along with the adamant Gujarat and Central governments, have deliberately precipitated the crisis to make the people flee away, without any responsibility to resettle them. We make it clear that the governments just cannot get away from their responsibility and task. People in the Narmada Valley will be resisting all the attempts to make the people destitute and helpless like the displaced people from other dams in the state and country. The Government of India and Maharashtra and Madhya Pradesh will have to answer to the people of Narmada Valley and from the country at large for this terrorism on its own people. http://www.narmada.org/nba-press-releases/july-2003/flooding.html. Also refer to another NBA Press Release dated 2 July, 2004 ["Narmada Submergence and Displacement: Unprecedented Human Tragedy, Challenge for New Government"] by Ashish Mandloi and Medha Patkar in this connection: The people in the Narmada Valley, struggling for the last 19 years are facing an expected yet unprecedented attack by the State which imposes nothing but destitution. This is obvious from the situation in two of the 30 big dams in the Narmada Valley: Narmada Sagar, in which the township of Harsud with a population of 22,000 is being forcibly evicted, while in the Sardar Sarovar, at least 150 affected villages in Madhya Pradesh, Maharashtra and Gujarat are going to be flooded this monsoon. http://www.oneworld.net/external/?url=http%3A%2F%2F www.narmada.org %2Fnba-press-releases%2Fjuly-2004%2Ftragedy.html

7. According to MS Patel, Secretary of Narmada [water resources and water supply], Government of Gujarat, the total cropped area for kharif season in Saurashtra is 4 million hectares. At present, water for irrigation is being provided by 113 dams for 0.3 million hectares. Even after the Sardar Sarovar Project is implemented, 0.4-0.5 million hectares would be irrigated. Therefore, 3.15 million hectares would still be dependent on rain. Therefore, even Narmada water cannot solve the problem. However, with the small structures in Saurashtra, villages would have

water for irrigation and drinking. *Op. cit.* http://egj.lib.uidaho.edu/egj14/maiti1.html

8. CVJ Varma. "Reservoirs for the Future: The Dharma of Dams". *Indian Express* [23 October, 2000]. Also see Shekhar Singh, "The Karma of Dams", *Indian Express* [25 October, 2000] in this connection.
9. See Aswini K. Ray, "Democratic Rights in a Post-Colonial Democracy", *Agora Project Working Papers* [Uppsala: University of Uppsala, 1996], pp. 101-12; and Ray, "Towards the Concept of a Post-Colonial Democracy: A Schematic View", in Zoya Hasan, S.N. Jha and Rasheeduddin Khan [eds], *The State, Political Processes and Identity: Reflections on Modern India* [New Delhi: Sage, 1989], pp. 127-49. Also see Prasanta Ray, *Conflict and State: Exploration in the Behaviour of the Post-Colonial State in India* [Kolkata: Sarat Book House, 1991], pp. 97-98.
10. See Ramaswamy R. Iyer, "A Judgment of Grave Import" [27 October, 2000]. http://www.narmada.org/sardar-sarovar/sc.ruling/iyer.article.html
11. See Stephen Hui, "De/colonizing Nature: Postcolonialist and Ecofeminist Perspectives on Human-Environment Relations". http://www.aquapulse.net/knowledge/nature
12. That tends to reconcile present demands with projected demands *i.e.*, natural resources cannot possibly be depleted only in order to cater to the present generation's requirements. Development should always be in motion so that it is able to focus ahead on moving targets of changed perceptions and priorities of a changed clientele.
13. http://www.ivambv.uva.nl/uk/werkvelden/werkveld6.htm
14. The United States of America had long since banned import of Kashmiri carpets on the pretext that these involved child labour and violated the enlightened American worldview of human rights. The USA—however—can afford to abuse democracy and human rights in Central Asia and still legitimize its politics of aggression.
15. See "People's Participation in R&R." http://www.mp.nic.in/nvda/people.htm
16. *Cf.* "A few state governments in India have of late waged a war of attrition with the Union Government over the contentious issue of providing cooked mid-day meals to underprivileged primary school children. This is primarily a central government-funded public welfare scheme where the center provides uncooked cereals [and transportation of foodgrains] free of cost. However, 'cash-strapped' state governments plead inability to provide cooked meals to children in the below poverty level category, and seek to provide uncooked cereals instead [that too on an irregular basis], although it costs about Re. 1 per child per day to

provide cooked meals for the stipulated 200 days a year." See Maiti, "Food Fight over Hunger". http://www.indiatogether.org/2003/mar/chi-hunger.htm

17. See "International Environmental NGOs and the Save the Narmada Movement". http://www.geocities.com/CapitolHill/6027/Narmada.html
18. Craig Gary and Marjorie Mayo [eds], *Community Empowerment: A Reader in Participation and Development* [London: Zed Books, 1995].
19. Social scientist Ramachandra Guha had written an article in *The Hindu* on 26 November, 2000, attacking novelist-turned-environmentalist Arundhati Roy for her stance *vis-à-vis* the Narmada Bachao Andolan. Guha concluded his article accordingly: "I am told that Arundhati Roy has written a very good novel. Perhaps she should begin another. Her retreat from activism would—to use a term from economics—be a Pareto optimum: good for literature and good for the Indian environmental movement." *The Hindu* published 30 letters on 17 December: 22 supported Guha while 8 expressed reservations. Interestingly enough, 20 out of the 22 pro-Guha letters were from men, a majority among whom happen to be academically distinguished, even holding doctorates. Of the remaining 8 letters, 5 were by women and only 3 by men. The author wishes to thank S. Ravi Rajan, Assistant Professor of Environmental Studies at the University of California, Santa Cruz, USA for this information.
20. See V. Venkatesan, "Of criticism and contempt". *Frontline*, Vol. 19, Issue 6, 16-29 March, 2002. http://www.flonnet.com/fl1906/19060270.htm
21. That differs from an *alternative* model of organic development [which takes into account grass-roots uplift in real terms].
22. See Maiti, "New Federal Roadmaps". http://www.indiatogether.org/2003/dec/opi-roadmap.htm
23. See http://www.e11th-hour.org/security/india.society.html
24. Excerpts from an interview with Keshav Bhai by Savita Kini and L.S. Aravinda of the NBA [during early 2000]. Transcript by Girish Bhat. Adapted by the author. See the website of the *Friends of River Narmada* http://www.narmada.org/ in this connection.
25. See James S. Coleman, *Foundations of Social Theory* [Cambridge, MA: Harvard University Press, 1994], p. 304.
26. See Rajesh Tandon, "Grass-roots Democracy", *Seminar* [March 1997], p. 39.
27. http://www.und.ac.za/und/ccms/socialsemiotics/designating.htm
28. See Gayatri Chakravorty Spivak, "Can the Subaltern Speak?" in Bill

Ashcroft, Gareth Griffiths, and Helen Tiffin [eds], *The Post-Colonial Studies Reader* [London: Routledge, 1995], pp. 24-28.

29. See Barry Smart, *Michel Foucault* [Chichester, England: Ellis Horwood, 1985]. Michel Foucault has demystified power. Foucault's analysis states that power is situated among a cacophony of social practices and situations. The discourses within these social formations are manifested in an economy of discourse. For Foucault then, power is directly tied into the economy of discourse itself . . . power can be transmitted along more sporadically. When someone asserts a statement, it becomes "power" when someone else [the other] takes the statement as "true." Power is not tangible, but rather depends on this economy of discourse . . . . Much criticism for Power/Knowledge is based on Foucault's assumptions about "truth" and its constituents. Foucault considers all knowledge arbitrary, including notions of truth, in order to keep power structures relevant and functioning. http://www.colostate.edu/Depts/Speech/rccs/theory54.htm

30. http://www.irn.org/

31. At the International Dam Decommissioning Strategy Workshop, Walker Creek Ranch, Petaluma, California, organized by River Revival: International Campaign for River Restoration and Dam Decommissioning [23-25 July, 1998].

32. See Sangvai, *op. cit.*, pp. 122-27.

33. *Cf.* Partha Chatterjee, "Agrarian Relations and Communalism in Bengal, 1926-1935", in Ranajit Guha [ed], *Subaltern Studies: Writings on South Asian History and Society* [Delhi: Oxford University Press, 1982], pp. 9-38. "But movements acquire their various ascriptive statuses, according to [Partha] Chatterjee, by virtue of an inner dynamic of cohesion; this reminds me of the process of identity formation that is so very important in the context of organizing and mobilizing social movements. We find Partha Chatterjee's 'perceptual distance' quite interesting since it draws us to the inevitable conclusion that the Indian crowds before and at independence were merely the other that was not at all hospitably incorporated into the principal format of the elite-dominated Indian national liberal movement or even the process of building the Indian State Nation. This distance was both real in terms of everyday politics as well as perceived in the sense of being deprived, even marginalised, from the momentous process of decision-making that eventually shaped the future of Indian polity. It is true that without a sense of identity a popular movement cannot even begin properly, let alone sustain itself over time. Such an identity is like a reference point that decides the level of efficacy of any particular movement. We would argue here that whenever the Indian crowds tried to identify themselves with any issue or institution, they were generally

manipulated by their elite leaders and diversified into channels of an abhorrent otherness." http://www.postcolonialweb.org/india/roy/maiti11.html

34. The author is grateful to Professor Thomas Fleiner, Director of the Institute of Federalism, University of Fribourg, Switzerland for this insight.
35. The author wishes to thank Professor Lidija R. Basta Fleiner, Director of the International Research and Consulting Centre of the Institute of Federalism, Fribourg, for this exposition.
36. See—in this regard—Subrata K. Mitra, "Legitimacy, Governance and Political Institutions in India after Independence," in Mitra and Dietmar Rothermund [eds], *Legitimacy and Conflict in South Asia* [New Delhi: Manohar, 1997]; Douglass C. North, *Institutions, Institutional Change and Economic Performance* [Cambridge: Cambridge University Press, 1990]; and Robert D. Putnam, Robert Leonardi and Raffaella Nanetti, *Making Democracy Work: Civic Traditions in Modern Italy* [Princeton, New Jersey: Princeton University Press, 1993].
37. That is indicative of accountability and transparency in the administration as well as a responsive and responsible government. See James G. March and Johan P. Olsen, *Democratic Governance* [New York: Free Press, 1995], in this regard.
38. Coleman, *op. cit.*, p. 114.
39. Mitra, *op. cit.*, p. 23.
40. See Sailendra Nath Ghosh, "Fundamentals of Nature Protection". http://www.india-seminar.com/2000/493/493%20comment.htm
41. *Cf.* Atul Kohli, *Democracy and Discontent: India's Growing Crisis of Governability* [Cambridge: Cambridge University Press, 1991]; Kohli, *The State and Poverty in India: The Politics of Reform* [Cambridge: Cambridge University Press, 1987], p. 29; and Kohli and Amrita Basu [eds], *Community Conflicts and The State in India* [Delhi: Oxford University Press, 1998].
42. *Cf.* Ali A. Mazrui, "The Frankenstein State and Uneven Sovereignty", in D.L. Sheth and Ashis Nandy [eds], *The Multiverse of Democracy: Essays in Honour of Rajni Kothari* [New Delhi: Sage, 1996]. Also see Maiti, *Problems of Governance in India since Independence: The Bengal Success Story* [New Delhi: Vedams, 2002].
43. http://www.wri.org/wdces/in80_104.html
44. *Cf.* R.N. Sharma, "The politics of urban space": In ideal typical terms, then, we may suggest that different types of economic policies correspond to different types of political arrangements. While social investment tends to be associated with corporate policy-making at national or regional levels of government, social consumption tends to

> be associated with competitive political struggles waged at the local level. Urban struggles develop around questions of social consumption; the corollary of this is that they are typically isolated from the labour movement and strategically limited in their objectives . . . . A strong emphasis is put on conflicts in the urban area revolving around new issues of consumption of collective goods such as education, health, public transportation and other services provided by the state and local authorities. This provision of collective goods by the state and its agencies opens up the eventuality of new inequalities and new class struggle. http://www.india-seminar.com/2000/491/491%20r.n.%20sharma.htm

3

GLOBALIZATION VERSUS GLOBALIZATION

> Fifty per cent of the world's hungry live in five countries: India, Bangladesh, Nigeria, Pakistan and Indonesia. Though we have heard these facts many times over, most of us can neither fathom the sufferings of the underprivileged, nor can we grasp the difficulties faced by millions of such people, barely clinging on to their lives.
>
> —Ronald Anil Fernandes, Paramount Welfare Educational Trust, Bangalore, Karnataka, India.

Key Words. Capacity-building, consumerism, discourse, global, human rights, hunger, *laissez-faire*, local, malnutrition, mode of production, public action, trade barriers.

Disquieting Debates[1]

We may increasingly appreciate nowadays that globalization is not only about processes but also about mechanisms that impact our daily lives and the manner in which we would prefer our lives to be impacted upon. This contention may appear to be somewhat irreverent and irrelevant but is merited with a certain quality of objectivity as well.

Consider the following: I am global as you are global while my practices may be local as your very own practices are also local. This is indicative of a tension that may not be resolved at the level of preconceived semantics, as the reality we happen to negotiate on a regular basis is informed by different fluxes.

So the nuances and criticalities of existence become all the more difficult to negotiate while rooted in one single destiny conditioned by one given and preordained order of values. We require more values and non-values in order to cohabit with more meanings and more non-meanings. So it is merely all about conjoining abstract signifiers with concrete signifieds as the fashionable glocal way of life.

We argue in this chapter that contemporary processes of globalization do not only happen to constitute polemic engagements with *laissez-faire* utopianism because of the political specifics available in the First as well as in the Third Worlds but that most of the benefits of globalization also accrue to the First World because of its dominant policy to resist *laissez-faire* market arrangements in the movement of goods and services and labour forces around the world—especially into its domain—and its sustained opposition to the norms laid down by the Washington Consensus.

The dynamics of globalization are more often than not perverted by the First World's studied reluctance to apply identical standards of *laissez-faire* to its borders and imports that it tries—with varying degrees of success—to impose on the Third World's legal structures and political arrangements. Only recently has the European Union agreed to discontinue subsidies extended to the agricultural sector of its member countries after the historic fiasco at the World Trade Organization ministerial-level meeting at Cancun.

New global bodies such as the World Social Forum have also emerged in the recent years to meaningfully negotiate with the World Economic Forum and its politics of hegemony that extends to identities, cultures, languages, material conditions of life, ethnicity, social baggages, epistemology [knowledge] and ontology [existence].

A Third World country like India may emulate the People's Republic of China so far as effective negotiations with globalizing processes are concerned. Like it or not, globalization is here to stay as an entrenched omnipresent phenomenon. So it should be customized to local needs, aspirations and ascriptions as far as feasible as one has always to bargain from one's relative position of strength.

Contemporary State mechanisms bent upon the compulsions of globalization may be compared to the double-faced Janus: they appear to pose virile facades in the rich and developed North while they also assume defeatist faces in the Less Developed Countries of the South [for *e.g.*: G8 vs. G88/OECD vs. SAARC].

The reality of globalization—therefore—necessitates a dialogue between the rich and the poor in the context of its essentialist homogenizing and/or exclusionary assumptions of an uneven power discourse as specters of Good Governance and Structural Adjustment Programmes [Gary and Mayo, 1995] haunt most Third World postcolonial democracies [Ray, 1989 and 1996], today.

While there are arguments that profiteering market forces make it difficult for welfarist governments to protect their citizens from transnational actors that are as elusive as their hot money [Rapley, 1996], there are also counter-arguments that institutions such as the International Monetary Fund, the World Bank or even the World Trade Organization actually protect citizens against the administrative lacunae of their concerned national governments [Keohane, 1998].

So the question is: should we approach globalization as the guest or the ghost *vis-a-vis* the State [the host]? This is in continuation of Jacques Derrida's hospitality theory. Globalization in fact appears to be a permanent fixture in the polyphonetic carnival of the present-day marketplaces of politics [following Mikhail Bakhtin].

There appears to be a consensus—however—that powerful markets tend to increasingly undermine political élites at home [Barber, 1996; Cox, 1993; McGrew, 1992; and Slater, 1996], while they also imperatively add financial muscle to MNCs/transnational corporates headquartered in the West.[2] But does this also suggest that national governments have been so thoroughly undermined today that the so-called Global Village[3] can eventually replace the State?[4] This means that we would finally move from reality to virtuality as netizens and not as citizens.

Globalization has been described [Kegley Jr. and Wittkopf, 1997: 249], as the "intensification of economic, political and cultural relations across borders" that is noticed in the following pieces of evidence: the average daily turnover in foreign exchange increased from $200 billion in the mid-1980s to approximately $1.2 trillion in 1996; net capital flows to developing countries grew from an annual average of $44 billion for the period 1983-88 to $197 billion in 1996; and Foreign Direct Investment increased from $10 billion to $91 billion [Echeverri-Gent, 1997].

However, it has also been noticed [Lee, 1996: 382] that "the worldwide gap between the rich and the poor has become a vast chasm. Both within and between countries, the rich grow richer at the expense of the poor." Lee adds that the share of income of the poorest 20 per cent of the global population has fallen from 2.3 to 1.4 per cent in the last 30 years while the share of the richest 20 per cent of the global population has increased from 70 to 85 per cent. More than 1 billion people live in countries where the average per capita income fell between 1980 and 1993.

Lee has even quoted the United Nations Development Programme administrator, Gustave Speth, who maintains that if the world continues down its current path, "economic disparities between industrial and developing nations will move from inequitable to inhuman."

John Echeverri-Gent [1997] has pointed out that if globalization, on the one hand, facilitates decentralization then, on the other, it also helps develop pockets of dynamic Free Trade Areas in large developing countries like China and India by reorganizing their economic geography, Foreign Direct Investments and global commodity chains. This process, however, creates large hinterlands of economic backwardness and entrenches economic inequality *within* the developing South. Globalization, therefore, intensifies regional disparities in the Third World.

John Rapley [1996] has found that Structural Adjustment Programmes have varied widely in the results they have yielded. While Latin America has partially benefited from structural adjustment, Africa has generally not been able to do. Rapley has also argued that Rolling Back the State *i.e.*, less government [as an imperative of contemporary globalization] does not always lead to enhanced economic growth.

Globalization, therefore, would appear to be an open-ended journey toward a globalized world order whose *weightless* economy [Huws, 1999: 32] may be described as one that defies both national and international borders so far as economic transactions are concerned. This is a situation where freight charges are nil and trade/tariff barriers are on their veritable way out.

Such a pilgrim's progress, however, is nothing new. Technological innovations during the past five centuries have steadily helped integrate the global community into an emergent global civil society. Transatlantic communications have developed from sailing boats to steamships, to the telegraph, the telephone, the commercial aircraft and now the Internet where even nationalism as a conventional political ideology has been reduced to an able rhetoric of "banal nationalism" [Billig, 1995].

The usual markers of national identity [for *e.g.*: ethnicity, language and physical locations] are conveniently appropriated by the Internet while at other times such benchmarks may not be so usurped, especially in Asian cultures where even the Internet is made to conform to the subtexts of cultural specifics against the backdrop of metanarratives called civilizations.

So a new basket of identities has developed and been deployed both in deliberate nationalism [what Michael Billig describes as "flag-waving"] and as everyday background noise. Billig uses this term to describe "the ideological habits which enable the established nations of the West to be reproduced." His primary example is the ubiquity of the American flag, with which he illustrates the methods by which "national identity in established nations is remembered because it is embedded in routines of life, which constantly remind, or 'flag', nationhood." However, he points out, it is precisely because these reminders are not consciously noticed [and thereby opened to questioning or interpretation] that they are powerful.

The so-called Internet Revolution is indicative of the hegemonistic battles waged on a daily basis around the world with reference to critical discourses of production, consumption, distribution and exchange. The World Wide Web was originally designed as a virtual space to permit efficacious and intuitive transfer of data across an array of proprietary networks.

Tim Berners-Lee [1996], who engineered the World Wide Web in 1990, writes that a goal of the Web was that if the interaction between person and hypertext could be so intuitive that the machine-readable information space gave an accurate representation of the state of people's thoughts, interactions and work patterns, then machine analysis could become a very powerful management tool, seeing patterns in our work and facilitating our working together through the typical problems which be set the management of large organizations.

It remains a fact that one of the steering imperatives behind the creation of the World Wide Web was productivity. With the privatization of the Internet backbone in 1991 and the one millionth dot com registration in 1997, the Web finally erupted as a virtual marketplace—not of information as former American Vice-President Al Gore conceived of it in 1993—but of products and services.

The power/knowledge discourse [following Michel Foucault] of the Internet hinges upon a negation of consumption as constitutive of production that [as Baudrillard (1995) has argued] is not coherent in a social system that constructs subjectivity on the post-postmodern assumptions of consumption. In his "On Consumer Society" Baudrillard subverts the traditional dichotomy of production versus consumption as follows:

> The truth is not that "needs are the fruits of production," by that the system of needs is the product of the system of production, which is a quite different matter. By a

> system of needs we mean to imply that needs are not produced one at a time, in relation to their respective objects. Needs are produced as a force of consumption, and as a general potential reserve within the larger framework of productive forces. [p. 201]

By positing consumption within the more general idiom of need and then assuming this as fundamental to the growth and development of a single economic system, Baudrillard makes it all but impossible to comprehend production and consumption as antipodal realities and consumption as being the localized consummation of a single need by the consuming subject [Kellner, 1989: 17].

Need, the motivation to consume, is the inherent subjective reaction triggered by capitalist societies. Preempting the World Wide Web, Baudrillard explicates a definitive space of consumption, the drugstore, to argue for the utopian specifics of modern capitalism within which the subject is defined as a consumer:

> The drugstore is the synthesis of profusion and calculation. The drugstore [or the new shopping malls] makes possible the synthesis of all consumer activities, not least of which are shopping, flirting with objects, idle wandering, and all the permutations of these. [p. 193]

Baudrillard indicates that in the process of conversion of commodities from objects of monetary exchange to objects of semiotic exchange, these spaces of consumption unite aspects of consuming subjectivity that were once marginal, perhaps even resistant to, the commonplace activities of consumption [p. 194].

In effect, Baudrillard contends that the subjective experience of consumption cannot be segregated from the general experience of everyday life, which Henri Lefebvre [1984] maintains is nothing less than the reproduction of capitalist relations of production [p. 86].

"Recreational uses of the medium, manifested in the form of nondirected search behaviour, can be an important benefit to consumers intrinsically motivated to use the medium"

[Hoffman, Novak and Chatterjee, 1995]. The differences intrinsic to a consumer's subjective experience of a shopping mall or a drugstore and that of the World Wide Web may be negligible while the "browsing" metaphor deployed to access the Web suggests this to be the case in point.

So arguing from Baudrillard's analytical point of view we find that the discourse of production that underpins both the analysis of the productivity paradox and Berners-Lee's description of the World Wide Web are founded upon institutional attempts to overhaul this subjective reaction in the direction of an almost fanatical self-abnegation of consumption praxes through the enforcement of hypertextual binaries.

The history of capitalist societies proves that such redefinitions worked earlier because the actual spaces within which production and consumption were traditionally located were themselves discrete spaces—individual consumption was held in abeyance by the very logical architecture of the capitalist mode of production:

> One of the primary motivations of capitalist production is the consumption of the individual worker's labour power, the only commodity whose "use creates value, a greater value than it costs". [Marx, 1990: 342]

To the extent that consumption takes place at all within the space of capitalist production, it happens as a result of the contractual obligation each individual worker enters into at the point of sale of his or her labour power. "If the worker consumes his disposable time for himself, he robs the capitalist" [Marx, 1990: 342].

But States have not ostensibly lost their importance and even Third World governments' capacities to tax and redistribute incomes, control their domestic economies and hegemonize civil societal activities have expanded in a significant manner [Aziz and Arnold, 1996].

This is notwithstanding the fact that "In any corrupt regime people enjoy the benefits of bypassing the government regulation. Under-reporting of income leads to tax savings which helps both the taxpayer and the assigning official who receives a bribe. But, this is not an unmixed blessing. In a society where corrupt officials can wield power of coercion and harassment, people are forced to pay bribe to avoid problems. Thus corruption entails benefits as well as cost" [Marjit *et al.*, 1999: 23].

However, the present-day transition of State efficacy—from welfarism to good governance—may be explained in terms of a paradigm shift that can even lead to deinstitutionalization of State apparatuses in postcolonial democracies as the conventional manner of looking at the Welfare State [as a sponsor of nation-building (Kothari, 1976) and State-Citizen interfaces] is subverted in the process.

James Manor [1996: 8-9] confirms that "In recent years, many Western aid and development agencies have increasingly emphasised the need to promote 'good government' in their programmes . . . . Many scholars . . . regard 'good government' agenda and the conditionality that goes with them as an example of latter day imperialism. Many also worry that some of these agenda entail considerable hypocrisy on the part of Western funders . . . . The contents of some 'good government' agenda are rather curious. Some place enormous stress on the need for market forces to predominate, which is not everyone's idea of 'good government'. Some mix that emphasis and pressure to enact structural adjustment programmes with pressure for democratization, decentralization, respect for human rights, legal reform, poverty alleviation, transparency and accountability. There is a degree of dissonance between some of these varied elements . . . . Capitalism requires the existence of state institutions, no matter how many free marketeers loosely claim that what it most needs is the disappearance of government. As economic liberalization proceeds, there is a greater need for contract law and for judicial and executive institutions to ensure that it actually makes an impact."

Globalization also involves a certain paradox—it requires good governance underpinned by Structural Adjustment Programmes that can, however, erode the popular bases of democratic governance [March and Olsen, 1995], and lead to collapse of entire regimes.

Malcolm Waters [1995: 99-101] points out that "In the third quarter of the twentieth century the corporate welfare state hit a multiple and widely recognized crisis . . . . The response to this multiple crisis was a process of disétatization or state-weakening . . . . State intervention by command was reduced but at the same time states sought to increase the scope and scale of the market. Many government services were opened to competitive tendering between the public and private sectors and, as is well-known, many state-owned industries were returned to the private sector. Many states stopped providing welfare in certain areas . . . . The crisis of the state contributes to the reflexivity of globalization."[5]

Globalization, therefore, would increasingly come across as the transition of world capitalism from one stage to another, safeguarding investments of global capital in this process. Globalization also increasingly requires disinvestment, prompting Anthony Giddens [1995: 140-41] to argue that "The relation between the decline of the welfare state and the changing character of the global order of states was to some extent masked by the very political successes of the New Right. The neoliberals led the attack on the 'overloaded' welfare state in the name of freedom of competitive enterprise from bureaucratic burdens and from enfeebled labour markets. Simultaneously, however, they not only defended the state and nation but called for a 'strong state' in the international arena. The paradoxical character of this position was soon noted by critics, and corresponded to the wider paradoxes of New Right political theory . . . ."

In *Millenial Dreams: Contemporary Culture and Capital in the North,* Paul Smith [1997] argues that while the economic imperative of capitalism, the realization of profit through the expropriation of surplus value from the worker, is no different than in Marx's time, what has changed is the "rhetorical and ideological situation" within which capitalism operates [p. 13].

Smith's historical demarcation is the collapse of socialist political regimes in Eastern Europe, the moment at which capitalism in the North apparently won its battle royale for comprehensive hegemony. According to Smith, the ideological and political institutions of post-Soviet capitalism function as having reached the pinnacle of economic development, synchronizing finally with the domination of time and space, what Smith calls the "isochronism" of present-day capitalism [p. 13].

The critically discursive structures originating from the specifics of isochronic capitalism are the result of a historical awareness of its post-Soviet hegemony and an ambitious, if not atrocious, idea that technological advances have in reality destroyed all the remaining spatial and temporal hurdles that so long obfuscated an economic system without limits and with infinite possibilities.

Smith's analyses do not conform to those postmodernist theories that declare the end of industrial capitalism [following Francis Fukuyama?]. He rather envisions a *modern* capitalism predicated upon the juxtaposition of a semiotic mythology with no connection to historical and/or material realities.

"Magical notions," Smith contends, "such as that of fully global space replete with an ecstatic buzz of cyber communication, or of an instantaneous mobility of people, goods, and services, or of a global market place hooked up by immaterial money that flashes around the globe many times a minute: these are the kinds of images that are regularly projected in the opening phase of millenial capitalism" [p. 13].

Available evidence suggests that average incomes have increased while the income gap between rich and poor countries has also widened [Albo, 1997; Altvater, 1997; Echeverri-Gent, 1997; Epstein *et al.*, 1996; Lee, 1996; and Wallis, 1996]. Both trends have been evident for more than 200 years: it is only now—however—that vastly improved telecommuni-cation systems have resulted in a growing awareness among citizens of poor countries of wide disparities in income levels and patterns of consumption. This has also caused forced migrations from the South to the North whenever and wherever possible.

Rich countries, as a result, have been left without any choice but to pass laws that discourage mass immigrations [Kalpagam, 1994]. It has even been observed that [Fix *et al.*, 1994] "Although there is no evidence to date of broad job displacement and the evidence regarding major wage effects is inconclusive, concerns have been raised about the impact of high levels of immigration on the growing wage inequality in the U.S."

This, however, tends to reduce the global economy to an exclusivist power arrangement that also draws on McDonaldization/Coca-Colonization—or cultural homogenization —benchmarked largely by one-way-traffic [*i.e.*, infiltration and withdrawal of global capital into the Third World at will but not likewise when infiltration of Third World labour into the North is concerned].

According to Eric Helleiner [1994: 173], "the globalization of finance has . . . aided the U.S. in preserving its policy autonomy in the face of growing external and internal deficits . . . the U.S. in fact actively cultivated the globalization phenomenon partly for this reason, beginning with its support of the Eurodollar market, carrying through opposition to capital controls in the early 1970s, and culminating in its enthusiasm for financial liberalization during the Reagan years. Globalization benefited the U.S. because of its hegemonic position in the new open global financial system, a position derived primarily from the unique attractiveness of U.S. and Eurodollar financial markets to foreign investors."

Rich countries religiously maintain their immigration barriers and discourage agricultural imports while most poor countries have not been quite successful to attract much Foreign Direct Investment due to misgovernance on the part of their national governments. Rich countries, however, may as well concede that politics is a fundamental informant of economic inequality since they are not likely to lower their agricultural and immigration barriers in the near future in order to facilitate protectionism at home. Rich countries may also review the performance of the Washington Consensus, which assumes that free markets necessarily promote economic convergence and underscores important issues [like the rule of law, property rights and transparent banking systems] to sustain dialogues between the North and the South.

Nicola Bullard, in "The Beginning of the End of the Washington Consensus" [1998a], observes that "In spite of the economic maelstrom threatening to engulf the world, this year's IMF and World Bank meetings were notably subdued. It was clear to everyone that the global economy was in trauma: Long Term Capital Management, one of the world's biggest hedge funds, had just been bailed out by what the *New York Times* described as 'Wall Street cronyism' [with some arguing that not to (do) so would have threatened world financial markets]. Asia's economies are showing little sign of recovery in spite of massive IMF intervention. Russia, suddenly and catastrophically, has been reduced to a cashless pariah [not that anyone dared speak about Russia—obviously its spectacular collapse is not a topic for polite company!]. Brazil, meanwhile, is desperately trying to keep the speculators from the door, and Japan is seemingly unable to muster the political will to restructure its failing banks. Things were looking bad, and no one knew what to do."

Rich countries may also on occasion encourage poor countries to Think Globally, Act Locally *i.e.*, design glocal—rather than global—development strategies that would be locally grounded within the larger context of globalization.

According to Bullard [1998b], "Redistribution of wealth and purchasing power to the four-fifths of the world who are not being given a chance to pull us out of this recession would give the [U.S.] economy a kick start, would ease the problem of overproduction, and provide all sorts of useful ways to recycle profits. It would also cool down global capital markets.

"However, creating this demand requires significant social reform in terms of asset and income distribution—it means land reform and wage and labour reform. Industrialisation via cheap labour and natural resource exploitation is no longer viable. We have reached the point where further economic growth can only be achieved by expanding domestic markets and by expanding our definition of what is productive to include public goods, culture, the environment, and human security. We are at a moment in history where economic necessity coincides with social justice."

However, the political élites of rich countries may even find it occasionally convenient to overlook their own immigration and tariff barriers since such barriers are considered absolutely vital to their own domestic political stability. The amount of clout rich countries command at multilateral platforms like the IMF or the WTO more often than not makes it difficult for developing countries to successfully negotiate and come to terms with such barriers.

Jan Aart Scholte [1996: 55] has analyzed that "Globalization has to date mostly been an extension of modernization. At the same time, the rapid rise and wide-ranging reach of this transformation of social space—the transcendence of territoriality—has brought great instability to capitalism, made traditional conceptions of sovereignty unviable, heightened worries about ecological sustainability, injected much confusion into the construction of identity and encouraged reactions against reason. To this extent, globalization has opened space for critical theory and a fundamental rethink of production, governance, ecology and community, as well as the nature and purpose of knowledge itself."

We infer that the globalizing State may well be compared to Janus: it has a strong face in the developed North where immigration and tariff barriers have been erected to discourage further redistribution in terms of income transfer entitlements among Third World immigrants. The United States has even imposed embargo on import of Indian carpets ostensibly because their production involves child labour *i.e.*, human rights violation!

But the State necessarily assumes a rather weak face in the developing South where governments have repeatedly failed to come up with good governance measures despite their modernizing, albeit non-Westernizing, civil societies [Huntington, 1968 and 1996].

However, the globalizing State is far from withering away: we may extrapolate it as an important actor that would continue to creatively interface with its public sphere [Habermas, 1992a and 1992b] and civil societies in terms of good governance, structural adjustment programmes, sustainable development and social capital formation/facilitation [Loury, 1987; Putnam *et al.*, 1993; and Coleman, 1994] in order to ensure third actor interventions and critical negotiations.

Entitlements and Capabilities

May we shift our stance somewhat to reflect that development may not always lead to freedom? Basic human rights [if guaranteed by the state apparatuses] may lead to capacities on the part of citizens. But what about capacities that do not sell at the globalized marketplace?

Who can ensure that all capacities and all sensitivities of the human self protected by entitlements may ultimately be merchandised successfully at the points of coincidence between demand and supply forces? Let us consider the following statement made by Richard Cobden:

> The progress of freedom depends more upon the maintenance of peace and the spread of commerce and the diffusion of education than upon the labour of Cabinets or Foreign Offices.

What type of literature will sell? What manner of pornography will thrive? What kind of political rhetoric will survive? What complexion of beauty will win pageants? What brands of aphrodisiacs will compete against what other brands of contraceptives? Such debates are in reality the substantiated polemics of a globalized mode of development that cannot always be engaged critically without subverting our stereotyped terms of discourse. Mention may be made here of the following observation by Ronald Anil Fernandes:

> One of the most neglected forms of human deprivation is malnutrition, particularly among children. Scientific evidence suggests that the risk of death from common childhood

diseases is doubled for a mildly malnourished child, tripled for a moderately malnourished child, and may be even as high as eight times for a severely malnourished child, when compared with the risks faced by a well-nourished child.

The Problem

The idea of human freedom is essentially rooted in the concept of human development, according to Noble Laureate Professor Amartya Sen's "Development as Freedom" thesis [that outlines an entitlement to capacity-building process]. And the idea of human progress is a construct that is designed around the axis of freedom. What is freedom? Is it only lack of societal constraint, withdrawal of discipline and punish, willing suspension of the panoptic Super Ego that they address as the "mainstream"? Or is freedom a concept much more fundamental, to be read into the critical texts of Rabindranath Tagore, Mohandas Karamchand Gandhi and Leo Tolstoy.

Sociologists claim that civilization is what we are and culture is merely an arrangement of artifacts that we happen to use during the course of our politics everyday life. But then civilization is also a system of values that is handed down generations as a movement of socialization that laymen identify as "progress."

Progress versus Development

But how can progress be distinguished from "development", if at all? A most prominent item on today's humanitarian global agenda, apart from mantras like good governance, social capital, neo-liberal communitarianism, grass-roots empowerment, civil societal capacity-building and gender sensitization, is certainly the notion of sustainable development.[6] This has become almost a catchword of sorts in the Third World, decolonized state nations that are more or less grappling to muster a political system around pluralistic identities of nationhood enmeshed in ethnicity, language, religion, region and mutual distrust. It is almost as if "softy states" are hanging loose and can only be brought back on to the fast track of development by way of external intervention and advocacy on the past of the Eurocentric West.

Development, it may be appreciated at this point, is not anything extrinsic like politics imposed from the above without any regard whatsoever to the end-users of limited political resources. Actors who are supposed to interface with their very own institutions are nearly always better comfortable if left alone with the material conditions of daily life that breed organic ethos of community existence. This is where the colonial masters went wrong in Asia, Africa and South America when they bled the colonies white and left behind a legacy of comprador bourgeois and crony capitalism that, in turn, fostered a repressive state apparatus and a perverted anti-people bureaucratic managerial state system that was not only anti-people but was also occasionally anti-progress.

What Richard Cobden[7] implies by "Cabinets or Foreign Offices" is actually this mechanistic attitude of the political élite [in capitalist systems] and party leadership [in socialist societies] that are smug in the cocoon of their mistaken convictions that people at the top echelons of power, authority and influence have necessarily a working knowledge of "the greatest good of the greatest number".

This is not a utilitarian or even a welfarist state approach—it is actually self-defeating as amply evidenced in the erstwhile USSR where an insane arms and space race with the United States [incidentally the only country in the entire world to have actually materially gained from the First and Second World Wars with minimum military casualties] led the once powerful communist country to a more or less incredible situation of mind-boggling bankruptcy.

Military hardware and nukes were being manufactured at the cost of basic consumer requirements like bread, potatoes and vodka, following Stalin's rhetoric of an entire generation making sacrifices [read being purged if found to be politically incorrect] for the cause of a better Russia of the future.

Moscow's huge and sprawling department store GUM was always nearly empty while the party's top brass were running around in their imported limousines, shopping in dollar shops selling Swiss chocolates and watches, Scotch whisky, French champagne and perfumes.

Add rampant corruption and repression to accept a second-hand political ideology not originating from the ground realities of people and you have ideal recipes for killing fields like the infamous Prague Spring.

Public Action

We are reminded of Professor Mohammad Yunus of Bangladesh[8] in this respect—the magician of the Grameen Bank ["rural bank"] microcredit revolution who even hugely impressed Hilary Rodham Clinton. What Professor Yunus still does is amazingly simple—he organizes self-help groups in the manner of cooperatives and tries to make them economically self-reliant in areas as humble as poultry, weaving, dairy and even small-scale production. But when such cottage industries are linked ["forward and backward integration"] in the larger context of market forces they become formidable in their control of the overall agrarian and even the urban economy. Peasant women in Bangladesh carry mobile telephones to communicate with distant markets, distributors and dealers! This may sound incredible but it is true nevertheless, proving the validity of Cobden's observation.

Operation Flood in Anand [Gujarat, India] and the Lijjat and Kissan enterprises are other such brilliant instances of people working toward their common good [based on innovative techniques like outsourcing of manpower and material resources, subcontracting or leasing of plant and machinery, breaking down the production process to delimit financial risk liability ventures somewhat akin to Adam Smith's exposition of the division of labour dynamics] without any outside intervention whatsoever.

One must remember that neither India nor Bangladesh tends to practise authoritarian regime maintenance. What was possible once in Beijing's Tiananmen Square when the People's Liberation Army crushed pro-reform students under tanks and armoured carriers is unimaginable in either India or Bangladesh [that secured its liberation in 1971 by way of Indian military cooperation]. So democracy is an essential requirement if "the progress of freedom" is to continue unabated.

Democratic Policy Prescriptions

By democracy we ordinarily mean popular authority or rule. As made popular by Jean Jacques Rousseau, one of the ideologues of the French Revolution [that effectively altered the course of European history by beginning the disintegration process of the medieval and feudalistic Age of Empires], the voice of God is heard in the voice of the People. This was a far cry from the autocratic self-styled pronouncement of French Emperor Louis XIV—"I am the State." It was no wonder that Louis XVI's wife Marie Antoinette [later sentenced to die to rather unceremoniously at the guillotine] had once expressed her wonder in such a naive fashion on hearing about the simmering discontent among the Parisian mob standing in endless queues or bread lines and more often than not starting violent riots among themselves—"If they cannot eat bread why don't they eat cake!"

This vulgar ignorance of the ruled on the part of their rulers is rather inimical to democracy. But we must remember that democracy as dynamic capacity-building agency in the post 9/11 world has all of a sudden underscored its long-ignored extrinsic quality. Democracy is not really insular, stretching from the East Coast to the West Coast of the US. If the notion of external sovereignty has suffered quite extensively since the height of the Cold War when the world was almost vertically divided into the NATO and Warsaw Pact countries [save the NAM states being led by Nehru, Nasser and Tito], the idea of external democracy has gained much popular and diplomatic acceptance.

Simply put, powerful nations can no longer ignore internal human rights or civil rights agenda *vis-a-vis* world public opinion. But this is what the US is consistently trying to follow as its most shortsighted foreign policy since the Malta Summit Conference when President George Bush Senior and CPSU General Secretary Mikhail Gorbachev officially declared the end of the Cold War, a historic event that even prompted Francis Fukuyama to write a banal work on the end of history and the last man.

Since the days of its Nineteenth Century isolationist Munroe Doctrine the US has put up apparently impregnable walls around itself that couldn't even be dismantled during the Marshall Plan for the Reconstruction of Europe after the Second World War or establishment of first the League of Nations [as an initiative of President Woodrow Wilson's Historic Atlantic Charter] and then the UNO, the International Monetary Fund, World Bank and now the omnipotent World Trade Organization that apparently dictates the movements of a new specter of the new millennium, namely Globalization. The US foreign policy has always been designed on lines of "muddle and meddle"—Vietnam, Korea, Bay of Pigs, Iran Contra scandal, Afghanistan and now Iraq.

The US boasts of democracy and swears by it, boiling with righteous motivation to export Yankee democracy around the underdeveloped world, but has, however, classified the JFK assassination archives for no apparent reason whatsoever. Clandestine covert operations, the strategic defense initiative [Star Wars], research in biological and chemical weapons—you name it and you would find the dirty trick invariably up America's [read the CIA and FBI's] sleeves.

In fact, it is the only nation to date that has used atomic weapons during a war, destroying Hiroshima and Nagasaki in the process to avenge the Pearl Harbor attack and crippling generations of Japanese children long after the holocaust as a result of toxic radioactive radiation carried forward genetically by succeeding generations.

Since the Gulf War fought by Senior Bush as the much-hyped Operation Desert Storm so graphically shown by CNN across millions of idiot boxes around the world, nobody knows exactly how many innocent Iraqi children have died from malnutrition, disease and hunger due to the US-imposed and UNO-condoned sanctions against Iraq. The US condemns Osama-Bin-Laden but should actively engage in soul-searching regarding its own virulent international terrorist status in our contemporary unipolar world where might is right in a Hobbesian state of affairs where human life, property and security are all indeed "solitary, poor, nasty, brutish, short."

The US, in brief, should radically reorient its foreign policy to address the dignity of human life and internal sovereignty of nation states around the world. Consider the killing of innocent hostages in Iraq during 2004 by militants on the ground that they were citizens of countries that were involved in the American war effort in the Middle East. This is a failure on the part of Indian diplomacy as well: we have failed to decisively take sides during a difficult period when things are increasingly falling apart on both sides of sharply defined ideological as well as civilizational divides. We have failed—unlike China—to critically negotiate with globalization on our own terms. India has not been able to gainfully bargain from her own position of proven competencies.

Clash of Civilizations?[9]

American Political Scientist Samuel Huntington had expressed apprehension way back in 1996 that the post-Cold War 21st Century would be marked by conflicts between Islam and the West, a throwback to the Crusades of the Middle Ages. This projection was also described in Western scholarship as the Jihad versus McWorld scenario, an eventuality that would test the resilience of the free world against the forces of fundamentalist insurgency . . . American [foreign] policy-makers should realize that it is high time they begin dismantling the country's strategy of cultural isolation and indifference.

It is a disquieting fact that an average urban student of the Third World knows more about the US than an average American undergraduate knows about other peoples and other cultures. Dissemination of multi-cultural knowledge should be facilitated both within and without the American academia, industry and social service sectors. Familiarity can also breed understanding and help expand worldviews of an entire people. The logic of globalization more often than not has worked in an discriminating manner, provoking even Western scholars to come up with insightful expressions like McDonaldization, Coca-Colonization and The US is us!

Moreover, the US should discontinue backing the wrong horses and should realize that Less Developed Countries in the Third World may be impoverished but are not, however, bereft of dignity. Likeminded liberal democratic countries like India should be cultivated as reliable long-term allies on a level playing field by a series of confidence building measures. The US should also discontinue its interventionist policies that have generated such universal animosity and condemnation. Not for nothing has the expression Ugly American become well-known!

Nobody has quite forgotten the acts committed by US Marines in Vietnam or the useless display of mind-boggling violence in Hiroshima and Nagasaki. The Third World has not yet come to terms with the missile attack on a children's hospital in Baghdad during the Gulf War, to cite an example. Have the Americans themselves forgotten the faces of helpless women and children at Kosovo only a couple of years back? Americans should realize that the lives of non-Americans are also valuable in the context of the entire human civilization, and should also engage in soul-searching to understand the roots of this anti-US attitude around the world.

The clash of civilizations has only just about begun—it is now the obligation of a more conscientious American people to learn from their mistakes of the near and distant past to salvage the future of their free and sanitized and once-impregnable World. They should talk less about Human Rights and should work more to safeguard Human Rights as the self-appointed policeman of the world. Those who do not learn from history, demonstrably and most regrettably, are often condemned to repeat it.

State, Market and Education

Economist John Williamson's prescriptions that had informed the Washington Consensus were fiscal discipline, redirection of public expenditure, tax reforms, financial liberalization, adoption of a single and competitive exchange rate, trade liberalization, elimination of barriers to Foreign Direct Investment, privatization of state owned enterprises, deregulation of market entry and competition and ensuring secure property rights.

The concept of distance education has taken a while to be accepted in the popular imagination in India and elsewhere

where it has been traditionally accepted since Independence that the State will pay for higher education irrespective of the market, merit or even financial status. But the pinch is now being increasingly felt in the job market where virtually "unemployable human resources" equipped with almost useless graduate or postgraduate degrees are being churned out year after year by our colleges and Universities. India is a welfarist country where subsidies [non-merit public expenditures] more or less benefit the privileged middle classes and higher education is considered to be a tool that facilitates proliferation of democracy. But "democratization of education" [read proletarianization of meritocracy] can never be a solution to the problem of unemployment and a stagnant job market.

Add unemployment and youth discontent to a serious population growth scenario and you get an explosive combination where the entire nation happens to sit on the top of a dormant volcano, apparently idling away time watching the World Cup of Cricket, while permanent employment and social security are fast becoming obsolete in a society where a job is supposed to be like your mother in terms of security and sustenance.

However, the open school or University system can address this simmering tension and disturbing state of affairs in an effective manner only if more professional courses are designed by professionals to accommodate our educated generalists, that is students with degrees in the humanities, literature and social sciences. One such option can be social work where the catchment area may cater to students from sociology, history, political science, anthropology, public administration and the like. The job market here is specific: the NGOs who sponsor the so-called third actor intervention, public action and civil societal advocacy.

Capacity-Building[10]

Science and commerce graduates may even be taught entrepreneurial and microcredit financing skills so that they may also contribute to the nation's self-help movement in the professional services sector.

The University Grants Commission's sponsored teachers' training programmes in India like refresher and orientation courses for college and University lecturers are more or less like academic picnics where precious public money is wasted in a meaningless manner over a period of three weeks or so. As such our generalist colleges and Universities produce manpower that is often not employable without any further skill enhancement in areas like computer literacy, management or any other technical training. But India's tax payers have to still bear the brunt of an expensive higher education system that almost entirely runs on subsidies and without any material returns to produce in exchange. Doctors and engineers and management professionals join the country's bureaucracy after their professional attainments, thus resulting in huge losses in terms of human resource management.

The UGC should seriously rethink its system of awarding scholarships, funding seminars, symposia, workshops, travel grants, book and equipment purchase and so on and so forth. Refresher and orientation courses are almost entirely useless as after completion of these programmes the only people who happen to benefit [at the cost of the people] are the teachers themselves so far as their Career Advancement Scheme is concerned and nobody else. High theory is flaunted at these programmes with no regard to the UGC's guidelines that undergraduate courses should primarily be brought into focus.

Let us face it: the commonplace and average student doesn't really need to read about Plato or Aristotle — he or she is much better off studying how commodities are produced for and exchanged in the market. This may sound unduly harsh but students or trained human resources are, in the very last recourse, commodities in the market to be bought and sold against a value defined and determined by forces of demand and supply.

State Versus Popular Initiatives

West Bengal's venture into microcredit for the rural poor has failed to make any real headway [unlike the case of neighbouring Bangladesh] but the state government, not with standing empirical and readily available evidence, continues to contest this charge. Amalendu Halder, project coordinator of the Loknath Divine Life Mission, a Kolkata-based NGO, has recently claimed that the failure was evident in "the many loopholes" in the below-poverty-line and the above-poverty-line official estimates. "The venture has dismally failed," he confirmed.

State government mandarins, however, shot this serious allegation down promptly enough [shaking out of their habitual inaction and indifference bred by an impersonal Weberian culture of red tapism] without any supporting data whatsoever. They said that the Loknath Mission and other similar NGOs operating in the emergent area of microcredit and self-help groups have not yet adequately familiarized themselves with the working of the various governmental schemes.

It is the most regrettable fact that civil servants in the Third World more often than not act as if they are the masters of the people rather than being their servants which, in constitutional terms, they actually are. This perverted phenomenon is a spillover from the colonial days when the questionable legacy of the "steel-frame of the administration" was passed down generations of bureaucrats. They were brainwashed at the administrative training college in Haileybury, England by the East India Company nabobs that they were about to return to India—the Brightest Jewel in the Crown—to assist the British in their self-appointed task euphemistically called the White Man's Burden. This was nothing else but a sustained exercise over a couple of centuries to systematically fleece this once-rich country and its defenseless people like nobody's business. This "drain of wealth" resulted in the man-made Famines of 1770 and 1943 when sheer hunger provoked cannibalism and human tragedies like selling off one's wives and daughters into prostitution.

Broadly speaking, the Swarna Jayanti Gram Swarojgar Yojana [a rural self-employment project jointly launched by the Government of India and the state government] has been in operation for two years. Potential beneficiaries either directly approach the district rural development cells manned by West

Bengal Civil Service officers for approval or their individual cases are forwarded by NGOs.

Haldar said the project faces subsidy and incentive-related financial irregularities that also bedevil many other schemes of the panchayats [three-tier institutions of decentralized local governance at the district level]. BPL groups receive subsidies ranging from INR 7500-10,000 per INR 100,000 loan granted by cooperative banks. There have been major complaints that bank loans so extended to self-help groups under this project are not free from irregularities and currying of political favour.[11]

State and Civil Society

Liberal democratic regimes like India or even the US can only be politically successful, deliver the common good and thereby continue in power in a more stable [read pro-people] manner if they are able to correctly read the obtainable ground realities and problems thereof. These problems are more or less popular in nature, and have a propensity to develop into discontent of the ruled actors against their ruling institutions. So the actors in power have to continuously shuffle and delicately balance priorities of human development, well-being and accessible freedoms like the ever-important agenda of human rights and civil liberties, a responsive and responsible administrative machinery, transparency at all levels of public expenditures and domestic and international peacekeeping projects rather than playing mutually harmful "spy versus spy" games.

Subrata Kumar Mitra [1997: 23] cautions that "If the wielders of power concede the point to those who challenge established values and norms, they risk losing their legitimacy. On the other hand, the failure to give satisfaction to the discontented might deepen their sense of outrage and alienation which can further reduce their legitimacy."

Powers-that-be ["Cabinets or Foreign Offices"] will do well to continually redress grievances of political actors at the grass-roots in a political manner by establishing and ably handling pro-people institutions. Only then organic identification would bind actors with institutions—only then the incipient involvement noticed at the level of "actors and institutions" would, arguably enough, transcend itself to the level of "actors in institutions", consolidating both the level and the quality of progress of freedom in the process.[12]

Polemics of Freedom

So the question we are left with while winding up is: do we prefer freedom backed up by minimum government or would we be merely satisfied with sobriety that is imposed on our lives and liberty by the dictates of high politics from the above. It is amply clear by the beginning of a new millennium already imperiled by the grim possibility of a nuclear war that civilized human beings organized as systems of politics across porous international borders can no longer afford to unquestioningly follow the policy prescriptions of their domestic governments, foreign offices and state departments.

More intense people-to-people contacts should be sustained on a long-term basis as such transnational networks can better work toward the so-called Track Two diplomacy between intellectuals and academics, social activists, policy analysts, development consultants and the common people [Maiti, 2001].

Consider the atrocities unleashed by the American Marines against Iraqi POWs or Al-Queda insurgents: these negate both the notions of freedom and sobriety and indicate a third space of force without any civilizational constraints whatsoever.

So the discourses of globalization continue to haunt us like the unknown specter or ghost of Jacques Derrida's hospitality theory. The flight of capital or hot money from the domestic economy overnight may appear to be spectral: but this is due to the fact that we often fail to accommodate the ghost as our guest on our very own terms of discourse. Certain formidable problems may often get sorted out if we can creatively interact with the forces of globalization while empowered with our own sets of intrinsic skill and knowledge sets. Such information should be gleaned from the politics of our everyday lives and not from elsewhere *i.e.*, from reality and not from virtuality.

It is the unknown citizen who should really be brought back into primary focus by Rolling Back the State—nowhere men and women such as you and me should be constituted as indices of basic empowerment, freedom and development.

Such a grandiose plan of action should necessarily be rooted in our understanding of present international debates centred around the movement of labour, immigration barriers, intellectual property rights and the right to ravage ancient civilizations at the drop of a hat in order to fulfil immediate economic as well as long-term statecraft objectives. This really seems to be utopian so long as human beings and their political societies continue to conform to the practised metaphors of power and periphery.

NOTES

1. The author is grateful to Professor Suranjan Das and Professor Arun Bandopadhyay of the Department of Modern History, University of Calcutta among other academics and practitioners in India and abroad for their critical observations on earlier drafts of this paper.
2. According to environmental activist Vandana Shiva, "Globalization of the economy is a new kind of corporate colonialism visited upon poor countries and the poor in rich countries." http://resurgence.gn.apc.org/articles/mander.htm Jerry Mander writes that "Economic globalization involves arguably the most fundamental re-design of the planet's political and economic arrangements since at least the Industrial Revolution. Yet the profound implications of these fundamental changes have barely been exposed to serious public scrutiny or debate. Despite the scale of the global reordering, neither our elected officials nor our educational institutions nor the mass media have made a credible effort to describe what is being formulated or to explain its root philosophies. The occasional descriptions or predictions about the global economy that are found in the media usually come from the leading advocates and beneficiaries of this new order: corporate leaders, their allies in government, and a newly powerful centralized global trade bureaucracy. The visions they offer us are unfailingly positive, even utopian: Globalization will be a panacea for our ills. Shockingly enough, the euphoria they express is based on their freedom to deploy, at a global level through the new global free-trade rules, and through deregulation and economic restructuring regimes large-scale versions of the economic theories, strategies and policies that have proven spectacularly unsuccessful over the past several decades wherever they've been applied. In fact, these are the very ideas that

have brought us to the grim situation of the moment: the spreading disintegration of the social order and the increase of poverty, landlessness, homelessness, violence, alienation and, deep within the hearts of many people, extreme anxiety about the future. Equally important, these are the practices that have led us to the near breakdown of the natural world, as evidenced by such symptoms as global climate change, ozone depletion, massive species loss, and near maximum levels of air, soil and water pollution." *Ibid.*

3. The global citizens' movement for sustainability insists that there are measures of human development other than ever-rising consumption of the Earth's resources. It demands new, resource-saving taxation systems and incentives to help regulate human activities. It wants fossil fuel and nuclear energy technologies to be rapidly superseded by renewable energy systems, such as solar, wind, wave, biomass and fuel cells, whilst assuring high levels of energy efficiency. It insists that farming can be put on a sustainable footing, transcending dependence on pesticides, fertilisers and gmos. It wants restoration of depleted forests to be undertaken all over the world, rather than in just a few isolated locations. It recognises the urgency of respecting the oceans and life within them. Above all else the global village means international co-operation for achieving sustainable, local economies that assure that most local consumption is met by local production. Trade could be increasingly dematerialised, with ideas rather than products being exchanged worldwide. The new networks of civil society will take us beyond protests against globalization towards joint positive action to implement an agenda of global sustainability, security and justice. http://resurgence.gn.apc.org/issues/girardet216.htm

4. Key government institutions must function effectively in order for a country to attain sustainable growth and benefit from globalization. Democratic governance must be more than just elections, although elections remain the vital force of democratic government . . . . Experience gained in the financial crises of the 1990s, including those in Mexico and Asia and the collapse of the Russian economy, has demonstrated conclusively that fundamental institutions rules, laws and norms of a modern market economy have to be carefully built. In addition, the government and/or the private sector have to provide the infrastructure essential for a market system . . . . Two aspects of building a modern market economy that are separated out here for additional emphasis are at the heart of efforts to open economies and create fair and transparent systems. Corporate governance is the set of rules public and private by which modern corporations govern themselves in a competitive market system. The lack of corporate governance was one of the key reasons for the recent Asian and Russian

economic crises. Similarly, effective anticorruption measures are increasingly regarded as essential to attract foreign investment, build a competitive economy and ensure fair treatment for all . . . . In today's high-tech information age, cutting-edge technology is an important means of lowering the cost, increasing the speed and improving the quality of business transactions and of basic services essential to daily life . . . . Building the world bilateral and regional trading systems requires constant attention and effort. Developed and emerging markets must all work to create a fair system that balances national interest with the long-run development of the global economy. http://www.cipe.org/publications/fs/ert/current/e35; 13.htm

5. The constraints of geography are shrinking and the world is becoming a single place. Globalization and the global society are increasingly occupying the centre of sociological debates. Widely discussed by journalists and a key goal for many businesses, globalization has become a buzzword in recent years. In this extensively revised and restructured new edition of *Globalization*, Malcolm Waters provides a user-friendly introduction to the main arguments about the process, including a chapter on the critiques of the globalization thesis that have emerged since the first edition was published. http://leeds.etailer.dpsl.net/Home/html/moreinfo.asp?isbn=0203136470

6. Almost every aspect of sustainable development will be affected by the quality of civil society, political participation and decision-making, and responsible and reliable governance. Because good governance is the fundamental requirement for progress and sustainability, furthering it is at the core of U.S. strategy to foster sustainable development. http://usembassy.state.gov/tokyo/wwwhgl0469.html

7. Cobden, Richard [1804-65]. British economist and statesman, known as the Apostle of Free Trade . . . . In Parliament Cobden favoured a *laissez-faire* economic philosophy, that is, minimum interference of government in business. He opposed factory reforms and trade unions and objected to the intervention of government in the affairs of foreign nations. His opposition to British foreign policy cost him his seat in Parliament in 1857. He was so respected by his political opponents, however, that Prime Minister Palmerston offered Cobden the post of president of the Board of Trade in his cabinet in 1859. Cobden rejected the offer, but remained politically active. The following year he negotiated an Anglo-French commercial treaty. His last important political action was to support the Union in the American Civil War, at a time when other British leaders were hesitant. He died in London on April 12, 1865. http://encarta.msn.com/ encnet/refpages/refarticle.aspx?refid= 761557174

8. When we started giving out tiny loans under a system which later became known as the Grameen Bank, we never imagined that one day

we would be reaching hundreds of thousands, let alone two million, borrowers . . . . Grameen Bank Provides credit to the poorest of the poor in rural Bangladesh without any collateral. At Grameen Bank, credit is a cost effective weapon to fight poverty and it serves as a catalyst in the overall development of socio-economic conditions . . . . There are now more than two dozen organizations within the Grameen family of enterprises. These include the replication and research activities of Grameen Trust, handloom enterprises of Grameen Udyog and fisheries pond management by Grameen Matsyho or the Fisheries Foundation. http://www.grameen-info.org/

9. See Prasenjit Maiti, "Clash of Civilizations?" The Humanist Washington DC: American Humanist Association, 2001]. This essay was provoked by 9/11 and its subsequent backlash in the form of tremors and apprehension of escalated violence and ethnic tension around the world. It is amply evident by now that that the US State Department has aggravated rather than alleviated the course of the most challenging North-South dialog since the conclusion of the Second World War and the Cold War by its deplorable diplomatic shortsightedness and megalomania that are not always entirely in good taste.
10. The contemporary view of capacity-building goes beyond the conventional perception of training. The central concerns of environmental management—to manage change, to resolve conflict, to manage institutional pluralism, to enhance coordination, to foster communication, and to ensure that data and information are shared—require a broad and holistic view of capacity development. This definition covers both institutional and community-based capacity-building. http://nrm.massey.ac.nz/changelinks/capacity.html
11. See Maiti, "Failure slur on self-help project". *The Telegraph* [5 November, 2002. Kolkata, India]. This news report was based on field surveys and interviews with NGOs, bureaucrats and newspersons. I've vindicated and concurred with Cobden's valid contention that the onward march of human civilization based on material development of the everyday conditions of life depends more upon the absence of irksome bureaucratic interventionism, proliferation of natural markets, expansion of consumer-friendly hinterlands and resource-rich catchment areas and the dissemination of information [knowledge being power] rather than upon the policy prescriptions drafted away from the periphery and implemented none to well to empower marginal man and woman at the grass-roots who are bereft of any meaningful access to the process of decision-making that affects their livelihoods in the long-run.
12. See Maiti, "A Human Ecological Analysis of the Narmada Bachao Andolan." *Electronic Green Journal* [Idaho: University of Idaho Library, 2001]. This paper written in support of the protracted Save the Narmada

Movement in India indicates how the government, its insensitive bureaucracy and repressive system of police administration and even the judiciary can actually defeat—albeit temporarily—popular aims and aspirations. The Government of India has of late decided to link up all the major rivers of the country so that river water from the Gangetic Basin of North India can flow into the comparatively arid regions of South India and facilitate both irrigation and hydroelectricity generation. However, experts are convinced that this move would not only considerably dry up the already reduced water volume of the Ganges [as a result of the water sharing treaty with Bangladesh across the Farakka Barrage in West Bengal] but would also result in annual floods and siltification of the different river basins of South India as well. The Supreme Court of India—the country's apex federal court—has already had set up a Water Disputes Tribunal to settle disputes and resolve bitter conflicts between states like Tamil Nadu and Karnataka in South India over the contentious issue of sharing water of the River Cauvery on a mutual basis as this river flows across both these states.

REFERENCES

Albo, Gregory [1997]. "A World Market of Opportunities? Capitalist Obstacles and Left Economic Policy." *Socialist Register.*

Altvater, Elmar [1997]. "Financial Crisis on the Threshold of the 21st Century". *Socialist Register.*

Aziz, Abdul and D.D. Arnold (eds) [1996]. *Decentralised Governance in Asian Countries* [New Delhi: Sage].

Barber, Benjamin R. [1996]. *Jihad versus McWorld.* New York: Ballantine.

Baudrillard, Jean [1995]. "On Consumer Society." J. Faubion (ed.), *Rethinking the Subject: An Anthology of Contemporary European Social Thought* {Boulder, Colorado: Westview].

Berners-Lee, Tim [1996]. "The World Wide Web: Past Present and Future." http://www.w3.org/People/Berners-Lee/1996/ppf.html

Billig, Michael [1995]. *Banal Nationalism* [London: Sage].

Bullard, Nicola [1998a]. "The Beginning of the End of the Washington Consensus." http://www.focusweb.org/publications/1998/The Washington consensus.htm

—— [September 1998b] "Regulation or Barbarism". http:// www.focusweb.org/publications/1998/Regulation or Barbarism.htm

Coleman, James S. [1994]. *Foundations of Social Theory* [Cambridge, Massachusetts/London: Harvard University Press].

Cox, Robert [1993]. "Gramsci, Hegemony and International Relations: An Essay in Method." S. Gill (ed.), *Gramsci, Historical Materialism and International Relations* [Cambridge: Cambridge University Press].

Echeverri-Gent, John [July 1997]. "Governance in a Globalizing World: Deconstructing Decentralization in India, China and the United States." Charlottesville: Department of Government and Foreign Affairs, University of Virginia [*mimeo*].

Epstein, Gerald *et al*, [November, 1996]. "Winners and Losers in the Global Economic Game". *Current History*.

Fix, Michael *et al*, [May 1994]. "Immigration and Immigrants: Setting the Record Straight". United States of America: The Urban Institute. http://immigration.about.com/newsissues/immigration/gi/dynamic/offsite.htm?site=http://www.urban.org/pubs/immig/immig.htm

Gary, Craig and Marjorie Mayo (eds) [1995]. *Community Empowerment: A Reader in Participation and Development* [London/New Jersey: Zed Books].

Giddens, Anthony [1995]. *Beyond Left and Right: The Future of Radical Politics* [Cambridge: Polity Press].

Habermas, Hans-Jürgen [1992a]. *The Structural Transformation of the Public Sphere: An Inquiry into the Category of Bourgeois Society* [Cambridge: Polity Press].

—— [1992b]. "Further Reflections on the Public Sphere". Craig Calhoun (eds), *Habermas and the Public Sphere* [Columbia: Columbia University Press].

Helleiner, Eric [1994]. "From Bretton Woods to Global Finance: A World Turned Upside Down". Richard Stubbs and G.R. Underhill (eds), *Political Economy and the Changing Global Order* [London: Macmillan].

Hoffmann, D., T. Novak and Partha Chatterjee [1995]. "Commercial Scenarios for the Web: Opportunities and Challenges." *Journal of Computer Mediated Communication*, 1 [3]. http://www.ascusc.org/jcmc/vol1/issue3/hoffman.html

Huntington, Samuel P. [1968]. *Political Order in Changing Societies* [New Haven/London: Yale University Press].

Huws, Ursula [1999]. "Material World: The Myth of the Weightless Economy". Leo Pantich and Colin Leys (eds.), *Socialist Register* [London: Merlin].

Huws, Ursula [November-December 1996]. "The West Unique, Not Universal". *Foreign Affairs*.

Kalpagam, U. [1994]. *Labour and Gender: Survival in Urban India* [New Delhi/London: Sage].

Kegley Jr., Charles W. and Eugene R. Wittkopf [1997]. *World Politics* [New York: St. Martin's Press].

Kellner, D. [1989]. *Jean Baudrillard: From Marxism to Postmodernism and Beyond* [Stanford: Stanford University Press].

Keohane, Robert O. [Spring 1998]. "International Institutions: Can Interdependence Work?" *Foreign Policy.*

Kothari, Rajni (eds) [1976]. *State and Nation Building: A Third World Perspective* [New Delhi: Allied].

Lee, Thea M. [November 1996]. "Trade Policy and Development: Spurring Good Growth". *Current History.*

Lefebvre, Henri [1984]. *Everyday Life in the Modern World* [New Brunswick: Transaction].

Loury, Glenn [1987]. "Why Should We Care about Group Inequality?" *Social Philosophy and Policy* [5].

Maiti, Prasenjit [January-April 2001]. "Toward Alternatives of Conflict Resolution in South Asia". *Journal of Social Sciences* [5 (1-2)].

Manor, James [1996]. "Recent Trends in the Study of State-Society Relations". Mette Halskov Hansen and Arild Engelsen Ruud (eds), *Weak? Strong? Civil? Embedded? New Perspectives on State-Society Relations in the Non-Western World* [Oslo: Centre for Development and the Environment, University of Oslo].

March, James G. and Johan P. Olsen [1995]. *Democratic Governance* [New York/London: The Free Press].

Marjit, Sugata *et al,* [May 1999]. "Harassment, Corruption and Economic Policy". Munich: CESifo Working Paper No. 189.

Marx, Karl [1990]. *Capital.* Volume 3 [New York: Penguin].

McGrew, A. 1992. "Globalization". Stuart Hall *et al* (eds). *Modernity and Its Futures* [Cambridge: Cambridge University Press].

Mitra, Subrata Kumar [1997]. "Legitimacy, Governance and Political Institutions in India after Independence". Mitra and Dietmar Rothermund (eds), *Legitimacy and Conflict in South Asia* [Manohar, New Delhi].

Putnam, Robert D. *et al,* [1993]. *Making Democracy Work: Civic Traditions in Modern Italy* [Princeton, New Jersey: Princeton University Press].

Rapley, John [1996]. *Understanding Development: Theory and Practice in the Third World* [Boulder, Colorado: Lynne Rienner].

Ray, Aswini K. [1996]. "Democratic Rights in a Post-Colonial Democracy". Agora Project Working Papers [Uppsala: The University of Uppsala].

—— [1989]. "Towards the Concept of a Post-Colonial Democracy: A Schematic View". Zoya Hasan *et al.,* (eds), *The State, Political Processes and Identity: Reflections on Modern India* [New Delhi: Sage].

Slater, David [1996]. "Other Contexts of the Global: A Critical Geopolitics of North South Relations". Elenore Kofman and Gillian Youngs (eds). *Globalization: Theory and Practice* [London: Pinter].

Scholte, Jan Aart [1996]. "Beyond the Buzzword: Towards a Critical Theory of Globalization". Elenore Kofman and Gillian Youngs (eds). *Globalization: Theory and Practice* [London: Pinter].

Smith, Paul [1997]. *Millenial Dreams: Contemporary Culture and Capital in the North* [London: Verso].

Wallis, Victor [January 1996]. "Socialism under Siege". *Monthly Review*.

Waters, Malcolm [1995]. *Globalization* [London/New York: Routledge].

SECTION II
NEGOTIATIONS

4

EMPOWERMENT AS DEVELOPMENT[1]

Hunger and poverty are not regional or national issues any more.[2]

Key Words. Affordability, capabilities, effective demand, entitlements, gender empowerment, market surveys, operation and maintenance of civic assets, poverty, purchasing capacity, Self-Help Groups, user groups, vocational training, well-being.

Urban development projects may often lay major emphasis on enhancing the quality and material conditions of life of slum residents by way of formation/facilitation of [women's] self-help groups. Non-Government Organizations may serve as field-level facilitators in this critical area of community development *vis-a-vis* skills upgradation courses and capacity-building programmes.

One of the principal objectives of poverty alleviation programmes is to uplift the standard of life of primary stakeholders [for *e.g.* slum dwellers in cities] in order to ensure their affordable access to primary civic services.[3]

Poverty alleviation programmes may first identify existing government schemes that share a similar pro-poor developmental focus. Such programmes may next focus on formation and/or facilitation of SHGs[4] that are expected to serve as dynamic and interactive platforms to mobilize and develop the community [especially women residing in local-level slums].[5]

Vocational training courses [especially for SHG members] may be subsequently implemented in order to equip the community with self-employment/income-generation skills and opportunities for livelihood enhancement as an integral condition of sustainable development[6]]. Poverty alleviation programmes may subsequently focus on local market surveys and backward as well as forward linkages for efficient marketing of products.

Development agencies such as NGOs may focus on formation as well as facilitation of SHGs that will be designed to act as local-level actors in order to organize the community [especially women]. Such dynamic women's groups may also be utilized so far as networking and outreach of different poverty alleviation schemes financed by the state and national governments are concerned.

Poverty alleviation initiatives may focus on training needs assessment and local market surveys in order to assess existing demand and supply forces with regard to domestic commodities or handicraft items [that may be produced at low cost investments]. Such commodities [as identified after surveys] should have an effective demand supported by purchasing capacities. Their nature should also be such so that they can be produced at low skills levels.

Poverty alleviation programmes may next concentrate on upgradation of existing skills or even creation of new skill sets *vis-a-vis* the community. Need-based skills may be assessed among community members, existing infrastructural lacunae identified and vocational training courses accordingly planned and implemented to facilitate income-generation activities.

A community-level coordination committee may be formed to monitor the demand for raw materials required in connection with production-related activities. Representative groups working in association with this committee may also be constituted for marketing purposes.

Such groups may be trained to monitor changing market trends so that they can reorient trained community members accordingly. This is imperative in order to continuously upgrade the dynamic database of market-related information to be shared among SHG members for best product-wise results in terms of total sales and the annual business turnover of concerned SHGs.

Representative groups may also act as user groups for operation and maintenance of civic assets. This necessitates institutionalization of group dynamics and its conversion from an informal to a formal mode of operation:

1. Formation/facilitation of self-help groups in order to mobilize the local-level women to participate in poverty alleviation initiatives and awareness-generation campaigns focused on best practices of solid waste management, primary health and hygiene, gender empowerment, formal/non-formal education and Operation & Maintenance of civic assets created/renovated under the project by way of demonstration effect and peer pressure.
2. Arrangement for/facilitation of short-term vocational training courses designed for both men and women so that primary stakeholders may themselves organize future platforms of interactive dialogue in order to decide what course of social development would be most efficacious for themselves.
3. Implementing participatory monitoring and evaluation exercises at the community-level in order to assess the quality of civil works being undertaken in urban slums and revise/reorient community liaison strategies *vis-a-vis* secondary stakeholders if required.

Plan of Action

Efforts may be made at the initial stage to involve community-based organizations as well as civil society organizations during training needs assessment and local market surveys for their logistic support and field-level inputs. Development agencies such as NGOs may assess the level of community preparedness to avail vocational training in slums where the community has already undergone such training in the recent past.

NGOs may also concentrate on slums where the level of community preparedness is not so high. Development agencies may lay emphasis on motivating the community in order to sensitize slum residents with regard to the likely future impact of vocational training and formation as well as facilitation of SHGs.

Community mobilization and participation events organized in consultation with local-level resource persons and/or key informants may be planned at this critical stage as rapport-building exercises in order to gain acceptance at the community-level. Entry points may constitute youth clubs and similar institutions. Such events may act as a forum where the local women can extensively interact with NGOs with regard to poverty alleviation programmes.

Methodology

Development agencies may next organize a joint meeting with community members interested to form SHGs. The concept, future impact and objectives of SHGs may be explained to such members during meetings and/or focus group discussions where the community's mindset with regard to poverty alleviation initiatives may be assessed by professionals trained in participatory poverty assessment techniques.[7]

A basket of participatory rapid appraisal tools such as the problem tree analysis, matrix scoring, priority ranking, resource and benefit mapping exercises may be utilized at this juncture in order to derive a clear picture of the community's felt needs and perceptions.

NGOs may next form and/or facilitate SHGs to obtain institutional financial support for community development activities. The level of community preparedness needs to be high in order to accept the rules and regulations of the group.

Mindsets of group members need to be assessed in a scientific manner before any SHG is developed as a thrift and credit group. A series of workshops may be organized after a few months of SHG formation and/or facilitation in order to reflect upon the lessons learnt and the way forward.

Self-Help Groups

SHGs are voluntary associations of the community, by the community and for the community. SHG members should share a common desire to work as an action group ready to exert peer pressure at the slum-level. Members should mobilize local women to launch small-scale savings and credit groups for their self-reliance and material well-being.

Vocational Training

Vocational training courses are required to improve the economic conditions of primary stakeholders so that their affordable access to basic urban services may be suitably enhanced. Such courses promote the confidence of community members [especially women] for decentralized participatory monitoring and evaluation exercises with regard to progress of physical works under different developmental projects. Vocational training courses are expected to empower local women with the twin objectives of gender mainstreaming and community development.

NGO Activities

NGOs should be able to identify and assess local-level resource persons, key informants and community-based organizations in order to implement SHG-related activities. Concerned government and municipal authorities should also be duly apprised of such activities in order to streamline and facilitate future plans of action.

Development agencies should also design, facilitate and implement poverty alleviation programmes in consultation and association with community members and/or representative groups.

NGOs may also be required to hold interactive sessions with resource persons, key informants, community-based organizations and civil society organizations to discuss the future impact of SHGs and/or vocational training courses in the short-run. NGOs may organize dialogue sessions with target groups such as the local women to discuss objectives of SHGs. Such interactions with SHG members may broaden their respective worldviews with regard to their future plans of action and ideas about their own development.

Development agencies may finalize the list of SHG members, draw up the group's rules and regulations in consultation and association with members, decide on monthly/ weekly subscriptions, help select/elect office-bearers *i.e.*, the president, secretary and cashier. Such activities contribute toward betterment of best practices of participatory development.[8]

NGOs may be engaged in a continuous monitoring and evaluation process of group activities by periodic attendance as observers during group meetings. NGOs should also try to organize different types of group games in order to facilitate intra-group dynamics. Development agencies may ensure organization of weekly group meetings, maintenance of accounts and documentation of meeting minutes. NGOs should be able to develop a sociable group culture so that the cohesion among members is sustained on a long-term basis. Social and human capital of the group should be continuously upgraded.

NGOs may arrange for professional training of group members in order to develop leadership qualities among them as a part of the overall capacity-building programme for SHGs. NGOs may also mobilize financial and material resources by their continuous networking and outreach activities.

Organizing regular examinations and monitoring sessions may assess skills upgradation of the trainees. Backward and forward linkages may also be put in place in order to merchandise products made by group members. Both organic as well as dynamic linkages should be established with other institutions to share information and pursue collective action for capacity-building of members and mobilization of resources. Development agencies may identify Government Schemes and disseminate such information to the community. NGOs may arrange for linkages with banks and/or formal/informal financial Institutions. Development agencies may also facilitate capacity-building programmes for group members in this regard.[9]

Ground Realities

There may be a low level of community preparedness among SHG members. Groups may be formed from among heterogeneous communities. There may be formidable political overtones affecting group members. Community-based organizations and NGOs may not be actively present at the slum-level.

Resource Persons and/or Key Informants may not always be available at the slum-level. The community may have certain reservations with regard to similar development projects in the recent past. SHG members may demand immediate and tangible results. Such are the ground-level problems that may adversely affect community development programmes.

Orientation Programmes

During the formation and/or facilitation of SHGs a series of orientation programmes may be launched by NGOs to train field facilitators. The following areas may be focused during such training sessions:

1. Development of communication skills among SHG members so that intra-group dialogues may be facilitated.
2. Development of leadership attributes among members so that future leaders may organically evolve from within the group.
3. Development of documentation skills so that meeting minutes may be duly recorded and a profile of group activities maintained.
4. Development of basic book keeping skills so that members may themselves be capable enough to maintain accounts.
5. Maintenance of ledgers may be taught by NGOs for the benefit of SHG members so that transaction of money is recorded on a regular basis.
6. Capacity-building of members by developing their worldviews, training them in sectors such as primary health and hygiene and basic skill sets required to sustain income-generation activities and poverty alleviation programmes.
7. Skills upgradation is required for SHG members so that their dynamic interactions *vis-a-vis* local market

potentials may be optimally utilized to generate sustainable livelihoods at the grass-roots.

8. Resource mobilization is critical so that SHG members may sustain the benefits of poverty alleviation initiatives.

Development agencies may streamline processes and mechanisms with regard to the daily functioning of groups by identifying the problems faced by group members, discussing such problems in an in-depth manner during group meetings, solving such problems in consultation with group members and implementing group-level strategies with regard to income-generation activities and/or self-employment programmes.

SWOT Analysis

Strengths	Weaknesses
1. High level of community preparedness in order to accept SHG rules and regulations	1. Low level of community preparedness
2. Active participation of SHG members in group activities	2. Inactive participation of group members
3. High level of motivation with regard to regular savings with a mission	3. Non-maintenance of funds and not updating accounts
4. Running the group in a synchronized and disciplined manner	4. Brief gestation period that adversely affects group dynamics
5. Maintaining a strict code of conduct among group members	5. Lack of knowledge with regard to SHG aims and objectives
6. Proven decision-making abilities	6. Lack of planning in the long-run
7. Established leadership attributes	7. Non-implementation of rules and regulations
8. Innovative ideas to solve various problems from different angles	8. Stereotyped worldviews and lack of creative ideas to solve problems
9. Unity and cohesion among group members	9. Lack of unity and integrity among group members
10. Communication skills among SHG members	10. Lack of communication skills
11. Willingness to learn from one another	11. Lack of capital for further expansion
12. Ability to preserve individual dignity and group identity	12. Political intervention and/or appropriation

Opportunities	Threats
1. Available skill sets of the group	1. Natural calamities
2. Group cohesion and unity	2. Intra-group complications
3. Availability of loans for self-employment purposes	3. Husband's/guardian's interference during formation of SHGs
4. Linkages with banks and/or financial institutions	4. Inability to network with banks and/or financial institutions
5. Review of local markets	5. Political intervention
6. Skills upgradation	6. Corruption

National Policy

The Government of India has made concerted efforts since Independence [1947] to provide financial support to the rural and urban poor at affordable rates of interest in order to solve their problems of poverty and unemployment. GoI laid stress on expanding banking networks throughout the country in order to provide credit to the poor. GoI also launched several subsidised wage and self-employment programmes for the benefit of the poor.

There still exists a considerable hiatus between the demand and supply of credit [as facilitated by formal financial institutions such as the nationalized banks] despite such sustained government-sponsored efforts. Reliance of the poor on informal and non-institutional sources of credit [such as usurious moneylenders] still remains high.

The limited impact of formal financial institutions in their effective outreach *vis-a-vis* the poor depends upon several factors as follows:

1. Extension of credit to the ["unbankable"] poor, in a small amount and for a short term, involves high transaction costs and is, supposedly, non-profitable for nationalized banks and/or formal financial institutions *i.e.*, commercially non-viable cost-benefit equations come into play.
2. Small-scale ventures and micro-enterprises at the grass-roots are generally considered to be ["non-

creditworthy"] risks that may involve high rates of default, as small clients are not usually able to run commercially viable business operations.

3. Small-scale potential clients do not generally have access to traditional collaterals such as immovable property to guarantee their bank loans.

Microcredit[10]

Micro-enterprise lending in India began as a response to the inadequate credit flow to the poor from the formal financial sector. An alternative path of sustainable development was developed and facilitated largely as a civil societal initiative by utilizing the services of NGOs. Self-help groups were formed by the poor and facilitated by NGO interventions in order to expand the networks of credit and cooperation among the poor. SHGs focus on providing savings [thrift] and credit services to the poor.

Such an alternative institutional framework has had a limited impact *vis-a-vis* issues and concerns of poverty alleviation so far. This is due to the fact that microfinance institutions are more often than not up against sustainability crises arising out of the absence of proper governance, regulatory mechanisms, ownership norms, legal entitlements and reliable sources of medium to long-term capital.[11]

ASIAN DEVELOPMENT BANK'S DEFINITION OF MICROFINANCE

Microfinance is the provision of a broad range of financial services such as deposits, loans, payment services, money transfers and insurance to poor and low-income households and their microenterprises. Microfinance services are provided by three types of sources:

1. formal institutions, such as rural banks and cooperatives;
2. semiformal institutions, such as nongovernment organizations; and
3. informal sources such as moneylenders and shopkeepers.

Institutional microfinance is defined to include microfinance services provided by both formal and semi-formal institutions. Microfinance institutions are defined as institutions whose major business is the provision of microfinance services.[12]

Intervention Strategies

NGOs may devise suitable strategies to finance self-help groups by developing and/or expanding networks with nationalized banks such as NABARD[13] and SIDBI.[14] SHG bank accounts may be opened and bank loans may be sought to set up corpus funds. Governmental financial institutions may be approached for seed money in the form of one-time grants under existing schemes for the urban poor.

Group members may utilize SHG funds either to set up individual or collective business enterprises where profits may be shared on an equitable basis. Such entrepreneurial ventures may have to be tied up at the city-level with banks and/or formal financial institutions, other like-minded SHGs working in related areas and government agencies working in the field of income-generation activities and poverty alleviation initiatives.

NGOs may also identify the potential areas of development for women, as SHGs generally comprise women members keen to enhance their individual as well as collective livelihoods by way of undergoing vocational training and skill enhancement courses designed to promote self-sustainability of the urban poor.

Development agencies may liaise with nationalized banks to formulate micro-level action plans under existing governmental schemes such as the Women Component Plan and the Indira Mahila Yojna to finance women entrepreneurs who may even set up permanent stalls at local markets in order to merchandise their products.

Temporary stalls at local-level fairs may otherwise be set up to sell SHG products. NGOs may also identify institutions that are interested in the welfare of women for networking and/or dispensation of credit through bankable schemes. NGOs may counsel women to avail of bank loan assistance.

Development agencies may also maintain and constantly update a database for gender disaggregated figures both for planning and achievements *vis-a-vis* poverty alleviation initiatives.[15]

Microcredit feasibility studies carried out by professional consultant agencies in this regard may examine pros and cons of capacity-building of decentralized microfinance institutions.[16] Such microfinance projects may also include built-in components to provide mentoring and pedagogic backup to local-level and small-scale microfinance institutions. Funds may also be made available by donor agencies to provide equity support to selected large-scale microfinance institutions on a pilot basis.

SIDBI'S LOAN ASSISTANCE ELIGIBILITY CRITERIA[17]

1. The MFI should be in existence for at least five years. It should have a demonstrated track record of running a successful microcredit programmes at least for the last three years. However, new MFIs willing to launch microcredit programmes may also be considered for assistance if senior microfinance professionals with relevant experience of at least three years manage such MFIs.
2. The MFI has achieved a minimum outreach of 3000 poor individuals [through individual lending/SHGs/ partner NGOs or MFIs] or has demonstrated the capability to reach this scale within a year or so.
3. The MFI should choose its clients irrespective of class, creed and religion.
4. The MFI should maintain transparency in its audited accounts and management of information system.
5. The MFI should have a relatively low-risk portfolio or else possess a viable plan to further enhance its recovery performance.[18]

TYPES OF ELIGIBLE INTERMEDIARIES

1. Societies registered under the Societies Act [1860] or similar State Acts.
2. Trusts registered under the Public Trusts Act [1920] or similar Acts.
3. Companies registered under the Companies Act [1956] including Section 25 Companies.
4. Non-banking finance companies providing financial services to the poor.
5. Specialised and other cooperatives such as Mutually Aided Cooperative Societies.
6. Any other type of institution that offers microfinance and related services may be considered on merit.[19]

Lending Channels

Microfinance institutions may on-lend directly to self-help groups and/or individuals or else route their financial assistance through their partner NGOs and MFIs. They may also adopt any other lending channel so as to effectively extend financial assistance to the poor.

ADB's Microfinance Strategy

Providing microfinance services efficiently to this excluded segment of the market remains a major challenge in the [Asian] Region. However, given that the Asian Development Bank has adopted poverty reduction as its overarching objective, ADB must respond to this challenge effectively. Supporting the development of sustainable MFIs that can reach the poor provides ADB an opportunity to respond to this challenge and make a significant contribution to its poverty reduction objective and the development of the overall financial system in its developing member countries.[20]

NETWORKING AND OUTREACH

1. Microfinance can be a critical element of an effective poverty reduction strategy. Improved access and efficient provision of savings, credit, and insurance facilities in particular can enable the poor to smoothen their consumption, manage their risks better, build

their assets gradually, develop their microenterprises, enhance their income earning capacity, and enjoy an improved quality of life. Microfinance services can also contribute to the improvement of resource allocation, promotion of markets, and adoption of better technology; thus, microfinance helps to promote economic growth and development.

2. Without permanent access to institutional microfinance, most poor households continue to rely on meager self-finance or informal sources of microfinance, which limits their ability to actively participate in and benefit from the development opportunities.
3. Microfinance can provide an effective way to assist and empower poor women, who make up a significant proportion of the poor and suffer disproportionately from poverty.
4. Microfinance can contribute to the development of the overall financial system through integration of financial markets.[21]

ADB's Policy

The goal of ADB's proposed Microfinance Development Strategy is to ensure permanent access to institutional financial services for a majority of poor and low-income households and their microenterprises. The purpose is to support the development of sustainable microfinance systems that can provide diverse services of high quality. Therefore, the strategy focuses on:

1. creating a policy environment conducive to microfinance,
2. developing financial infrastructure,
3. building viable institutions,
4. supporting pro-poor innovations, and
5. supporting social intermediation.[22]

Self-Help Groups

SHGs and decentralized MFIs at the local-level may constitute units of action research that may ensure enhanced livelihood patterns of the urban poor by promoting the larger cause of sustainable development in the context of good urban governance practices.

So far as poverty alleviation initiatives at the grass-roots are concerned, it is critical to devise viable strategies in order to fund SHGs and extend logistic support to decentralized MFIs so that the latter can efficaciously serve as community-level nodal agencies to cater to microcredit requirements of the urban poor, especially women. Such strategies may have to conform to guidelines of donor agencies in this regard.

Flow Chart

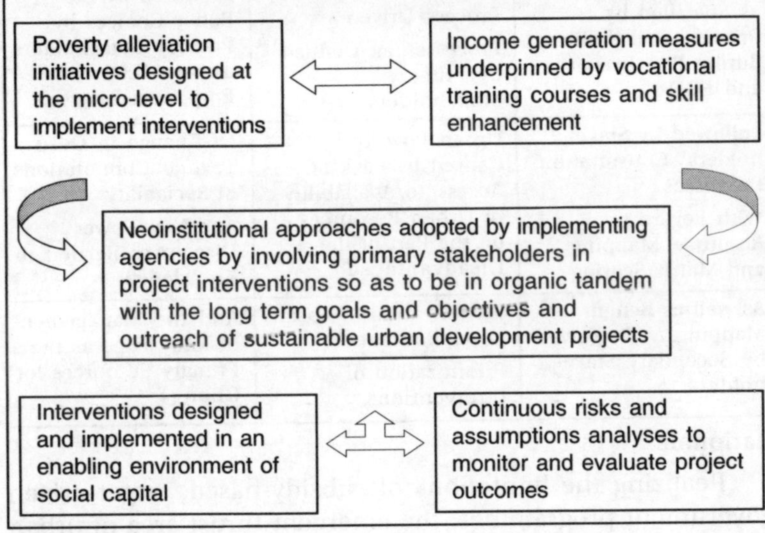

Way Forward

Urban poverty is no more defined exclusively in terms of low levels of income. This concept is now measured against lack of community-level access to basic services such as water supply and sanitation facilities.

NGOs working in the area of poverty alleviation may focus on improving the material conditions of life and enhancing livelihoods of urban communities. Local market interventions may be planned and implemented in this regard to cater to daily consumables and provide convenient access to basic facilities and services.

Effective access to community-level [decentralized] microfinance institutions is a precondition to implement income-generation activities. Microfinance may be made available not only to the consumers but also to the local-level entrepreneurs. Microfinance may also be accompanied by measures to share risks and enhance capacities of financial institutions.

SRO Model		
Strategies	Resolutions	Outcomes
Any Developmental Intervention Related to Core Competencies as Specified by Primary Stakeholders during PPA Exercises and FGDs	Qualitative Shift of Interventions from Progress Driven to Process Driven Processes as Defined by Primary Stakeholders	New Power Dynamics at the Grass-roots Informed by the Policy Choices by Primary Stakeholders as New Actors and Empowered Agents
Followed by Stake-holders' Consultation Processes With Regard to Resource Mapping and Matrix Scoring	Urban Poverty is Caused by Lack of Access to/Availability of Urban Resources on the Part of the Disadvantaged	Of Change in Deep Textual Connotations of Sociability And New Power Discourses Related to Knowledge
As well as Benefit Mapping as Perceived by Secondary Stake-holders	Identification of Local Level Bottlenecks Prioritization of Interventions	And the Management of Knowledge as the Primary Resources for Change

Rationale

Realizing the limitations of subsidy-based, target-driven government programmes, the emergent thrust area of urban development constitutes a self-sustaining revenue-based model underpinned by market mechanisms for dissemination of products and services [related to provisions for basic amenities pertaining to water and sanitation needs of the community]. Such efforts should be strategized/synergized with provisions for flexible access to microcredit.

Strategy

NGOs may on-lend microfinance assistance to women's groups in slums and set up steering committees at the city-level to monitor loans disbursed at competitive market rates for the sake of viability of microfinance projects. Women's groups may be required to open savings accounts in local bank branches that may be operated by joint signatories selected among group members [especially the office-bearers].

One signatory from each group may be required to represent the group at the steering committee-level. NGOs may coordinate steering committee [review and evaluation] meetings. Microfinance assistance for a stipulated period may be disbursed in fixed amounts to group accounts while collaterals may constitute a precondition for such loans.

LogFrame Model

Sl. No.	Goals	Objectives	Risks	Assumptions
1.	Poverty Alleviation	Access to Urban Resources	Population Pressure	Systemic Compulsions
2.	Income Generation	Livelihood Alternatives	Globalization Impacts	Depleted Capacities
3.	Gender Empowerment	Redefining Entitlements	New Material Conditions of Life	Lesser Purchase
4.	Civic Engagement	Capacity Building	Relative Deprivation	Lesser Payoff
5.	Public Action	Voices/Choices	Populism	Adversity
6.	Social Capital	Communitarianism	Fragmentation	Snowball Effect
7.	Institutional Networks	Local Actors	New Vested Interests	Demonstration Effect
8.	Enabling Environment	New Economic Categories	Non-viable Class Dynamics	Domino Effect
9.	Change Management	Paradigm Shift	New Culture Root Paradigms	Carnival Effect
10.	Development Alternatives	Changes in Power Equations	Otherness	Polyphony

Revolving funds may be safeguarded by loan recoveries at a fixed rate of simple interest. Microfinance assistance may be extended to self-help groups even after withdrawal of project-related interventions in order to ensure sustainable development.

Microfinance-Poverty Reduction Nexus[23]

Financial service	Results	Impact on Poverty
Savings Facilities of microfinance institutions (MFIs)	More financial savings Income from savings Greater capacity for self-investments Capacity to invest in better technology Enable consumption smoothening Enhance ability to face external shocks Reduce need to borrow from moneylenders at high interest rates Enable purchase of productive assets Reduce distress selling of assets Improve allocation of resources Increase economic growth	Reduce household vulnerability to risks/ external shocks Less volatility in household consumption Greater income Severity of poverty is reduced Empowerment Reduce social exclusion
Credit Facilities	Enable taking advantage of profitable investment opportunities Lead to adoption of better technology Enable expansion of microenterprises Diversification of economic activities Enable consumption smoothening Promote risk taking Reduce reliance on expensive informal sources Enhance ability to face external shocks Improve profitability of investments Reduce distress selling of assets Increase economic growth	Higher income More diversified income sources Less volatile income Less volatility in household consumption Increase household consumption Better education for children Severity of poverty is reduced Empowerment Reduce social exclusion
Insurance Services	More savings in financial assets Reduce risks and potential losses Reduce distress selling of assets Reduce impact of external shocks Increase investments	Greater income Less volatility in consumption Greater security
Payments/Money Transfer Services	Facilitate trade and investments	Greater income Higher consumption

SJSRY[24]

The Swarna Jayanthi Shahari Rozgar Yojana [SJSRY] is an Urban Poverty Alleviation Programme [UPAP] of the Government of India. It was launched in December 1997, with the objective of increasing employment opportunities for below poverty line citizens in urban areas.

Components

The Swarna Jayanti Shahari Rozgar Yojana has five components such as:

1. Urban Self-Employment Programme [USEP].
2. Development of Women and Children in Urban Areas [DWCUA] programme.
3. Thrift and Credit Societies [TCS] programme.
4. Training Component.
5. Community Structure Component [CSC].[25]

Additional Programmes

There are two more additional programmes for smaller towns:

1. Urban Wage Employment Programme.
2. Infrastructure Component.

Stakeholders

Banks, NGOs, training institutions, the government and below poverty line households are the principal stakeholders of SJSRY.

Community Structures

Community Development Societies, Neighbourhood Committees, Neighbourhood Groups and Below Poverty Line households are the community structures that generally play a major role to implement SJSRY.

Urban Self-Employment Programme

Under this programme, individuals devise an income generation project plan and apply for a loan. A successful plan may receive a subsidy from the government and a loan from a local bank branch. The loan is 80 per cent of the project cost [maximum] while the subsidy is 15 per cent [maximum]. The other 5 per cent is borne by the individual. The maximum project size supported is Rs. 50,000 per individual.[26]

Development of Women and Children in Urban Areas

Under DWCUA, groups of women devise a project plan. A successful plan may receive a subsidy from the government and a loan from an area bank branch. The loan is 45 per cent of the project cost [maximum] while the subsidy is 50 per cent [maximum]. The other 5 per cent is borne by the group. The maximum project size supported is Rs. 2,50,000.[27]

Thrift and Credit Societies

The Thrift and Credit Societies programme brings together 10-20 women from Below Poverty Line families to carry out saving and lending activities. The government gives a lump sum grant to the group after it has been functioning for one full year. The grant is determined at the rate of Rs. 1,000 per member and is to be utilized as a revolving fund.[28]

Training Component

This component sponsors skill development in a variety of service and manufacturing trades as well as in local skills and local crafts. After being trained, beneficiaries should be able to set up self-employment ventures or secure salaried employment with enhanced remuneration. Training institutions such as ITIs/Polytechnics/Shramik Vidyapeeths/Engineering Colleges and other suitable training institution run by the government, private or voluntary organizations may be utilised and provided support for this purpose [but they must be registered with the concerned government department].[29]

Community Structure Component

This component provides a budget for working with other government agencies and departments to address needs of the eligible population beyond jobs and income.[30]

Prosthetic Assistance[31]

Prosthetic assistance is extended to the orthopedically handicapped, blind and deaf and dumb with financial support from GoI [Ministry of Social Justice and Empowerment]. The following aids are provided to persons with disability [PWD] under administration of the state government:

1. Artificial limbs, crutches and hand-driven tricycles are provided to orthopedically handicapped persons.
2. Harmonium and books [Braille System] are provided to the blind.
3. Hearing aids are provided to the deaf and dumb.

The following criteria need to be fulfilled to receive financial assistance under this scheme:

1. The applicant should belong to an economically backward category.
2. The candidate should be the resident of his/her state for more than ten years.

PWD Scholarship[32]

This scholarship is awarded by the Department of Relief and Welfare. Candidates should not exceed the age of sixteen years and should be enrolled at any recognized educational institution below Class IX. Financial assistance for educational purposes will be provided from Class XI onwards. Tenure of the scholarship usually extends to the academic years of study. Other conditions remaining the same, the scholarship will be renewable on successful completion of study.

The following criteria need to be fulfilled to receive financial assistance under this scheme:

1. The applicant's candidate should be an Indian citizen and resident of his/her state.
2. The candidate should be blind, deaf and dumb or orthopedically handicapped.
3. The candidate must not be in receipt of any financial help either from the state government or GOI.
4. He/she should sign a declaration to avail of the scholarship.
5. The candidate's monthly family income should not exceed Rs. 500.

Disability Pension[33]

Economically vulnerable persons with disability are also eligible to avail disability pension. The person needs to be declared "unrehabilitable" by a qualified medical board. The person should be the resident of his/her state.

Economic Rehabilitation of the Physically Handicapped[34]

The National Handicapped Finance Development Corporation extends financial assistance to persons with disability for the following purposes:

1. To set up small-scale business enterprises in the service sector. Loans will be sanctioned up to Rs. 2.5 lakh for this purpose. Loans will be sanctioned up to Rs. 20 lakh to set up industrial units.
2. Loan will be sanctioned for higher studies/professional training to cover tuition fees, books, miscellaneous expenses and hostel facilities.
3. Loan will be provided for skill and entrepreneurial developmental programmes.

There are three different schemes under the administration of the Bustee Service Cell as follows: [1] National Social Assistance Programme, [2] Swarna Jayanti Shahari Rojgar Yojana, and [3] Financial assistance provided by the District Industrial Center [Department of Sericulture and Handloom] to needy artists.

National Social Assistance Programme[35]

NSAP has three components, namely National Old Age Pension Scheme, National Family Benefit Scheme, and National Maternity Benefit Scheme.

National Old Age Scheme[36]

A person aged sixty-five years and above can avail financial assistance under this scheme. Family income of this person should not exceed Rs. 4,000 per annum. Each eligible candidate will receive Rs. 100 per month. Altogether GoI will provide 75 per cent of the total amount while the state government will provide 25 per cent of the assistance. Panchayats and municipalities implement this scheme by involving voluntary agencies as much as practicable.

National Family Benefit Scheme[37]

After the death of the head of the family (he/she should be the only earning member), Rs. 10,000 is given to the family at a time on the basis of the Ward Councillor's recommendation. The family income of the person should not exceed Rs. 11,800 per annum.

National Maternity Benefit Scheme[38]

Under this scheme, Central Government assistance is provided as lump sum cash assistance to women of households below the poverty line, subject to the condition that the maternity benefit is restricted to pregnant women for up to the first two live births provided they are of 19 years of age.

Widow Pension[39]

The pension amount is Rs. 150 per month for widows below poverty line. There is no age bar involved.

Annapurna[40]

This GoI scheme provides that foodgrains up to 10 kgs per month will be provided free of cost to such destitute and aged persons who are otherwise eligible for old age pension under the National Old Age Pension Scheme but are not in receipt of the same and whose sons do not reside with them. The Ministry of Rural Development in association with the Ministry of Food and Civil Supplies will implement this scheme.

Local Market Surveys

Development agencies may plan to carry out local market surveys in and around low income group areas where women's self-help groups have been formed in order to facilitate urban poverty alleviation initiatives.

Such micro-level surveys may be contextualized against the macro-level issue of sustainable development underpinned by issues and concerns of income-generation, self-employment and gender empowerment.

Urban development projects more often than not aim to decentralize Operation and Maintenance of civic assets in such a manner that project beneficiaries [primary stakeholders] may efficaciously supervise collective utilities without relying excessively on external financial assistance.

This may be made possible if a sense of ownership or trusteeship is developed among the community in the low-income areas *vis-a-vis* public utilities such as water supply and sanitation, sewerage and drainage and solid waste management.

Such trusteeship may be organically developed by [1] imposing user charges or fees on end-users of community assets[41] and [2] expanding available networks of social capital [mutual trust and cooperation] at the community-level.

It is to be appreciated in this connection that decentralized O&M may only be practicable if [1] end-users are convinced that the services accruing to them merit regular payment of predetermined user fees to concerned authorities and/or agencies, [2] project beneficiaries are included at the policy-making stages as an imperative benchmark of community empowerment, [3] awareness-generation campaigns are planned and executed in areas such as primary health and hygiene, O&M of community assets and enhancement of livelihood patterns, and [4] poverty alleviation initiatives are launched under project interventions to facilitate "affordable access" to upgraded basic urban services and promote overall community development.

Self-help groups and decentralized microfinance institutions at the local-level may constitute able intervention measures that are able to ensure enhanced livelihood levels of the urban poor and promote sustainable development in the context of good urban governance practices.

Women's SHGs may opt for vocational training courses in order to develop product and/or service-related skills that may be initially marketed at the local-level with financial support [grants/soft loans] from nationalized banks.

It is essential to survey local markets in order to assess the demand for goods and services before inception of vocational training courses. This is required for the sake of merchandizing goods and services in conducive market conditions supported by effective demand [underpinned by purchasing capacities].

Local market surveys may constitute field-level indicative exercises that will enable development agencies to decide on vocational training courses. SHG members may be subsequently persuaded to undergo specific training courses for the sake of maximum impact at the level of market interventions.

NGOs and SHG members may subsequently visit local markets on the basis of empirical knowledge derived from surveys. They can even negotiate with the traders to initially push sell their goods by exerting pressure as an interest group. Samples of products made after completion of vocational training courses may be displayed to businessmen in order to ensure quality control.

SHG members may appoint local community-based organization members on a contractual basis to periodically carry their products to nearby markets for distribution to designated dealers. This may expand networks of cooperation at the community-level and help institutionalize interfaces between SHG members and the community in general. This may also help in increased circulation of capital at the level of the decentralized economy and enhance livelihood standards.

Emphasis may be laid more on service-oriented rather than product-related vocational training due to the fact that interventions at the level of services are better placed to succeed than product-related interventions. The logic of globalization generally ensures that branded goods utilize the advantage of economies of scale supported by quality control and packaging of products.

Exceptions occur in the case of services, as the commodification of services generally depend on the concerned packaging *i.e.*, an upmarket beauty parlour that engages trained local women can still perform reasonably well against competition.

This is also valid in the case of low-cost products such as readymade garments for daily wear and inexpensive condiments, handicraft and fast food items that require low-cost investments and whose production units may be downsized, depending on changing expenditure patterns and/or trends of income.

Training Needs Assessment

1. Situation analyses of the low-income areas [with regard to the available businesses and services, existing and potential skills, levels of community preparedness and enterprise as well as awareness related to literacy, caste, religion, gender dynamics and political overtones] may be carried out with regard to income-generation activities and poverty-alleviation programmes.
2. Infrastructural facilities in and around the low-income areas may be examined in order to ensure effective implementation of proposed interventions [formation and/or facilitation of self-help groups and vocational training programmes].
3. Inventory of vocational training needs at the community-level should be prepared in consultation with potential project beneficiaries so that a participatory approach to urban development issues may be institutionalized.

TNA Strategy

Training needs assessment may require concerted field facilitation efforts in order to mobilize the community so that primary stakeholders [prospective project beneficiaries] are adequately motivated to realize their latent potentialities. Development agencies may catalyze community resources and assist capacity-building of primary stakeholders so that self-belief is stimulated and possibilities of poverty-alleviation initiatives and/or income-generation activities made concrete during the course of participatory development as mandated by the stakeholders' consultative process.

Initiation of vocational training in low-income areas may be preceded by the formation and/or facilitation of self-help groups. The community should be guided as and when required but at no point of time should community priorities be subverted to cater to secondary stakeholders' plan of action. Mutual accommodation may be encouraged to institutionalize the community-NGO interface and enhance the cause of sustainable development.

Participatory Poverty Assessment

A Participatory Poverty Assessment is an instrument for including poor people's perceptions and views in the diagnosis and analysis of poverty and the formulation of poverty reduction strategies. PPAs are generally carried out as policy research exercises, linked to governmental policy processes, aimed at understanding poverty and priority poverty reduction actions from the perspective of poor people. More recent PPAs have emphasised their importance in terms of improving the effectiveness of public actions aimed at poverty reduction. PPAs can strengthen more conventional poverty assessment processes through:

1. broadening stakeholder involvement and thereby increasing general support and legitimacy for anti-poverty strategies;
2. enriching the analysis and understanding of poverty by including the perspectives of the poor;
3. providing a diverse range of valuable information on a cost-effective, rapid and timely basis;
4. creating new relationships between policy-makers, service providers and people in poor communities.[42]

Conclusion

The urban poor should have the right to information dissemination and freedom to choose between viable alternatives. These are entitlements that cannot be translated into capacities in the absence of a level playing ground. Both the voices and the choices of the poor may be factored in development-related interventions:

> As countries refine their poverty reduction strategies, the role of human capital, including health and nutrition, is

> receiving considerable attention. People become poorer as a result of bad health or health crises, but being poor also makes people less healthy and more exposed to risk.[43]

NGOs may initially focus on those low-income areas where the community is relatively better mobilized. The axes of civic participation such as civil society organizations and/or community-based organizations may be subsequently identified in order to plan developmental interventions in consultation with Resource Persons and/or Key Informants. Interventions may be scientifically implemented and supported by a plan of action that may be replicated elsewhere if required:

> Social capital refers to the institutions, relationships, and norms that shape the quality and quantity of a society's social interactions. Increasing evidence shows that social cohesion is critical for societies to prosper economically and for development to be sustainable. Social capital is not just the sum of the institutions, which underpin a society—it is the glue that holds them together.[44]

Urban poverty hinders popular participation, as slum dwellers and/or residents of low-income group areas are nearly always engaged in earning their livelihood. Moreover, they cannot generally afford to pay for Operation and Maintenance of physical infrastructure.

Willingness to pay for O&M of civic assets on the part of the urban poor may be ensured by NGOs if the economic condition of primary stakeholders is improved by way of poverty alleviation initiatives.

Self-help groups are expected to serve as a forum to organize the urban poor [especially women] for the purpose of income-generation activities and O&M of collective assets. NGO's way forward in this regard may be conceptualized as follows:

Development and Outreach			
Sl. No.	Plan of Action	Interventions	Outreach
1.	Formation/ Facilitation of Self-Help Groups	Conversion of SHGs into Representative Groups	Conversion of Representative Groups into User Groups
2.	Training Needs Assessment and Market Surveys	Capacity-Building in order to Train the Trainers	Facilitating Interactive Dialogues for Trainers to Share Lessons Learnt
3.	Inception of Vocational Training Courses for SHG/User Group Members	Planning Networks for Trained SHG Members and Developing Market Linkages	Organizing Seminars/ Workshops for Primary as well as Secondary Stakeholders

This is despite the fact that development generally emerges out of chaos and can seldom be planned in a rigid manner. Field-level lessons should be utilized to coordinate between theory and praxes as each case is unique and requires innovative solutions to situation-specific problems.

Redefining entitlements is a process that intrinsically challenges predominant assumptions in the context of growing pressure of population and fragmentation of urban resources. New material conditions of life are redefined and differently molded in this process.

Lesser payoffs in terms of minimum tangible benefits to primary stakeholders may take place as a direct spin-off of the multipliers of poverty reduction programmes. This is somewhat similar to the diminishing marginal utilities of consumption and over-utilization of resources that finally lead to satiety.

Poverty alleviation initiatives and income generation measures may lead to gender empowerment for a certain section of the community. This may or may not lead to formation or facilitation or even enhancement of the available stock of social capital so far as the target groups among the community are concerned.

New culture root paradigms may get entrenched in this critical process as functions of new societal arrangements and perceived specifics of realigned identities and different matrices of power. Such may be the case when new local markets are sought to be explored in the face of established global markets.

Such a state of affairs would require new institutional networks that may work in a milieu of change management predicated by development alternatives. This necessitates a new regime of discourse where the terms beget different signifiers and alternating signifieds.

Voices and choices of the people would become confused otherwise in a cacophony generated by the multitude or the Tower of Babel of policy alternatives. Such an overwhelming otherness would provoke dystopic and dysfunctional social pathologies that would be without any incipient tenets of hospitality whatsoever.

Systemic compulsions of the new international economic order ushered in by the World Trade Organization and the General Agreement on Trade and Tariff may be viewed as in-built disruptions that only add background noise to disturb channels of communication between the market and the consumer who is prepared to utilize significant and limited resources in order to access utilities.

Depleted capacities of primary stakeholders occur as a result of the systemic imperatives of globalization. The government schemes that we have discussed in this chapter may sound workable in theory but are more often than not viable in reality due to this fact.

Populism is another disabling factor that plagues liberal democracies such as the Indian political system. We come across policy decisions that are not commercially tenable in the market but are implemented nevertheless due to the compulsions of so-called pro-people and pro-poor politics.

Local actors may be able to reorient a new brand of politics in their favour by manipulating primary resources available at the grass-roots. But we have to deal with local as well as macro-level politics simultaneously in order to coordinate between the compulsions of subalternist and elitist power approaches.

Our communitarian approach to social realities may ultimately serve to restore the community at the center of our developmental focus but at a significant cost. This cost is the one incurred during informed exercises pertaining to social choice. Focus group discussions on urban poverty more often than not lead to insightful deliberations as conceptualized in the following model:

> So it would appear that the incidence of poverty and the eradication of poverty are often to be studied in a context of change management as conceived by the above model. It is a fact that urban poverty is generally a reflection of existing political equations that are available at the level of microphysics of power.

Obtainable social realities would suggest that poverty becomes institutionalized as a phenomenon in the interest of powerful social actors who are able to obtain the maximum mileage out of the sense of relative deprivation that afflicts civil society.

Poverty is also a function of social asymmetry. Inflation and stagnation of the currency may adversely affect the population in uneven ways. This is due to the fact that social clusters are located along the economic hierarchy in different degrees of embeddedness.

Public action and civic engagement in an enabling environment may or may not entrench channels of cooperation among primary stakeholders. Such vertical divisions among society are caused by differing axes of participation and priorities.

Benefit mapping of poverty alleviation initiatives will sustain the long-term goals and objectives of development agencies due to the fact that such exercises extend credibility to such community-level interventions. Such interventions may continue to be process driven rather than being progress driven as this works out to be more viable at the grass-roots level in the long-run.

So poverty alleviation initiatives may be neoinstitutional in their approach *i.e.* from actors and institutions the developmental focus of NGOs may shift to the actors in institutions paradigm. This would ensure identification with institutional mechanisms on the part of primary stakeholders in an organic manner. Such a process of identification ensures that interventions are more in tune with the ground-level realities of impacting upon the urban poor:

> The effects of poverty on health are often exacerbated by social discrimination and exclusion from health, education, and other services. Women and girls often face discrimination in health and special obstacles in accessing health care. When services are difficult to reach, travel costs may be more prohibitive for women than for men. Women generally earn less than men and have less control over how household resources are spent. Cultural norms may also restrict women from travelling long distances, especially alone, to obtain health services. Poor communities typically face multiple health risks related to their location.[45]

The neoinstitutional approach to alleviate urban poverty may also facilitate good urban governance practices in terms of better accountability, better transparency and more efficacious service delivery mechanisms *vis-a-vis* the municipal authorities.

The governmental schemes mentioned earlier in this chapter may only succeed if there are channels of organic involvement operational between the primary and secondary stakeholders *i.e.* if policy-level choices become institutionalized as the voices of the community.

Any intervention designed by secondary stakeholders may be implemented in consultation with primary stakeholders. Such informative dialogue sessions may begin during the stage of planning for physical works for the urban poor as mandated by developmental projects.

Either the community as a whole or its representatives may be required to attend focus group discussions where urban planners, civil engineers and social entrepreneurs are present to represent the secondary stakeholders. Problems of lack of access to or availability of water supply and sanitation services may be discussed in such platforms. It is to be understood that lack of access to the facilities of life constitutes measurable poverty indicators.

Such service delivery lacunae existing at the grass-roots may be identified by the secondary stakeholders in association with the primary stakeholders in order to formulate workable micro plans that evolve from participatory exercises.

Micro plans are informed by ground realities: so these have a higher rate of probability to succeed when implemented. Minute details of urban planning may be factored in micro plans by the community if decided on the basis of consensus. Priority ranking of available and required resources is essential in this regard.

Urban poverty is predicated by intrinsic problems that are defined by local anatomies and social pathologies. Either distribution channels do not function or else the initiative to consume more is absent due to lesser income levels and rising inflation rates.

The urban poor are rendered increasingly vulnerable either way in terms of entitlements and/or capabilities. Such a state of affairs leads to marginalization of the poor in more critical ways than ever before.

So we conclude that empowerment can subsequently be translated into development if the voices of the community are reflected in an able manner *vis-a-vis* realities of the market. Demand and supply forces will ultimately decide whether defined pockets of urban poverty are able to transform themselves into economically embedded zones of well-being sustained by resolute voices among the open-ended carnival of choices.

NOTES

1. The author is grateful to his colleagues and fellow professionals at Action Aid, Asian Development Bank, Kolkata Urban Service, CARE, Infrastructure Professionals Enterprise, Institute of Social Sciences, Kolkata Environmental Improvement Project, Kolkata Urban Services for the Poor, Price Waterhouse Coopers, Small Industries Development Bank of India, The Energy and Resources Institute, Women's Interlink

Foundation, World Vision as well as different [bilateral] donor/funding agencies, NGOs, CBOs, CSOs and SHGs for several theoretical research and field-level [empirical] insights developed in the course of this chapter.

2. See review of Amartya Sen, *Poverty and Famines: An Essay on Entitlement and Deprivation* [1984]: Human beings are deprived of food in many ways. Sen points out that food availability decline is only one possible cause of occurrence of a famine. Famines can occur even if the food output is sufficient in a region, for example in a situation when certain groups of people become richer and purchase more food leading to a steep rise in the prices, while the poor find the food increasingly unaffordable. Sen conceptualizes these issues in the framework of entitlement and ownership. Obviously, a person gets starved when his exchange entitlement set is a null set *i.e.,* he owns nothing worth exchanging for bundles of food. A famine occurs when a large number of people in a country or a region suffer from such entitlement failures at a same time . . . Sen discusses two alternative methods to measure poverty—the Income method and the Direct method. Both methods essentially represent two alternative conceptions of poverty analysis. The inequality approach to poverty is also found to be very common. Can poverty analysis be put into a policy framework? Sen answers this question in the negative pointing out its difficulties. Sen says that a policy definition is based on a fundamental confusion. But at the same time, Sen fails to answer the question of how then the problem can be solved. http://www.economics-finance.com/Poverty_and_Famines_An_Essay_on_Entitlement_and_Deprivation_0198284632.html
3. Poverty and social impact analysis [PSIA] implies an analysis of the distributional impact of policy reforms on the well-being or welfare of different stakeholder groups, with particular focus on the poor and vulnerable. PSIA has an important role in the elaboration and implementation of poverty reduction strategies in developing countries. It promotes evidence-based policy choices and fosters debate on policy reform options. http://lnweb18.worldbank.org/ESSD/sdvext.nsf/81ByDocName/PovertySocialImpactAnalysis
4. Formation of SHGs, empowerment of its members and making them sustainable are being taken up as strategic interventions by governmental organizations and non-government organizations. http://www.manage.gov.in/pvtext/Abstracts.htm
5. See Giovanna Prennushi, Gloria Rubio and Kalanidhi Subbarao, "Monitoring and Evaluation". http://www.worldbank.org/poverty/strategies/chapters/monitoring/moneval.htm
6. See E. Barbier, "The Concept of Sustainable Economic Development", *Environmental Conservation*, 1987. "The primary objective of the

Sustainable Development is to reduce the absolute poverty of the world's poor through providing lasting and secure livelihoods that minimize resource depletion, environmental degradation, cultural disruption and social instability". http://sdnp.delhi.nic.in/

7. See "Participatory Poverty Assessment" [Community Driven Development]. http://lnweb18.worldbank.org/ESSD/sdvext.nsf/09ByDocName ProjectPreparationImplementationParticipatoryAssessmentsParticipatoryPovertyAssessment
8. Participation of the stakeholders, create conditions for consensus and potential conflict resolution; Peoples participation not only make, programmes and policies more acceptable, they make them cost-effective and enhance ownership; and The stakeholders once brought into a participatory mode, undertake significant follow-up activities on their own accord and enhance social mobilization. These are key contribution to sustainable development. http://www.ecouncil.ac.cr/rio/national/reports/asia/bangladesh/ban4.htm
9. Linkages seek to establish synergy with different institutions, agencies and cooperatives for mutual benefit.
10. The term microcredit is used ambiguously for representing microfinance . . . . But considering the various needs of the poor when undertaking income generating economic activity and their social uplift, the terminology, which is widely accepted by the practitioners of lending to the poor, is MICROFINANCE. This is something of a more powerful weapon for poverty alleviation than microcredit, as it encompasses various financial needs of the poor other than the credit. Microfinance Institutions [MFIs] are defined as institutions whose major business is the provision of microfinance services. http://www.alternative-finance.org.uk/cgi-bin/summary. pl?id=152&language=E
11. See Piyush Tiwari and S.M. Fahad, "Microfinance Institutions in India", in this connection. http://www.gdrc.org/icm/conceptpaper-india.html
12. http://www.adb.org/Documents/Policies/Microfinance/microfinance0100.asp
13. The microfinance initiatives spearheaded by NABARD date back to the mid-1980s, and have helped in assisting the rural poor, especially women, in contributing meaningfully to the process of economic growth in the rural areas. Research studies conducted by NABARD showed that the most important and immediate banking needs of the poor were to keep safe their occasional surpluses in the form of thrift. They also needed consumption loans to meet emergent lifecycle needs. The banking service and products needed to be hassle free. Based on its experiences and the findings of these studies, NABARD initiated a pilot project in 1992 that aimed at financing 500 SHGs across the

country, through the already existing banking network. The bank financed about 600 SHGs by 1993. http://www.nabard.org/index.htm

14. http://www.sidbi.com/english/products/sfmc/microfinance.asp
15. http://harcobank.nic.in/wwc.html#t1 http://harcobank.nic.in/wwc.html
16. "If it were widely available, institutional commercial microfinance could improve the economic activities and the quality of life of hundreds of millions of people in the developing world". See M.S. Robinson, "Addressing Some Key Questions on Finance and Poverty", *Journal of International Development* [Special Issue (1996), Vol. 8, No. 2, p. 154]. However, it is generally concurred that microcredit extended to the poor who are without the capacity to repay can actually aggravate their poverty.
17. http://www.sidbi.com/english/products/sfmc/microfinance.asp *Op. cit.*
18. www.sidbi.com/english/products/sfmc/sfmcinstitutions.asp
19. Small Industries Development Bank of India, an apex financial institution for promotion, financing and development of small-scale industries in India, has launched a major project christened "SIDBI Foundation for Micro Credit" as a proactive step to facilitate accelerated and orderly growth of the microfinance sector in India. SFMC is envisaged to emerge as the apex wholesaler for microfinance in India, providing a complete range of financial and non-financial services such as loan funds, grant support, equity and institution-building support to the retailing microfinance institutions so as to facilitate their development into financially sustainable entities, besides developing a network of service providers for the sector. SFMC is also poised to play a significant role in advocating appropriate policies and regulations and to act as a platform for exchange of information across the sector. Operations of SFMC in the next few years are expected to contribute significantly towards development of a more formal, extensive and effective microfinance sector serving the poor in India. www.sidbi.com/english/products/sfmc/sfmc.asp
20. http://www.adb.org/Documents/Policies/Microfinance/microfinance0601.asp
21. http://www.adb.org/Documents/Policies/Microfinance/microfinance0100.asp
22. *Ibid.*
23. *Ibid.*
24. http://www.janaagraha.org/campaigns/sjsry.htm#bank
25. http://www.janaagraha.org/campaigns/sjsry.htm

26. *Ibid.*
27. *Ibid.*
28. *Ibid.*
29. *Ibid.*
30. *Ibid.*
31. *Ibid.*
32. *Ibid.*
33. *Ibid.*
34. *Ibid.*
35. *Ibid.*
36. *Ibid.*
37. *Ibid.*
38. *Ibid.*
39. *Ibid.*
40. *Ibid.*
41. That may be kept at nominal levels to begin with and then incrementally raised by utilizing the feedback derived from stakeholders' consultative processes. Market dynamics may be taken into consideration at later stages of determining user charges for the sake of commercial viability and long-term [strategic] sustainability of O&M at the community-level.
42. See "Participatory Poverty Assessment", *op. cit.*
43. See M. Claeson, C. Griffin, T. Johnston, M. McLachlan, A. Soucat, A. Wagstaff and A. Yazbeck, "Health, Nutrition and Population" http://www.worldbank.org/poverty/strategies/chapters/health/health.htm
44. http://www.worldbank.org/poverty/scapital/whatsc.htm
45. http://www.developmentgateway.org/node/130661/

5

PARTICIPATION AS DEVELOPMENT[1]

In UWEP Integrated Sustainable Waste Management [ISWM] has become the core concept for understanding and planning waste management in developing cities. ISWM interrelates with strategic planning and management concepts and tools development in complementary sectors like Environmental Sanitation and Integrated Water Resource Management. With regards to the development objectives and beneficiaries UWEP-Plus continues to contribute to a better environment and livelihood for the urban poor. It builds the local capacities to take away obstacles in the development process. In terms of results, the participative ISWM planning will not only capacitate the local stakeholders, the validated methodologies and mechanisms will facilitate ISWM planning in other cities. The pilot projects will not only improve the local infrastructure to evacuate and treat waste and wastewater, on its operational experience will be built in other cities. The substantive research will not only deliver the knowledge for better local management of water and nutrient cycles, it will create arguments for national sector policy making and the importance to support good waste management practice from the global environmental perspective.[2]

Key Words. Bio-medical waste, hazardous waste, house-to-house collection, institutional mechanisms, O&M, participatory management, safe practices, segregation at source, self-help groups, service delivery, urban poverty, user charges, user groups.

Solid Waste Management strategies adopted by development agencies/voluntary organizations/Non-Government Organizations[3] may introduce long-term environmental impact and infrastructural improvements in critical areas of urban management, town planning and specific developmental issues and concerns such as municipal, hazardous and biomedical waste management.

Community-based solid waste management systems based on participatory approaches may also focus on critical issues and concerns such as delivery of comprehensive stakeholder as well as community awareness-generation campaigns, including informal education and training to scavengers working at the landfill sites, extension of door-to-door waste collection services, segregation of biodegradable and non-degradable wastes at source, facilitating market cooperatives to manage waste collection systems and promotion of public-private partnerships.[4]

The Ministry of Environment and Forests [Government of India] has been funding research in multi-disciplinary aspects of environmental & ecosystems protection, conservation and management at various universities, institutions of higher learning, national research institutes and non-governmental organizations. The primary objectives are to develop strategies, technologies and methodologies for better environment management and also create infrastructure and a pool of trained manpower to shoulder the responsibility of environmental management in the country. Environmental Research particularly aims at attempting solutions to the practical problems of resource management and provides necessary inputs for the twin objectives of conservation of natural resources and restoration of environmental quality.[5]

The Research Division after consultation with other divisions in the Ministry, experts on subject and gauging other emerging areas; has decided thrust areas for the next 5 years *i.e.*, up to 2005. The following . . . areas have been proposed for priority action by this Ministry [such as] Development of biological and other interventions for pollution prevention and control, including waste recycling:

1. Development of microbial and other biological methods for treatment of solid and liquid waste, and hazardous industrial effluents.
2. Improvement of processes for low or no wastes.
3. Heavy metals uptake by aquatic and terrestrial plants and other remedial measures for separation of heavy metals.
4. Waste recycling, product recovery and use with emphasis on such wastes as red mud, fly ash, phospho-gypsum, useful metals.[6]

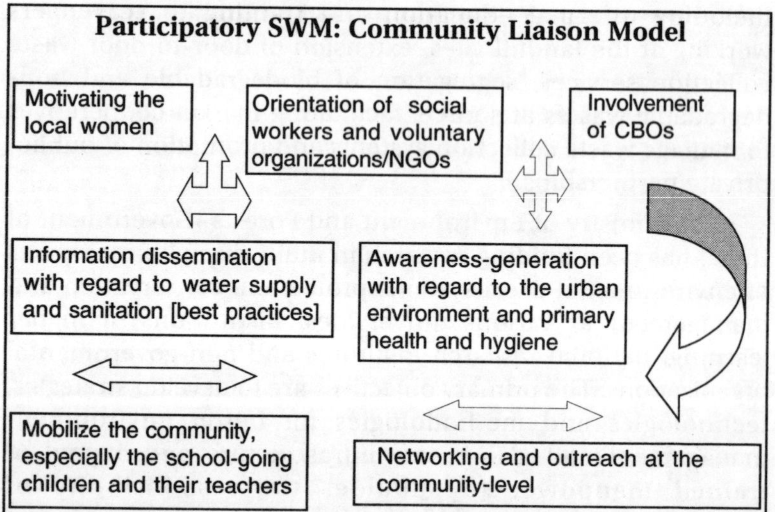

Revenue Streams

Cost recovery mechanisms may be tactically evolved and extensive baseline assessment as well as household sample surveys undertaken to ascertain willingness to pay for solid waste collection, transportation and final disposal services. Development agencies working in this area may deal with.

1. Solid waste collection and segregation at the primary *i.e.*, household-level in order to separate biodegradable and non-degradable wastes.[7]
2. Rational utilization of machinery and manpower in order to optimize utilization of civic resources.

3. Awareness-generation programmes and information dissemination campaigns for primary as well as secondary-level stakeholders.
4. Replacement of open vats and informal dumping points with closed containers that may be lifted by dumper placers on a daily basis.
5. Modernization of the municipal transportation fleet and introduction of mechanized road sweepers and payloaders.
6. Introduction of the direct loading system with the help of dedicated vehicles so that waste is never disposed of on or along roadside pavements.
7. Maintenance of transportation workshops in order to better service the fleet earmarked for solid waste management.

Partcipatory SWM[8]

In case of segregation of solid waste at source, households may be mobilized by Voluntary Organizations/NGOs to separate biodegradable and non-degradable wastes in color-coded litterbins/disposable bags provided for this purpose. House-to-house campaign with regard to collection of segregated waste may be carried out by development agencies.

Biodegradable waste can be finally disposed of in containers and transported to compost plants/sanitary landfill sites. Non-degradable [recyclable] waste may be transported to a local sorting point where rag pickers may be deployed by the concerned municipal authorities in order to generate new livelihoods that may transform waste to wealth by means of recycling of material resources.

Citizens—in order to avoid littering of waste [that leads to health hazards induced by exposure and/or contamination]—may be suitably mobilized by NGOs and VOs to dispose of household waste during scheduled clearance hours and not to dispose of further wastes after completion of the daily round[s] of door-to-door collection service maintained by the municipal authorities/contractor agencies.

Publicity campaigns, outreach exercises and awareness-generation programmes may be designed by professional public relations agencies and subsequently launched by development agencies in consultation with local-level Community-Based Organizations/NGOs/Civil Society Organizations and the concerned civic authorities in this regard.[9]

Development agencies may be engaged in best practices[10] of waste segregation in hotels and restaurants, clinical establishments, railway stations, airports, ports, crematoriums, commercial complexes, wholesale and retail market outlets, residential complexes, educational institutions, urban slums and offices as well as at the grass-roots/household-level in order to segregate biodegradable and saleable non-biodegradable wastes such as polythene bags, plastic goods, glass, metals and hazardous wastes [toxic chemicals and acids].[11]

Papers, cartons and packages may be recycled. Plastics [such as shredded bottles and packages] should not be allowed to be disposed of at the landfill sites.[12] Bio-medical wastes should be transported in covered trucks. Hazardous wastes such as dry cells of batteries, pesticide containers, corrosive chemicals, paints and varnish should be disposed of with proper caution.

SWM Outreach

Development agencies may enter into partnerships with NGOs and CBOs that are in a position to influence group dynamics and community-level interactions. The first step would be to build rapport with local-level formal and informal groups by way of organizing community events that may mobilize primary stakeholders to share a common platform from where their concerns may be voiced and dealt with subsequently.

Such community mobilization events may be cultural or related to sports and/or primary health and hygiene issues. These events may serve to address the collective psyche of prospective/potential beneficiaries. Community-level activities may also streamline an interactive process, utilizing which

Awareness-Generation Campaigns			
Issues	Intervention Strategies	Primary Target Groups	Key Messages
Disposal of solid waste in and around catch pits located near community stand posts	Discussions with CBOs, community meetings with local women	Community [especially local women]	Prevent disposal of solid waste near water stand posts as this leads to unhygienic conditions
Accumulation of wastewater near broken stand posts[13]	Focus Group Discussions with local women	Local women	Water stagnation breeds mosquitoes that spread diseases such as malaria
Disposal of household wastes within bylanes or around municipal handcarts	Community meetings in association with local CBOs/ information dissemination targeting local children/ poster displays at prominent locations	Community in general and local women in particular	Littering of waste leads to unhygienic conditions that help spread [contagious] diseases

identified representative groups would adopt a proactive role in the overall decision-making process and micro-planning of SWM-related activities and implementation strategies.

Within a stipulated period during the morning solid wastes from households should be collected directly either by development agencies or municipal authorities by using handcarts and fibre reinforced plastic baskets. Roadside waste should be swept and disposed of in the containers positioned for that specific purpose.

Arrangement for door-to-door collection of solid waste may be introduced on the basis of subscriptions from the primary stakeholders involved in this process. NGOs may focus on the following issues and concerns in this regard:

1. Willingness to Pay for better civic services.
2. Primary Health and Hygiene.
3. Participatory Operation and Maintenance of civic infrastructure.[14]

WTP underscores the projected revenue earnings of concerned municipal authorities in terms of user charges [fees] in accordance with the guidelines pertaining to O&M of civic assets [and affordable access to the same on the part of primary stakeholders/project beneficiaries].

Better supervision of municipal personnel indicates optimum utilization of manpower presently available *i.e.*, streamlining human resources and avoiding "free rider costs" [non-merit expenditures or subsidies] incurred *vis-a-vis* non-performing assets. Underemployment of the municipal staff may not continue while facilitation of their capacity-building process happens to be in progress.

Such critical benchmarks examine the "value for money" concern of urban good governance as a central issue of sustainable development underpinned by the stakeholders' consultative process.

Perceptions of the community regarding developmental interventions may well be mixed. The community may be generally skeptical so far as the long-term tangible benefits of urban development projects are concerned. So the strategy to be followed to build initial rapport with the community depends on the level of acceptance of development agencies on the part of primary stakeholders.

Community participation activities organized to facilitate initial rapport-building with regard to solid waste management may also depend on the physical layout of different urban localities [especially slums]. For instance, a sit-and-draw competition may help to organize the community in small-size slums that have more or less homogeneous populations.

Community liaison events such as friendly football matches as well as health and/or eye check-up camps may be more effective in large slums with heterogeneous populations [and skewed identities], as it is more often than not difficult to disseminate information efficaciously to a complex and mixed population.

Communities that are characterized by complex demographic compositions and mixed cultural baggages in terms of ethnicity, religion, caste, language, origin and socio-economic backgrounds may directly impact the process of initial rapport-building activities undertaken by development agencies in slums.

Logistic support from local-level CBOs may also determine the kind of developmental interventions to be designed for initial rapport-building exercises. Such exercises may also depend on the formal and informal groups capable of influencing the community by way of interventions and molding public opinion. Personality attributes of key informants, opinion leaders and resource persons are critical in order to gauge whether rapport-building activities are at all required or not at the grass-roots-level.

If the local-level opinion leaders are able to mobilize the community and organize primary stakeholders to initiate dialogues with regard to micro-planning and implementation of developmental activities [physical/civic works] then rapport-building events may not be at all necessary.[15]

The kind of activities to be undertaken by developmental agencies for initial rapport-building exercise should also ensure gender mainstreaming exercises in order to broadbase participatory SWM exercises as far as practicable and incorporate voices and choices of that section of the community most severely affected by unsafe waste disposal practices.[16]

Social Capital

Community mobilization and participation activities on the part of developmental agencies also seek to build and sustain a stock of social capital[17] at the community-level that would facilitate monitoring and evaluation of physical works. Social capital would also ensure that the community continues to look after its collective assets after withdrawal of developmental interventions.[18]

Social capital has been identified as a critical factor in community-driven efforts to provide basic services, particularly for the poor. Through increased coverage, provision of more appropriate and affordable technology, and improved operation and maintenance by users, community-built and operated service delivery systems are expected to perform better and in a more sustainable fashion than those built and managed by governments. Research sponsored by the Social Capital Initiative [SCI] has investigated the role of social capital in the provision of community-based water[19] and sanitation projects.[20]

Communitarian Approach

Community participation strategies usually operate at two levels: [1] the communitarian level where the community is brought back into developmental focus in order to build and sustain a proprietary sense among primary stakeholders[21] and [2] the neoinstitutional level where "actors and institutions" are transformed into "actors in institutions" *i.e.*, end-users of institutionalized civic services are mobilized enough to identify their personal agenda with community interests.

These are in effect utilitarian tools to motivate the community to become proactive and safeguard collective concerns at the corporate level:

> Two community-based systems for solid waste management [SWM] for a squatter-slum area in K West Ward, Mumbai, [Gilbert Hill-Gamdevi Dongri], will be designed and pilot tested. The results will be presented to community members for decisions on implementation. The policy changes will also be discussed with the Mumbai Municipal Corporation [MMC] to facilitate the implementation of the systems. One is a simple primary collection system for which residents must employ sweepers or themselves to carry wastes to designated points for removal by the MMC. In the second option, wastes will be separated at source into organics and inorganics, and the organics will

be composted at small sites in the settlement while the recyclable materials will be sold or given away to waste pickers, and the residuals will be taken to the MMC collection points. Both options require educating the residents through a system of community workers about the practical benefits of clean environs and community operation. The second option demonstrates the resource values in wastes and the potential for "greening" the environment by using the compost. Both options will generate jobs within the community, and both require improved relationships with the MMC garbage collection service. The implementing institution will gain experience in training community workers for environmental interventions and develop expertise in the social aspects of SWM.

. . . Because there is very little research experience in India[22] on the perceptions, motivations and behaviours of people with regard to solid waste, the project will in fact be developing methods to investigate these issues. The links between solid wastes, drainage, sanitation, water supply and the concept of "greening" will be part of the investigation. One of the products of waste recycling, bio-organic soil enricher, can potentially be used in and around the slum for growing ornamental plants, herbs and vegetables, and other plants.

Anticipated results are that the community-based primary collection system and the community-based primary collection with source separation and waste reduction will each be suitable in different parts of the slum. The first system should result in the cooperation between residents [responsible for regular cleaning and taking wastes to collection points], the sweepers who will be paid by the residents and the municipal corporation [removing wastes and cleaning drains]. Residents' committees will be created to monitor progress. The second system will separate organic waste from other waste for composting. The compost will be used for the greening of Gilbert Hill. Indirect benefits, such as improvement in health of residents, adding value to organic and inorganic waste, changes in community perspective on waste, are expected in the coming years.[23]

WatSan Outreach

Context-bound and situation-specific community mobilization and participation programmes may be adequately strategized in order to streamline development-related interventions and facilitate an interactive dialogue process between project consultants/executive agency and primary stakeholders.

Such liaison and awareness-generation programmes serve to build empathy at the stakeholders' level and facilitate dialogic rather than pedagogic interfaces at the project implementation, monitoring and evaluation levels. Community mobilization is not an end but a means to secure rapport-building that—in its turn—may well ensure acceptance of consultants at the community level. This acceptance would finally serve the following purposes:

1. Needs assessment with regard to civic services/ community assets and physical works, vocational training programmes and income-generation activities [to suitably implement poverty reduction initiatives].
2. Awareness-generation with regard to primary health and hygiene and safe [*i.e.* eco-friendly] community practices.
3. Monitoring and evaluation of physical works carried out for the community by the community itself.

Awareness generation is one of the principal facilitating tools by virtue of which any given community may be schooled in terms of quasi-technical specifics related to its needs for basic civic services like [drinking] water supply and sanitation. Awareness generation programmes may also be instrumental to facilitate "affordable access" to such services.

The rapport-building and institutional mechanism [user friendly] approaches deployed by development agencies in this regard may constitute a basket of tools such as optimum utilization of word of mouth publicity by identifying vocal opinion leaders in the urban slums and low income group residential areas, organizing health camps, sports events, street plays, sit-and-draw competitions/quiz contests/debates for children [in order to involve their family members, especially mothers who, in turn, would facilitate informal group mobilization within the community], blood donation camps, posters and other print media campaigns, promotional films and other such public events that may even involve celebrities.

Plan of Action

The aim of initial community liaison exercises would be to stimulate interest among the community with regard to the need to follow hygienic practices. The community in general and the primary stakeholders in particular need to be motivated to discontinue unsafe hygiene practices by ensuring affordable access to sanitation marts and efficient municipal service delivery mechanisms.

The need for safe drinking water, solid waste management, sanitation, sewerage and its inter-linkages with hygiene and health may be stressed by NGOs in this connection. The convenience and privacy accruing due to proper sanitation facilities may also be highlighted. Effective demand for cleaning agents and sanitation-related urban infrastructure may also be focused on by development agencies.

The initial community and social development messages may be kept precise. These may highlight problems faced by the community in their everyday life such as overflowing and/or clogged drains, choked latrines and lack of adequate water supply.

Communication materials may relate to the daily issues and concerns of primary stakeholders. Dynamic tools may include radio, television, videos, films, street theatre and puppet shows while static tools may comprise illustrated pamphlets, leaflets, hoardings, billboards, kiosks, glow signs and posters.

Poverty is one of the principal reasons that reduces efficacious as well as affordable access to basic civic infrastructural services in urban slums due to the financial restrictions on the ability of the primary stakeholders to pay for the municipal services being rendered, thus putting the financial burden of subsidies on the utilities that constitute an integral part of urban management-related institutions and arrangements.

Most urban slums have little or no infrastructure facilities while the people living in these slums more often than not either do not have the financial capability to pay for such basic facilities or else share a common indifference toward the concept of introduction of user charges.[24]

So the very first intervention on the part of development agencies may be the formation of slum units to maintain the existing infrastructure and carry out daily operation and repair-related activities. The unemployed local youth may run such decentralized O&M units against user fees.

The next basket of poverty alleviation initiatives may impact at different levels such as the local market scenario level, vocational training and [available] skills upgradation level and market linkages as well as technical and/or financial backup services level.

WatSan: Community Participatory Model

WatSan involves Community Awareness *vis-a-vis* Primary Stakeholders/Beneficiaries

Community Awareness leads to Affordable Access to Civic Resources

Affordable Access ensures Optimum Utilization of such Resources

Optimum Utilization necessitates O&M of Resources

O&M requires Poverty Alleviation Initiatives

Income-Generation Programmes may be launched to Alleviate Poverty

Self-Help Groups/User Groups may be formed and facilitated to cohere Public Action

Women and Rag Pickers may be united to pool Financial Resources

Community may be mobilized and made aware to exert Peer Pressure

Community - Awareness - NGOs - Interventions - Participation - Development

Methodology

Participatory development initiatives strategize interactive dialogues between primary and secondary stakeholders in order to optimize project-related physical as well as socio-economic interventions.

Primary stakeholders are communities that may be impacted by the onset of development initiatives while secondary stakeholders are the executing/implementing/funding agencies, donor countries/organizations and consultants who hold professional and ethical stakes in the outcome of projects.

The Stakeholders' Consultative Process is in fact is an interactive dynamic that involves learning from one another.

Participatory Development: SWOT Analysis

Sl. No	Strengths	Weaknesses	Opportunities	Threats
1.	High level of community preparedness	Inactive participation of primary stakeholders	Available community-level resources	Low levels of literacy and general awareness
2.	Active participation of the community in participatory M&E activities	Lack of O&M funds	Linkages with nationalized banks/ financial institutions	Intra-community conflicts
3.	Motivation with regard to thrift and credit societies	Brief gestation period preceding vocational courses	Review of local markets	Dysfunctional decentralization
4.	Coordination among user [O&M] groups	Lack of knowledge about community empowerment	Skills enhancement	Inability to network and outreach with similarly affected local-level communities
5.	Creative manner of conflict resolution	Lack of vision	Financial assistance	Delegated activities
6.	Policy choices	Lack of regulatory mechanisms	Gender sensitization and empowerment	Indifference
7.	Leadership qualities	Lack of resources	Awareness campaigns	Lack of interest

SCP tends to underscore community-level best practices/field-level lessons learnt[25] and highlights both innovative and pragmatic solutions to problems of crises management [in the short-run] as well as sustainable urban development and management strategies [in the long-run].

Group Games

Such games may be facilitated by NGOs in order to streamline group dynamics and mobilize group leadership aptitudes as well as attributes and raise the stock of existing social capital at the community-level. Intensive debates and discussions may accompany these games as and when required.

Game 1

How do you intend to work for the uplift of your community?

1. By forming self-help groups.
2. By forming thrift and credit societies.
3. By forming user groups.

Scope of Game 1

Game 1 will examine the level of any given community's motivation with regard to community development works. This is essential during the inception stage of NGOs' community mobilization and participation campaigns that will finally develop into poverty alleviation initiatives. The attitude and orientation of primary stakeholders needs to be assessed before the community as a whole [or its representatives] may be taken on board with regard to income generation activities and/or poverty alleviation programmes.

Strategy Involved in Game 1

The logical mode of progression in this regard is to first form/facilitate women's water user groups that shall be in charge of Operation & Maintenance of water supply and sanitation services in urban slums. Such WUGs may later be upgraded to form informal women's groups that will serve as a platform for future community organizational endeavours such as self-help groups and primary thrift and credit societies.

Game 2

How do you intend to enhance your material conditions of life?

1. By attending STVT courses.
2. By micro-credit assistance.
3. By internal SHG loans.

Scope of Game 2

This game seeks to evaluate the entrepreneurial mindsets of the community by focusing upon different critical areas of developmental interventions. The ideal mode of progress in this area will be to proceed from self-help groups to short-term vocational training courses informed by training needs analyses. Funding support may either be generated internally in terms of SHG loans or externally by way of microfinance assistance by accredited microfinance institutions at competitive rates of interest.

Strategy Involved in Game 2

Prospective beneficiaries—especially local community women identified and selected from particular Nagarpallis—may be mobilized by NGOs to attend community meetings, focus group discussions and participatory rapid appraisal exercises in order to streamline poverty alleviation initiatives at the community level.

Game 3

How do you plan to resolve community conflicts with regard to equitable access to collective resources?

1. By political intervention.
2. By SHG/user group intervention.
3. By CBO/CSO intervention.

Scope of Game 3

This game seeks to explore ways and means of conflict resolution at the community-level. It is a fact that such conflicts are more often than not provoked by unequal access to collective resources.[26] The solution may be

1. to broadbase service delivery mechanisms or else;
2. to devise innovative measures by which community members may gain access to such resources.

Strategy Involved in Game 3

It may be advisable not to involve political leaders in such conflicts although popular representatives may be approached to intervene occasionally. Women's groups, user groups and/or self-help groups may be involved to resolve such conflicts. CSOs and local youth clubs may also be approached in this connection.

Game 4

What is your idea of an SHG?

1. One that extends soft loans to members.
2. One that facilitates income-generation activities.
3. One that promotes O&M of collective resources.

Game 5

What is your idea of external interventions?

1. Those that will ultimately withdraw in the future.
2. Those that will help capacity-building of primary stakeholders.
3. Those that will promote group equations.

Scope of Games 4 and 5

Games 4 and 5 will adjudge the levels of comprehension of community members and seek their feedback with regard to self-help groups and external interventions that may be both planned and facilitated by SHGs in the broader context of participatory development in accordance with the guidelines laid down by bilateral donor/funding agencies.

Strategies Involved in Games 4 and 5

Games 4 and 5 will involve the community in interactive dialogue sessions underpinned by group dynamics. These games will also monitor and evaluate reaction patterns of participants in terms of SWOT [strengths, weaknesses, opportunities and threats] analyses.[27]

Such assessments of the community will—in turn—help NGOs better come to terms with potentialities of the primary stakeholders and design developmental interventions and awareness-generation programmes accordingly. NGOs' group games will overall delimit community strengths in order to focus on community opportunities.[28]

Conclusion

So it is evident that a participatory approach to solid waste management may well facilitate the waste to wealth process during the course of which community-level liabilities are transformed into collective urban assets that can serve to upgrade the civic infrastructure and ensure more sustainable and healthy cities, better material conditions of well-being and an enhanced quality of everyday life.

Delegated Dialogue Model

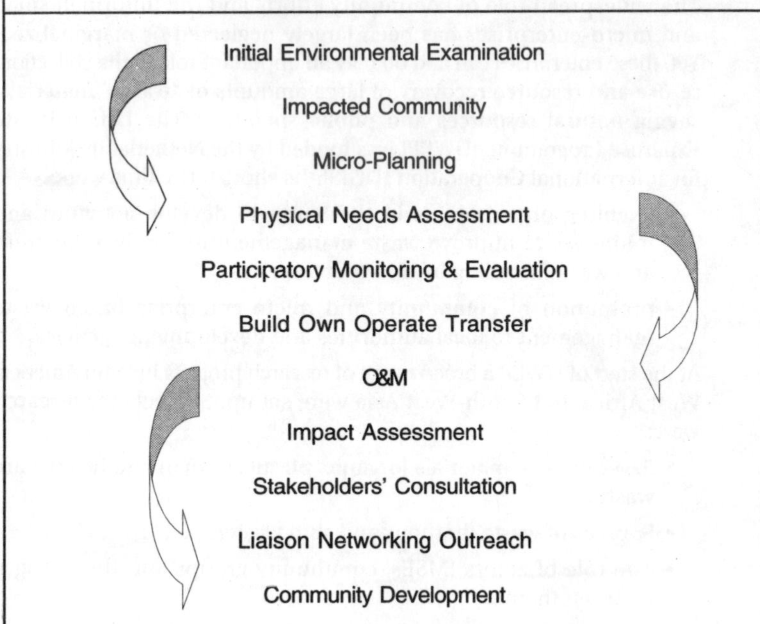

Empowerment at the grass-roots may also indicate a wider arrangement of delegated roles and responsibilities on the part of the concerned municipal authorities. Such role redefinitions and reversal of culture root paradigms may induce further best practices of urban good governance based on social capital, better civic networks, accountability, transparency and a pragmatic plan of action based on the choices and voices of the primary as well as secondary stakeholders.

NOTES

1. The author wishes to thank colleagues at The Energy and Resources Institute and fellow professionals at the Kolkata Environmental Improvement Project for various technical insights and lessons learnt during theoretical/action research, process documentation and field facilitation activities such as cleanliness drives, awareness-generation campaigns and community-consultant liaison meetings.
2. The decreasing ability of the public sector to fully cope with the growing magnitude of the waste management and related environmental health problems has shifted the emphasis towards solutions from private sector enterprises. Privatisation is considered as the grand solution. The widespread role of community efforts and the [informal] small and micro-enterprises has been largely neglected or marginalized. Yet, these enterprises can and do play an important role in the collection, re-use and resource recovery of large amounts of "waste" materials, saving natural resources and public spending. The Urban Waste Expertise Programme [UWEP] was funded by the Netherlands Ministry for International Cooperation [DGIS]. Its short-term aims were:
    - enabling organisations in the South to develop activities and initiatives to improve waste management in low-income areas and waste handling by micro-enterprises.
    - promotion of community and micro-enterprise based waste management to local authorities and development agencies.

    At the start of UWEP a broad range of research projects in Latin America, West Africa and South-West Asia were set up. Subjects for research were:
    - Several waste materials [organic, plastic, human and health care waste].
    - Sources of waste [harbour and ship waste],
    - The role of actors [MSEs, community groups and the linkages between them].
    - The processes [waste collection and separation at source].
    - The financial aspects of waste management and recycling.

    The results of these studies formed one of the starting points for the execution of pilot projects with partners in Bamako [Mali], Batangas

Bay [the Philippines], Bangalore [India] and La Ceiba [Honduras]. http://www.waste.nl/uwep.htm

3. A study on solid waste issues in Dhaka was carried out by JICA in 2000. Recommendations were put forth regarding the creation of a master plan, procurement of collection vehicles, construction of incinerators for the treatment of medical waste and establishment of composting facilities, among others. Low-to-middle income households make up most of the population of Dhaka. Hence, Dhaka designated Rampura Residential Area [low-to-middle income households, population—53,000, per capita generation of waste=0.5 kg/person/day] [total generation: 26.5 tons/day] as a model area under the Kitakyushu Initiative to strengthen community waste management programmes through the organization of a public awareness-raising campaign for residents, which primarily covered health and environmental impacts of solid waste disposal, as well as the impacts of hazardous wastes from hospitals and other community activities. Together with this is the inclusion of the provision of financial, technical and advisory support to the community organization for enhancing participation in the improvement of waste collection, separation and primary disposal systems in the pilot area. The project aimed to bring changes in community behaviour and assist Dhaka City Corporation in reducing burdens for solid waste management. The community is largely unaware of the hazardous impact of the waste; therefore, many households dispose of the waste in drains, ditches and in the open street. Building on the recommendations from JICA, Dhaka proposed the development of a project enhancing linkages with support organizations and the promotion of environmental improvement activities at the community-level. Targets included the improvement of public awareness through local and mass media campaign, and improvement of the level of stakeholder participation in at-source separation, house-to-house collection and primary disposal of solid waste. In the implementation of this project, Dhaka worked together with two NGOs, namely the Bangladesh Integrated Environment Development Forum and AID Bangladesh, who were engaged by DCC to provide house-to-house collection services in 39 wards and have recently started services in different areas of Dhaka. BIEDF has engaged eight rickshaw vans for collection activities. Door-to-door collection begins at 12 AM and continues until 7 PM. There is a conservancy supervisor who monitors the project and reports to the project authority. However, for more effective house-to-house collection, other conditions must be met to address the issue of proper solid waste management. This holistic approach has been taken as a pilot project under the Kitakyushu Initiative. The city has reported increased awareness and cooperation of the general public with regard to separation at source,

proper disposal and recycling through an awareness-building programme with focus on surveys of the residents in Rampura Ward, organization of trainings and community briefing sessions, rallies, development of pamphlets, education of conservancy workers in the proper handling of waste, and counselling to hospital and commercial sectors for effective management of solid waste. The project has not only facilitated public participation in the project area, but has also provided an example to other NGOs and CBOs to start community-based, participatory door-to-door collection systems in other parts of the city. Through the above activities, the impacts and results of the project included the following: [i] increase in public awareness and cooperation of residents in separation at source, proper disposal, recycling, and monitoring of the project; [ii] improvement of the hygienic condition of the area [including foul odours and number of flies and mosquitoes]; [iii] proper mitigation for toxic and industrial wastes through discussions and meetings with hospital and commercial industries; [iv] improved awareness and understanding of Dhaka City Corporation workers, NGOs, and staff of community-based organizations [CBOs] to ensure efficient use of resources; [v] strengthened linkages between CBOs, NGOs and government agencies to increase overall capacity and efficiency; [vi] proposal for the development of a model mini-transfer station [MTS] to ensure proper waste disposal in the community [first of its kind in Bangladesh]; [vii] employment of young persons from the community as conservancy workers. A project site for MTS has been designated in Rampura. Land will be provided to BIEDF free of cost. However, funds for infrastructure development of station have yet to be assured. Once the station is established, the vans now collecting waste from households and nine different containers and bins, can dispose of this waste at a central location. This will minimize scattered waste around containers and bins, and will ease the flow of traffic and pedestrians, as well as facilitate the segregation of waste, promote organic waste treatment methods such as composting and bio-gas production, and discourage the contamination of ground water by waste materials. Similar successful efforts have also been conducted by Sheltech Consultants in Dhanmondi Residential Area [high-income households], as well as Waste Concern [NGO] in the area of composting. These experiences have served as reference for this project. Monitoring teams consisted of community volunteers, NGO and governmental personnel. In December 2003, an inception report by the Japan International Cooperation Agency [JICA] to conduct a study on Solid Waste Management in Dhaka City placed focus on "developing a model for community participation in solid waste management." Background information from the Kitakyushu Initiative pilot project is referred to with regard to NGO coordination throughout the municipality. http://www.iges.or.jp/kitakyushu/Pilot%20Projects/Dhaka%20[Collection]/Dhaka%20[Collection].htm

4. Two papers are particularly useful on this subject. The first is a study carried out on the experience of the Bangalore Urban Platform in Karnataka, India. This study was an input for Tangail municipality in Bangladesh, and the Chairman from Tangail joined the research team to gain some experience directly. This contributed to the enthusiasm in Tangail to adopt a "platform" approach. The second report is the handbook developed in Bangladesh, which gives guidance and links this to reviews of the experience in Tangail .... In Bolivia, research on the Manizales experience in Colombia provided a stimulus for local environmental planning. In addition, at the local level, a resource list of local environmental resources was put together and published .... Use of the information centre to promote "environment brigades" and using competitive debates in schools helped to increase awareness. This is described in "local partnership approach" which analyses the Bangladesh experience in partnership .... Solid waste management was a common issue and action area between the three countries. It is particularly important as it is often the area that is most feasible to get started with action .... In Bangladesh, solid waste management was a very important component in Tangail. The organization of community level management worked well. This is described in the main reports on Bangladesh, Local Partnership Approach and also partly in Learning Lessons from The Bangalore Urban Poverty Alleviation Programme—Participatory Approaches to Urban Development .... A number of relevant issues arise from the SINPA experience. First, the linking of capacity building with planning worked very well. The focus tended to be at times more on getting plans and implementation moving. Capacity building became, as originally intended, a means to the end of improving development .... Significant research was carried out in Argentina linked to the Sinpa Bolivia programme. This analysed the experience of Cordoba. A further study was carried out to compare experience in a number of Latin American cities .... The whole programme was an exercise in using participative approaches. In general, they worked well, but it became clear that the balance between participation and product was very important to avoid "participation fatigue". http://www.ihs.nl/sinpa/capacitybuilding/training.htm
5. http://envfor.nic.in/divisions/re/thrust.html
6. *Ibid.*
7. See Peter Harper's [Centre for Alternative Technology, Wales, United Kingdom] comments in this connection: In order to reduce household waste by 80% you start with fewer and more discriminating purchases (not very popular, but not repulsive, and could be encouraged). Once

the stuff is in the house you obviously have to separate out the solid recyclables: cans, bottles, newspaper. This is typically around 40% of the total, is popular, is encouraged from on high and widely practised. Most of the rest is kitchen and garden waste, packaging paper and card, and plastics. Householders can't do a great deal with plastics themselves; although they have a bad environmental image in a landfill they squash down to less than 10 per cent and they take some CO_2 with them. So let them go: they are a 'pip'. The rest is relatively easy to compost, and home-composting is in one of the intermediate-popularity categories: promising! Local authorities don't like organic waste because in bulk it smells and causes all sorts of health problems, so generally they will encourage householders to compost it: this is even more promising. As well as environmentalists wanting to remove them as potential pollutants, gardeners are going to be interested in the plant nutrients (nitrogen, phosphorus, potash, etc.) contained in household organic wastes, because if reclaimed they could save the cost of fertilisers and soil improvers. If we rank all the household organic wastes, including the liquid ones, in order their nutrient content we get:

- Kitchen waste
- Garden waste
- Urine
- Faeces
- Grey water
- Paper and card

It is encouraging that the two richest items are also ones that are familiar and easy to handle. This is a potential cherry. It is noticeable also that of the liquid wastes the one which is free of pathogens and easiest to collect is also the richest in nutrients: another potential cherry here? In fact if we add the first three together we have got 95% of the nutrients flow through the house: the rest of the liquid wastes—hard to collect and very much against the grain of popular taste!—we can reject as 'pips'. Notice here the important part played by 'doing the numbers'. The biological difficulty in releasing the promise of these potential cherries is that the three clean wastes are far too rich: in order to be composted effectively they need to be combined with a bulky, fibrous material poor in nutrients but rich in carbon. But—another cherry coming up—this is just what we have at the end of the list, readily available and very easy to collect, which most paper banks will not take, and which occupy huge volumes in landfill: packaging card and miscellaneous waste paper. It turns out that paper and card compost extremely well. In fact they considerably improve the quality and quantity of ordinary domestic compost. You can also combine urine and cardboard effectively and the composted product is indistinguishable from fine soil. Picking cherries and spitting out the pips is a preliminary process. Then you go on to designing the hardware, securing the institutional support, stitching up coalitions of interested parties, training, informational campaigns and so on. It is rarely just a simple piece of hardware, but a complex mixture of technique and life-style. There is an important role for eco-villages here as test beds, precisely because they are not afraid of life-style changes. They can try things out, make improvements, get the bugs out. They should be the laboratories of techno-social innovation in the field of sustainability. Their very diversity is a strength because they can sample many different styles and standards of living. The wealthier, bourgeois communities will be more in tune with mainstream western culture, and the radical, low-cost Bohemian communities could develop stronger cherries with longer-term potential and wider global application. Something for everyone! http://genoa.ecovillage.org/genoceania/newsletter/archive/articles/pages/cat_wales.html

8. The development of community-based composting in Jakarta represents an example of sound practice for composting in a developing country. Aid from Australia, Germany, the Netherlands, and New Zealand helped to initiate pilot projects in Jakarta in the 1980s. Later, the Harvard Institute for International Development [HIID] and the Centre for Policy Implementation Studies, supported by the Government of Indonesia and the Jakarta City government, worked on a model for operating small-scale, neighbourhood composting in Jakarta. Starting around 1992 several small composting enterprises were set up in Jakarta. The Jakarta experiments incorporated sound practices in small-scale composting in similar cities, while enhancing the role of the informal sector. The project trained individuals already involved in materials processing and taught them the basics of composting. A second element was compost market stimulation through training the intermediate buyers of recyclables to understand the physical and commercial properties of the compost. In the pilot project, measures were taken to protect the workers' health, but it is uncertain if these precautions will be observed when and if private entrepreneurs take over the model and operate it as businesses. Sound practice would follow up the pilot projects by creating the urban infrastructure both to facilitate more enterprises and to monitor the labour conditions. The Jakarta research project provides a good example of how cities can begin to examine possible sound practices in the composting of municipal solid wastes. An assessment of small-scale, multi-source composting projects in Jakarta and Bandung, done in 1994, suggested that such composting can achieve important reductions in wastes and contribute to the improvement of the neighbourhood environment. Critical to the lasting

success of such projects are good management and market research, and a consistent institutional support system. http://www.unep.or.jp/ietc/ESTdir/Pub/MSW/SP/SP4/SP4_4.asp

9. The Canadian Urban Institute [CUI] participated in a 1998 capacity development initiative organized by Vancouver-based International Centre for Sustainable Cities [ICSC] in Hat Yai, Thailand. The purpose was to build the capacity of the Thai municipalities of Hat Yai and Songkhla related to sustainable solid waste management, by using participatory strategic planning techniques. The workshop transferred the experiences of Canada and of the CUI's projects in the Philippines. The workshop contributed to: building the capacity of local authorities to undertake action planning using participatory, multi-stakeholder approaches; undertaking an assessment of the current state of solid waste management systems and service delivery in the municipalities; brainstorming on key issues affecting the solid waste management problems and challenges of the cities; and identifying priorities and strategies for addressing solid waste management issues. An action plan was drafted with priority areas that included waste separation and waste disposal, public participation, education and awareness . . . . The aim of the project was to build the capacity of the municipalities of Hat Yai and Songkhla to deliver services under a strongly decentralized government system and to manage their solid waste management in a sustainable way, using participatory strategic planning techniques. The project contributed to CIDA's priorities in Thailand at promoting good governance at the local level and the development of linkages between Thai and Canadian institutions. The initiative achieved the following results: Increased capacity of local authorities to undertake action planning using participatory, multi-stakeholder approaches. Assessment of the current state of solid waste management systems and service delivery in the municipalities. Identification of key issues affecting the solid waste management problems and challenges of the city. Identification of priorities and strategies for addressing solid waste management issues and development of an action plan with priority areas that included waste separation and waste disposal, public participation, education and awareness.
http://www.canurb.com/programs/int_programs_asia_thailand.php

10. See "Best practice—waste management and minimization": The starting point for any successful actions are a good knowledge of waste streams and what happens to them. The University of Bath demonstrates best practice in this, with a lot of data, definitions, guidance and other information on its Intranet. Once the waste data is completed, it is likely to highlight a number of strategic options which could be taken, including:

- Setting and achieving target
- Getting better data from/relationship with contractors
- Compaction
- Segregation/recycling
- Waste minimisation initiatives.

Many commercial organizations have found setting and achieving targets—and assigning responsibility for achieving them to be a powerful means of reducing waste generation and costs. Consultation with the people who can influence success—including cleaners and students—is also important. The most ambitious target would be that set by Massey University in New Zealand, which aim to be a zero waste campus by 2015. It's not always easy to get data from waste contractors but it can be done. One secret is to have a nominated manager at the waste contractor. Another is to follow the examples of Derby, Bradford and Leeds Metropolitan Universities—summarised in a HEEPI case—and introduce a 'pay by weight' contract. This involves weighing each waste container collected. The better information this creates allows better matching of collection with demand, with consequent financial savings. Over the last 3 years, Derby has reduced the average number of bin empties per week by approximately 20 per cent and the average monthly number of bins on site by 13 per cent. Reducing the bulk of waste by compressing enables trucks to pick up more materials (potentially reducing transportation costs and saving time, money and fuel, and therefore vehicle emissions), reduces the storage constraints which sometimes makes it difficult to achieve greater separation of waste, and 'stretches' landfill capacity. These generally outweigh the higher energy consumption and financial cost of running the compactor. UMIST, for example, recently invested in a mobile compaction unit, which is capable of carrying 15 tons of waste. Bins are emptied into this rather than a waste contractor's skip. This greatly reduces the number of uplifts needed and therefore travel by contractor's vehicles—certainly more than enough to compensate for the additional fuel used by the compactor. Segregating waste into different streams usually increases costs. Although prices for recycled materials have been volatile and often low in recent years it is important to do it because:

- Increased recycling and reuse means reduced costs of waste disposal, especially if these increase as predicted
- It is a high profile issue for students, especially those coming from Northern Europe or North America
- There is likely to be continuing Government and public pressure to increase the rate of recycling and reuse.

Some institutions (*e.g.* Bradford and LMU) do this by working through their waste contractor, who is allowed to keep any income from recycling as an incentive. Derby took a different approach by sub-contracting collection of recyclable materials to local enterprises.

The ultimate ambition of waste management within any sector or industry is to be able to produce minimal—or even no waste—whilst being able to go about its normal business operations. However in practice this is difficult to achieve and requires the support of all parties from senior management to students. Sheffield College has also achieved considerable success in waste minimisation through a targeted programme. This has included:

- Reusing paper for printing out draft documents and a segregated waste paper
- Collection boxes for empty beverage cans
- Ordering engine oil centrally and charging departments for use, which has halved consumption.

http://www.heepi.org.uk/waste/waste_best_practice.htm

11. See "PREVENTING URBAN WATER POLLUTION": The majority of people now live in cities. These urban environments are characterized by suburbs that contain many acres of hard surfaces. Natural vegetation such as forests and fields slow rainwater down, allowing it to soak into the surface. In contrast, streets, roofs, parking lots and manicured lawns, all provide hard, impervious, surfaces that prohibit rain from soaking into the ground. Since the excess rain water cannot soak into the ground, it accumulates and rushes into storm sewers and waterways. There is a common misconception that water traveling into storm sewers ends up treated at the local wastewater treatment plant. Because of this misunderstanding, *many citizens use storm drains and ditches as places to dispose of all kinds of pollutants.* Thus, storm drains carry large amount of pollution away from urbanized areas mixed with the excess storm water. Street litter, fertilizers, pesticides, herbicides, pet and yard waste, motor oil, anti-freeze, household hazardous wastes, and paint are just a few of the pollutants that find their way into storm drains. This water travels from storm drains into local streams, ponds, and lakes, and ultimately into local streams and rivers. Because storm drains can be a major source of pollution to our waterways, it is important to keep polluting materials out of them . . . . Many household products we use daily contain toxic materials that can threaten public health and the environment. Drain and oven cleaners, paint thinners, and bathroom cleaners are just a few of the items we use that can cause serious health and environmental problems . . . . Fertilizers contain large amounts of chemicals that are good for lawns and plants when used properly. The main chemicals contained in fertilizers are nitrogen

and phosphorus. These two chemicals can cause accelerated growth of aquatic plants in leading to oxygen depletion and large fish kills . . . . Pesticides and herbicides contain toxic materials that pose both environmental and human health risks. Humans, animals, aquatic organisms, and plants can be severely threatened by these chemicals. The toxins found in pesticides and herbicides can runoff lawns and gardens into storm drains and streams whenever it rains . . . : When improperly used, paint can poison people and animals. Lead is an especially harmful content of some paints . . . . Anti-freeze can seriously deplete oxygen from water, and can be harmful to all plant and animal life, including humans . . . . Motor oil can damage or even kill aquatic vegetation and animal life. An oil slick—contaminating two million gallons of drinking water—can develop from one quart of oil . . . . Large quantities of street litter ends up floating in streams, rivers and lakes. Street litter is often made of plastics. Plastics take hundreds of years to biodegrade and can be harmful to birds and animals who mistake them for food . . . . Yard waste can clog storm drains making it difficult to carry away excessive amounts of water during storms . . . . If left on yards, pet waste can release untreated bacteria and other harmful materials into streams. http://www.cjnetworks.com/~sccdistrict/resubwt.htm

12. See "Say 'NO' to Plastic Carry Bags": Thin plastic carry bag has become an intrinsic part of our lives and the urban landscapes. It is one of the most ignored environmental and health problems. Almost everyone including chemists, grocers, vegetable/fruit vendors, restaurants, fast food centers and super markets, put everything we buy in plastic carry bags, as they find it cheaper, easier and cleaner to get them. Even the temples give away "Prasadams" in them. The colourful plastic carry bags can be seen littered around carelessly. They cause more harm when they are strewn allover. But people, unmindful of their hazardous nature, are liberally accepting plastic bags and discarding them all around carelessly. Being non-biodegradable, they choke the earth for hundreds of years, making the soil unfertile, apart from polluting ground water through leaching of toxic substances. They choke open drains, sewer lines and even the stray cattle foraging them for food. The carcinogens—the agents which cause cancer—is likely to be generated during chemical reactions that take place in plastic materials, *inter alia* due to temperature variations. They are reported to enter human body, through food items like sambar, pickles, fatty or liquid items, packed in non-food grade and coloured plastic bags. The regular intake of such food items containing carcinogens, is very hazardous to health over a period of time. Though there may not be any immediate effect on health, it would be too late, once the effects of carcinogen start showing up, say after about 20 years. Basically

there are three main routes for disposal/utilization of enormous quantity of domestic plastic waste being generated these days. One is incineration *i.e.*, burning under controlled conditions for reducing its volume and providing a stable landfill. The second is recycling of plastic waste, which may be difficult to recycle more times, hence the recyclability of the plastic bags reduces. Because of practical problems and the cost factor in segregation and collection, the domestic plastic waste is invariably disposed along with other domestic garbage, for dumping in open landfills, unmindful of its environmental consequences. In the light of environmental and health risks, the cost factors and other problems involved in the management of domestic plastic waste, it is desirable to reduce the quantum of waste generated, by minimizing the use of plastic carry bags and by reusing them in our daily lives. This can be achieved by increasing the thickness of carry bags, so as to make them expensive and to discourage their liberal dispensation, use and disposal. Then whatever is discarded will be collected by the rag-pickers because of their high value realization. The Government of India, keeping in view various aspects of the problem, notified "Recycled Plastics Manufacture and Usage Rules 1999" in September 1999 to regulate the manufacture and use of carry bags and containers made of recycled plastics. The carry bags and containers made out of recycled plastics shall be marked as "Recycled" along with indication of the percentage of recycled material used. http://www.hyderabadgreens.org/plastic.html

13. http://www.iwahq.org.uk/template.cfm?name=iwa_news_37

14. See "Participatory stakeholder framework" [Vol. 1 of 1]: This environmental assessment for the Nepal Health Sector Programme Project discusses likely environmental impacts regarding health care waste management and establishes a strategic framework for action plans to improve waste management including proposed measures to mitigate negative impacts. Health care waste is categorized as follows: infectious waste [bandages and cotton and paper tissue with blood], pathological waste [including body parts, fetus and placentas], sharps [injection needles, scalpels], pharmaceutical waste [outdated and spilled medicines], genotoxic waste [including waste from cancer treatment], chemical waste [discarded solid and liquid chemicals from laboratories, insecticides], waste with high content of heavy metals [broken mercury thermometers, chemicals for developing x-ray photos], pressurized containers, and radioactive waste. The framework presents a risk assessment of the present state of health care waste management and presents findings according to each step in the management process: waste generation, waste segregation, containerization, internal transport and storage, external transport, treatment, disposal, and wastewater. Risks cited at every step were: the absence of incentives

to minimize the volume of waste; risk of infection from the steam sterilization of needles, syringes, and surgical gloves; the absence of regulation of particular hazardous materials such as mercury, and other heavy metals, chlorinated compounds; the lack of awareness of the need to consistently segregate medical wastes from domestic waste; the absence of lids and lack of plastic lining of waste containers, increasing the risk of spreading infectious micro-organisms both during waste transport and cleaning of the containers; cases where waste is transported manually implies a risk of infection to the sweepers if they are not wearing protective clothing; the transport of waste in uncovered vehicles posing a risk as well as a nuisance to the public; the dumping of waste out in the open before being transported to the dumpsite where scavengers [including children] scrounge around for recyclable material; the generation of noxious gases from burning wastes in open fire; the burial in the ground of pathological waste; the decomposition of the organic content of waste in the ground, generating leachate that will flow into the river; the absence of sanitary landfills in Nepal with that could protect against groundwater pollution; and the risk of discharge of treated and untreated wastewater may pose risk to people collecting water for households, fields and gardens, washing, playing, for religious purposes, and spreading ashes from cremation. To minimize some of these risks the report suggests: "green" procurement [purchasing substitute items posing less risk to the environment], waste reduction, recycling, and reuse; quantitatively assessing waste products; waste segregation, handling, transport, treatment, and disposal practices, pollution prevention; and training staff and educating the public about proper waste management. http://www-wds.worldbank.org/servlet/WDS_IBank_Servlet?pcont=details&eid=000160016_20040623172255

15. See "Community Participation in the Management of the Urban Environment—Senegal": The municipality is involved in different actions, and is represented at the meetings of each continuous assessment committee. It approves the establishment of the routes for the early collection of solid waste in the neighbourhoods involved in the programme. The committee is based in the relevant district health centre. It signs the approved contracts with those requiring private refuse collection. A contract is signed with a cart driver, who is supplied with a horse-drawn cart for which he is responsible. The cart driver ensures a door-to-door refuse collection on a determined route. The contract only requires two hours of early collection from the cart drivers and would like such a link between employment and environment not to distort the cart driver's vocation as road hauliers. Around 450 households have been provided with private sanitation infrastructures, of which nearly 200 are linked to water treatment

plants through a narrow drainage system. Up to 65 per cent of demand has been met, which represents 15 per cent of requirements. The population co-finances this equipment at a rate of about 70 per cent; in the long run, the costs will be entirely covered by the beneficiaries. Cost recovery is ensured by the management committee, which countersigns the contracts for the beneficiaries of the sanitation infrastructures. The costs recovered by the programme are invested into a community revolving fund [savings account], which will allow other inhabitants requesting such infrastructures to benefit from the project. The development of private sanitation has enabled us to confirm the ability of the neighbourhood representatives on the continuous assessment committee to administer the supply of work created by the construction sites. Youths from the neighbourhood have been trained by the programme and organised into several micro-enterprises working in enhancing the value of refuse [recycling, compost and urban agriculture]. http://www.unesco.org/most/africa6.htm

16. Egyptians rate inadequate solid waste management as the top priority urban environmental issue. Sub-standard solid waste management [SWM] systems have serious impacts on public health and economic development. The open burning of solid waste contributes to air pollution and increased respiratory problems. Illegal dumping of trash in public areas attracts pests and vermin increasing the probability of vector borne diseases. The improper management of solid waste and its commingling with medical and hazardous wastes lead to serious health problems and lost workdays. In contrast, clean cities promote a healthier workforce, attract investment, and support tourism. SWM services in Egypt have historically been provided directly by governorates. However, they have not been efficient or effective. The Prime Minister's office has targeted nine governorates for SWM privatization with an emphasis on service improvement and cost control. National, municipal, and local laws and ordinances need to be harmonized, proper privatization procedures need to be followed and new support systems need to be established in the areas of contract management and monitoring, public awareness, citizen complaints, and legal and regulatory enforcement. Stakeholders need to be consulted early on in the harmonization process to ensure their concerns and issues are considered and given an opportunity to review and comment on the effort's conclusions to ensure that they are practical and useful. The Governorates need technical advice on the privatization process and the establishment of institutional systems to ensure that privatization results in more effective and sustainable SWM services for their citizens . . . . GreenCOM's activities in the field of solid waste management include design and installation of signage, production

of public awareness and educational materials, and capacity building with various constituencies.

- GreenCOM contracted with a local ad agency to develop public awareness materials for a solid waste management campaign featuring a cartoon sunflower girl character named Khadra. The message of the campaign was "Cleanliness is Part of Faith," and 265 signs were installed, including street signs and lighted lamp pole signs placed in high traffic areas in Cairo, Alexandria, Qalyoubia, and Hurghada governorates, underground metro billboards in Cairo; signs posted on buses in Cairo on heavy usage routes; and large billboards in high visibility locations in Cairo. In addition, 5,000 school posters with tips on reducing, reusing, and recycling were placed in schools nationwide, and pocket and wallet-sized calendars and agendas distributed.
- Working closely with Abt Associates, the technical assistance providers to the Alexandria solid waste management privatization project, GreenCOM developed a strategy for public awareness campaigns to prepare the citizens of Alexandria for the Integrated Solid Waste Management private contract being implemented by the French company Onyx.
- A Solid Waste Management Learning Supplement was developed for secondary technical schools. Solid Waste Management Learning Supplements were distributed to all secondary technical schools in Egypt, 1640 supplements in all. Another 200 sets were distributed at teacher training workshops in Alexandria and the Red Sea. The workshops demonstrated effective use of the multi-media materials accompanying the supplement, including a CD-ROM, a video of industry success stories, overhead transparencies, hands-on classroom activities, and background papers. In addition to Alexandria and the Red Sea governorate, workshops were also held in Aswan, Sohag, Qena, Damietta, and Daqahliya governorates, with a total of 316 teachers from 107 schools attending. http://www.greencom.org/greencom/project_profile.asp?id=41

17. Social capital refers to networks of trust and cooperation at the community-level. See "Social Capital in Water Supply and Sanitation": One billion people lack access to clean water and two billion to adequate sanitation. Lack of clean water and sanitation is the main reason diseases transmitted by human waste are common in developing countries [World Development Indicators 1998]. Social capital contributes to the sharing of information about sanitation as well as the building of community infrastructure. Synergy between the state and civil society can improve infrastructure design and maintenance by securing

financial resources and ensuring that projects respond to community needs . . . . Before community members convene to debate common goals and how much they are willing to pay to meet them, it is important that communities' choices and priorities are well-informed. This often means that some information-sharing and education on health and sanitation needs to take place. Social capital both within and beyond the community can facilitate the knowledge-sharing process . . . . Ownership and management of water supply projects are very important. Water should be managed at the lowest possible level. http://www1.worldbank.org/prem/poverty/scapital/topic/water1.htm

18. See "Urban Social Capital and the Environment": In urban areas, water, waste and energy efficiency used to be the exclusive domain of municipalities. But today existing infrastructures are overwhelmed with growing urban populations and city governments are without adequate resources to manage and protect the environment . . . . Meanwhile, urban communities face numerous environmental dilemmas, many spurred by industrial pollution, such as acid rain, surface and groundwater contamination, and the disposal of solid and hazardous wastes. http://www1.worldbank.org/prem/poverty/scapital/topic/env1.htm

19. Monitoring water quality in developing countries, in view of the continually revised environmental aspects of development projects as well as the wide variety of water quality problems, can be a difficult assignment for most hydrologists. These guidelines were developed by UNESCO, WHO and UNEP personnel in an attempt to simplify and standardize the large variety of sampling programmes, data management and field operations. http://www.un-urbanwater.net/resources/pollution.html

20. See "Social Capital, Water, Sanitation and Waste Management": Social capital affects the community-driven delivery of basic services by facilitating group efforts based on cooperation and collective action. The studies reviewed by Kähkönen indicate that the lack of involvement by local communities contributes to the failure of many government-run and supply-led water and sanitation projects, and to the less-than-satisfactory performance of many large-scale irrigation systems. In reaction to these outcomes, the community-driven development [CDD] approach gives more control of decisions and resources to community groups. In water and sanitation projects, community members are expected to act collectively to design, construct, operate, and maintain the systems together. In irrigation projects, this focus translates into a shift from engineering designs to the organization of farmers. Research on water projects by Isham and Kähkönen in Central Java, Indonesia, and on solid waste management by Pargal, Gilligan

and Huq in Dhaka, Bangladesh suggest that social capital works in several ways to affect the ability of households to work together for the provision of these services. First, these studies show that pre-existing social capital promotes participation of community members by reducing the cost of collective action. Second, these studies indicate that social capital is associated with the level and the nature of household participation. In this respect, the indicators of social capital found most relevant in the literature reviewed by Kähkönen include the social and economic homogeneity of users, the number and density of community groups, networks and associations, and the degree of mutual trust between community members. Most of these variables were found to be relevant in water projects in Central Java. In the case of Dhaka, the social capital indicator found to be most closely related to formation of voluntary solid waste management efforts was the strength of norms of reciprocity, followed closely by norms of sharing among neighbourhood residents. Significantly, household education level was also found to be strongly associated with the likelihood of collective action for solid waste management. Large irrigation systems present certain characteristics that differentiate them from water and sanitation projects. Kähkönen's review shows that irrigation systems require high levels of cooperation and collective action since they represent common pool goods that are rival and non-excludable. The rival nature is reflected in the fact that the use of water by one farmer reduces the amount available to other farmers. Simultaneously, the non-excludable nature of these systems makes it unfeasible to keep certain farmers from using the system or from taking more water than the allotted amount. These undesirable effects can only be avoided through monitoring by the community or a water user association. SCI studies suggest that the effects of social capital on community cooperation and participation will depend on the way the CDD process is defined and implemented, and on the nature of the project, including the choice of technology. Collective action acquires a different dynamic depending on whether community participation is internally or externally promoted, and on the way that participation is advanced. The projects studied in Indonesia by Isham and Kähkönen were externally initiated by concerned agents such as NGOs and government agencies User participation in service design was found to be relatively low in all projects, while final decisions were often made by nonusers. In Dhaka, in contrast, Pargal, Gilligan, and Huq found that participation was high and decisions were taken by all concerned households. Generally, households will have a tendency to free ride on others' efforts, which makes operational rules and monitoring systems important for project effectiveness. Isham and Kähkönen found social capital to be positively and significantly correlated with rules governing water system design and construction. Moreover, they found that pre-existing social capital tends to decrease the need for monitoring of community members and to make the monitoring process easier. The effects of social capital can nevertheless be curtailed by operational rules if the CDD framework is not adequately applied. The level of participation and decision-making in water service design was found to be low, especially in projects where the rules counteracted the community-driven approach by giving the government the right to make the final decision on technological choice. Importantly, even in cases where village leaders were making the final decisions, they did not seem to represent the technology preferences of households any better than outsiders. The role of social capital in community cooperation is influenced, in many cases, by the choice of technology. Isham and Kähkönen show that in water projects, social capital seems to have a positive and significant effect only for piped water systems. This finding is explained by the fact that design and construction of piped systems require more joint effort than designing and constructing wells. Moreover, studies reviewed by Kähkönen indicate that while some innovative, low-cost engineering designs make certain service delivery systems more affordable to the poor, they may demand more intense maintenance and thus increased community cooperation. This is the case, for example, of the condominial system—a low cost waterborne sanitation system-pioneered in Recife, Brazil. SCI research indicates that social capital is associated with a high level of system performance, in large part because mutual trust and shared norms are observed with higher levels of participation. More specifically, in water projects in Central Java, Isham and Kähkönen found that social capital improved system performance by counteracting users' incentives to free-ride and ignore operational rules, while fostering more sustained collective action for operation and maintenance [O&M]. Evidence from this research and the literature reviewed by Kähkönen indicate that social capital influences the content of the rules, but if these rules do not adequately promote and ensure user involvement in service construction and O&M, the effects of social capital on system performance may be reduced. Moreover, this research suggests that although social capital influences rule-compliance, monitoring remains important for system performance. Community participation does not by itself guarantee a system's performance or sustainability, however. In addition to the levels of sustained collective action among users, Kähkönen's review suggests that the performance of rural water projects that have followed the CDD approach varies substantially due to other critical factors such as action or inaction of the public agency, and coordination between residents and the public agency. The qualitative evidence available in the literature supports the assumption that establishment of a users' committee contributes to improved project outcomes through, for instance, better O&M. Isham and Kähkönen show, however, that more than the committee itself is needed. They indicate that in Central Java, some water committees had insignificant or even detrimental effects on project outcomes due in large part to the lack of mechanisms to organize and train these committees properly. At a general level, the impact of CDD projects can be measured by its demonstration effect, as other communities witness the results of collective action by their neighbours. Pargal, Gilligan and Huq found that this demonstration effect was high in the case of the initial community-managed waste disposal efforts in Dhaka. The literature reviewed by Kähkönen also documents high demonstration effects in urban sanitation projects in countries such as Brazil and Pakistan. Moreover, a unique characteristic of the CDD approach is that while relying on pre-existing social capital, it also affects future levels of social capital by increasing interaction and mutual trust. The very process of establishing a system, provided that an adequate CDD framework is applied, might strengthen social networks, build trust, reinforce norms of reciprocity, and even encourage participation in other civic and social organizations. Social capital is not the only factor influencing the emergence and sustenance of collective action for basic service delivery, or the success of community-driven efforts. At various levels, the CCD approach is a joint effort of the government and the community. The community-government cooperative effort makes the policy environment an important factor in the success of collective action for basic service delivery. Even in efforts led by NGOs, the government plays a fundamental role in creating an enabling environment for community-based efforts via policy, legal and regulatory frameworks. More precisely, the extent to which the state ensures, among other things, the enforceability of contracts, the respect of the rule of law, and civil liberties, will have an impact on collective action and the long-term sustainability of community-based projects. Kähkönen's review indicates that collective efforts at service delivery cannot be effective without, for instance, a policy environment that is relatively conducive to community management and that grants farmers or community members a legal right to organize. If associations are not recognized as a legitimate form of organization, their leaders do not have standing to represent members before administrative or judicial bodies. At the same time, the formal courts may not be able to enforce any decisions made by the group and the group will have difficulty in making association officials accountable for their actions. Vertical linkages between community groups and government agencies also facilitate the provision of basic services. Cooperation and coordination between the communities and the government is critical for system performance. Both parties need to trust each other and honour their commitments to carry out the assigned tasks. In community-based water projects, government and NGO officials are expected to design and construct the services with the users. In the case of irrigation systems, local farmers' associations are part of a larger irrigation scheme, and actions of the government are bound to affect the performance of community management and irrigation systems. Farmers need to be able to trust the government bureaucracy, while government officials need to respect farmers' decisions and control of the system at the community level, in order to maintain and strengthen generalized trust. http://www.iris.umd.edu/socat/topics/water.htm

21. The communitarian approach also seeks to reorient the collective in terms of operation and maintenance activities. See "SOLID WASTE MANAGEMENT—Enhancing municipal and private sector partnerships": Solid waste management is a major concern in urban areas in developing countries. Adequate collection and disposal is beyond the resources of municipal authorities. Urban authorities lack the means to manage the rapidly growing amounts of solid wastes. Having no alternative, residents dump their refuse on roadsides and open drains thus contributing to poor environmental health and low quality of life in their communities. Those involved in solid waste management must acquire skills to plan and carry out their work. They must also learn from each other, sharing experiences and drawing lessons to better manage solid waste in their own areas. To respond to this need, Network for Water and Sanitation International [NETWAS] in Nairobi, in collaboration with Sanitation in Developing Countries [SANDEC] and the Swiss Centre for Development Cooperation in Technology and Management [SKAT] of Switzerland have developed a course which aims to develop skills in planning and management of solid waste and provides a forum for participants to learn from the experiences of others. http://www.netwasgroup.com/courses/courses/2005/1

22. India is undergoing an economic, social and political transformation brought about by urbanization and globalization. While this ongoing transition poses numerous challenges including urbanization of poverty, it also offers significant opportunities to accelerate economic growth and improve the overall quality of life for its citizens. Whether this potential is realized depends critically on how Indian cities are managed. Strengthening Urban Management (SUM), through capacity building, is therefore a key area by which cities can meet the challenges of urban development. This entails the creation of a conducive and enabling environment for urban institutions to effectively perform their functions, and for city managers to acquire the knowledge, skills

and expertise necessary to plan, manage and govern their cities. http://www.worldbank.org/wbi/urban/asci/index.html

23. See "Community Based Solid Waste Management in Slums [Bombay, India]": The project will design a community based solid waste management system for Gilbert Hill [the second largest slum in Bombay]. Two approaches to waste management will be tested. The first is a community-based primary collection system by which residents cooperate in collecting wastes and delivering them to transfer points for collection by the municipal authority. The second is community-based primary collection with source separation and waste reduction through composting and trade in inorganic materials for recycling. Project activities will serve to determine people's attitudes to and perceptions of solid waste problems and their capacity to participate in various technological and organizational options; to investigate the nature and quantities of solid wastes from households, shops, enterprises, stables and other sites in Gilbert Hill and to test suitability for composting; to provide training and community education on solid waste management; to test and compare two approaches to solid waste management; and to negotiate with the Mumbai Municipal Corporation for the policy changes needed to implement selected programmes. http://web.idrc.ca/en/ev-4269-201-1-DO_TOPIC.html

24. See "Marketing of Solid Waste Management Services in Tingloy, the Philippines: A study on affordability and willingness to pay": It is vividly illustrated in literature and implemented in projects all over the world that an impressive range of initiatives and actions within cities in Third World countries, together with partners in international support programmes, have been improving the practice of environmental and solid waste management. This, however, stands in contrast with the one factor that allows waste problems to steadily magnify, namely one's attitude, perhaps reluctance, towards waste. Without changing one's behaviour towards waste oneself creates, it will be genuinely impossible to combat the solid waste problem in the near future. With this in mind a marketing study was conducted, the results of which are presented in this working document. Based on a developed methodology for measuring the demand for solid waste services and, compatible herewith, the determination of voluntary solid waste fees, a participatory demand assessment and a questionnaire were implemented in Tingloy, the Philippines. Using the methodology, it was aimed at identifying the most preferred solid waste management alternative for the island. By working closely with the official bodies in Tingloy, interest and support for a community based solid waste system were gained. On that basis the survey could find its way to the residents of Tingloy. In the end, the survey accomplished an awareness raising among the population of the island's

urban area and contributed to a better insight in the needs, preferences and socio-economic situation of the residents. http://www.globenet.org/preceup/pages/ang/chapitre/capitali/cas/a.htm

25. The six-year Urban Waste Expertise Programme [UWEP], 1995-2001, funded by the Netherlands Ministry for International Cooperation seeks to enhance local expertise through research and pilot projects, workshops, training and exchange visits, and dissemination of documented knowledge and expertise generated in the course of the programme. A further aim of the programme is to promote waste policies which facilitate the integration of small businesses and micro-enterprises into existing public and private sector waste management systems; this is to be accomplished through regional meetings and policy conferences with local authorities and development organizations. http://www.waste.nl/

26. See Maurice Schiff, "On the Inefficiency of Inequality": A number of studies have examined the implications of preference interdependence. This paper models individual utility as depending either on the level of other people's consumption or on the difference in consumption levels. It assumes that the impact of an increase in other people's consumption on individual utility diminishes with the level of consumption, raising individual utility when that consumption is very small and lowering it when that consumption is very large. Based on that plausible assumption, the paper shows that, whether individual utility depends on the level of other people's consumption or on the difference in consumption levels, (1) welfare declines with inequality, (2) equilibrium inequality is inefficient, and (3) the optimal intervention leads to a more equal distribution. Implications for the role of development institutions are examined. http://econ.worldbank.org/view.php?type=5&id=37043

27. See "Reduce, Reuse, and Recycle": Source reduction, often called waste prevention, means consuming and throwing away less. Source reduction includes purchasing durable, long-lasting goods and seeking products and packaging that are as free of toxics as possible. It can be as complex as redesigning a product to use less raw material in production, have a longer life, or be used again after its original use is completed. Because source reduction actually prevents the generation of waste in the first place, it is the most preferable method of waste management and goes a long way toward protecting the environment . . . . Source reduction, often called waste prevention, means consuming and throwing away less. Source reduction includes purchasing durable, long-lasting goods and seeking products and packaging that are as free of toxics as possible. It can be as complex as redesigning a product to use less raw material in production, have a longer life, or be used

again after its original use is completed. Because source reduction actually prevents the generation of waste in the first place, it is the most preferable method of waste management and goes a long way toward protecting the environment .... Recycling turns materials that would otherwise become waste into valuable resources and generates a host of environmental, financial, and social benefits. After collection, materials [*e.g.*, glass, metal, plastics, and paper] are separated and sent to facilities that can process them into new materials or products. Recycling is one of the best environmental success stories of the late 20th century. Recycling, including composting, diverted 68 million tons of material away from landfills and incinerators in 2001, up from 34 million tons in 1990. By 1999, more than 9,000 curbside collection programmes served roughly half of the American population. Curbside programmes, along with drop-off and buy-back centers, resulted in a diversion of about 30 per cent of the nation's solid waste in 2001.... You think you have done everything possible in recycling your household, school, or office materials. Deep down, however, you suspect there's more to recycling than setting out your recyclables at the curb. In order to make recycling economically feasible, we must "buy recycled" products and packaging. When we buy recycled products we create an economic incentive for recyclable materials to be collected, manufactured, and marketed as new products. Buying recycled has both economic and environmental benefits. Purchasing products made from or packaged in recycled materials saves resources for future generations .... Another form of recycling is composting. Composting is the controlled biological decomposition of organic matter, such as food and yard wastes, into humus, a soil-like material. Composting is nature's way of recycling organic wastes into new soil used in vegetable and flower gardens, landscaping, and many other applications .... Common household items such as paints, cleaners, oils, batteries, and pesticides contain hazardous components. One way to help determine if your household waste has hazardous components is to read the labels on products. Labels that read danger, warning, caution, toxic, corrosive, flammable, or poison identify products that might contain hazardous materials. Leftover portions of these products are called household hazardous waste [HHW]. These products, if mishandled, can be dangerous to your health and the environment. Although we cannot completely stop using hazardous products, we can make sure that leftovers are managed properly. The best way to handle HHW is to reduce the amount initially generated by giving leftover products to someone else to use. To deal with household hazardous waste, many communities have set up collection programmes to prevent HHW from being disposed of in MSW landfills and combustors. These programmes ensure the safe disposal of HHW in facilities designed to treat or dispose of hazardous waste. More than 3,000 HHW collection programmes exist in the United States. http://www.epa.gov/epaoswer/non-hw/muncpl/reduce.htm

28. See "COLLECTION AND TRANSFER": Efficient, sanitary, and customer-responsive collection of solid wastes is at the heart of a well-run waste management system. Collection services are provided to residents in virtually all urban and suburban areas in the United States, as well as some rural areas, either by private haulers or by municipal governments. The types of collection services have expanded in many communities in recent years to include the special collection or handling or recyclables and yard wastes. Even though disposal costs continue to grow rapidly across the United States, the costs of collecting wastes continue to outpace disposal as a percentage of overall service costs for most communities . . . . Each community should clearly define the goals for its collection system, periodically review the system's performance in meeting these goals, and regularly review and adjust the system's goals to conform to the community's changing needs. To define collection system goals, consider the following issues, the level/quality of service your community's needs, the roles to be played by the public and private sectors, the community's long-term waste management and source reduction goals, preferences for and constraints on available funding mechanisms, existing labour/service contracts that may affect decision-making . . . . The municipality should determine appropriate roles for the public and private sectors. The collection system may be operated by [1] a municipal department, [2] a contracted private firm or firms or [3] a combination of public and private haulers. Regardless of the management options chosen, a clear organizational structure and management plan should be developed . . . . Decisions about how residents prepare waste for pickup and which methods are used to collect it affect each other and must be coordinated to achieve an efficient, effective system. Decisions about the following must be made: Solid waste set-out requirements: guidelines and ordinances specify how residents should prepare solid waste and recyclables for collection should be developed. Point and frequency of collection: how often to collect waste and from what points [curbside, backyard, etc.] must be decided . . . . As in all organizations, good personnel management is essential to an efficient, high-quality waste collection system; hiring and keeping well-qualified personnel is crucial. Because collection jobs are physically demanding, carefully assess each applicant's physical condition. To retain employees, management should provide a safe working environment that emphasizes career advancement, participatory problem-solving, and worker incentives . . . . Maintaining good communications with the public is important to a well-run collection system. Residents can greatly affect

> the performance of the collection system by cooperating with set-out [how waste is presented for collection] and separation requirements, and by keeping undesirable materials, such as used oil, from entering the collected waste stream . . . . Collection and transfer facilities should develop and maintain an effective system for cost and performance monitoring. Just as the goals of a collection programme guide its overall directions, a monitoring system provides the short-term feedback necessary to identify the course corrections needed to achieve those goals. http://web.indstate.edu/recycle/Usersumch4.html

6

MEASUREMENT OF DEVELOPMENT[1]

"A sustainable community is one in which improvement in the quality of human life is achieved in harmony with improving and maintaining the health of ecological systems; and where a healthy economy's industrial base supports the quality of both human and ecological systems."[2]

Key Words. Community, development agencies, impact assessment, indicators, infrastructure, Operation and Maintenance, policy choice, stakeholders, sustainable strategies, user groups.

Sustainable urban development happens to be one of the major concerns of the new millennium at the policy choice level as this underpins an array of growth, risk and assumption factors predicated by a mode of production that is in a state of perpetual flux itself due to fluid forces and relations of production.

Such a state of affairs entails that global bodies such the UN-Habitat[3] and UNDP[4] start exploring viable alternatives to sustain cities and their hinterlands, as these are the growth centers and conurbations that largely determine the direction of the world economy. Urban development, therefore, emerges as a serious business that needs to be addressed in terms of workable strategies. One such methodological tool that is readily available is the Infrastructure Impact Assessment strategy that periodically takes stock of urban development projects.

IIA refers to the exercises by which beneficial impacts of urban development projects may be assessed. To ensure that project facilities are managed efficaciously and that benefits accrue to target groups, IIA programmes are mandated by urban development projects. Such programmes monitor the delivery of services as planned under development projects and measure benefits as they accrue.

IIA generally comprises (i) the preparation of indicators and analyses of benchmarks and (ii) monitoring & evaluation studies to assess the benefits of development projects. This is done by carrying out periodic sample surveys in order to determine the changes in key social and technical indicators over time.

Monitoring is the systematic collection of data to provide management, donors and other stakeholders with an indication of project progress. Evaluation is the systematic and objective assessment of an ongoing or completed project, including its design, implementation and results. Evaluation leads to more informed decisions, allowing those involved in the project to learn from experience and to be accountable to donors and stakeholders. Both Monitoring and Evaluation should be used to demonstrate accountability and to understand the dynamics of the programme. The differences in the objectives, methodology and purposes of Monitoring and Evaluation are shown in the table on page 192. It is important to keep in mind that Monitoring does not replace Evaluation.[5]

Stakeholders' Consultative Process involves different issues and concerns of IIA. In order to scientifically implement project-related activities it is imperative to develop a time-frame of proposed activities to be carried out during project cycles. Any development agency's social action plan will elaborate and schedule the activities to be undertaken in accordance with the aims and objectives of SCP as mandated by the scope of physical works of different urban development projects.

SCP is in fact an interactive dialogue process that handles issues such as resource mapping, benefit mapping, needs assessment, priority ranking and participatory development so that physical interventions may become all the more effective and sustainable at the community-level.

Willingness to Pay underscores the projected revenue earnings of municipal authorities in terms of user charges/

fees so far as Operation & Maintenance of civic assets [and affordable access to the same on the part of primary stakeholders/project beneficiaries] are concerned. Better supervision of existing urban infrastructure indicates optimum utilization of manpower presently available *i.e.* streamlining human resources and avoiding "free rider costs"/non-merit expenditures incurred on non-performing assets [that leads to underemployment] in the process. Both these benchmarks examine the "value for money" concern of urban good governance as a central issue of sustainable development underpinned by the stakeholders' consultation process.

Differences between Outcome Monitoring and Outcome Evaluation[6]

Objective	Outcome Monitoring	Outcome Evaluation
	To track changes from baseline conditions to desired outcomes.	To validate what results were achieved and how and why they were or were not achieved.
Focus	Focuses on the outputs of projects.	Compares planned with intended outcomes achievement. Focuses on how and why outputs and strategies contributed to achievement of outcomes. Focuses on questions of relevance, effectiveness, sustainability and change.
Methodology	Tracks and assesses performance (progress towards outcomes) through analysis and comparison of indicators overtime.	Evaluates achievement of outcomes by comparing indicators before and after the intervention. Relies on monitoring data to information from external sources.
Conduct	Continuous and systematic by Task Managers, Project Managers and key partners.	Time-bound, periodic, in-depth. External evaluators and partners.
Use	Alerts managers to problems in performance, provides options for corrective actions and helps demonstrate accountability.	Provides managers with strategy and policy options, provides basis for learning and demonstrates accountability.

Impact assessment of development projects in terms of new civic infrastructure created is also an exercise related to physical progress measurement of engineering interventions and designs at the level of implementation.

It is important to understand that impact assessment studies also include in their purview the issues and concerns of participatory development. Non-Government Organizations and other voluntary organizations/development agencies that engage social entrepreneurs focused on capacity building rather than mere service delivery in terms of philanthropic humanitarianism [especially during disaster and (tactical) crises management] may interact with the primary stakeholders at the grass-roots who are perceived by the secondary stakeholders as potential and/or prospective project beneficiaries.

Such interactions may include a basket of participatory rapid appraisal tools and strategies such as focus group discussions, personal interviews, community meetings, transacts, priority ranking and matrix scoring.

Needs assessment exercises of physical resources as perceived by the primary stakeholders will be based on such participatory observation methods. These exercises will also be predicated by resource mapping of the proposed project area by consultants.

Micro planning will be developed next in association/ consultation with the primary stakeholders. Resource Persons, Key Informants and/or Community[-Level] Representatives will take part in such grass-roots planning in order to make such exercises as broadbased as feasible.

Development agencies cannot aspire to capture the aspirations of the community without getting involved in such empathetic interactions. It should always be kept in mind that development is intrinsic to local-level realities. It is imperative to be attuned to the local for development to succeed at the macro-level of society.

Engineers will attend all such community-level interactions in order to sensitize themselves with the priorities and perceptions of the community. Such choices may also be informed by gender orientations to development.

IIA indicators may be both quantitative and qualitative in nature in order to include process indicators, progress indicators and qualitative indicators. These will provide primary [field-level] data to monitor the project, evaluate progress of physical work and guide the implementing agencies as well as consultants so far as effective utilization of resources is concerned. IIA indicators may also evaluate the impact of the project on the quality of life of primary stakeholders before and after the project and examine the increased level of community participation and awareness-generation *vis-a-vis* project interventions:[7]

> Indicators are new professional tools for management of housing and urban programmes. The Arabic equivalent of the word indicators is pointers, indicating the outcomes or path to choose, "what approach is more effective" from amongst a possible range of policy solutions. The indicators are in the nature of a diagnostic tool that facilitates the assessment of the current health of the activity that is being assessed, such as the housing conditions, reach out and quality of basic services, income distribution pattern, economic environment or efficacy of governance. The utility of these "pointers" depends upon the quality of the data and the capacity of the users to analyse and interpret them and link them to the specific task in hand. Some of the indicators which have been in use for a considerable time are well-understood. Classic examples are GDP growth rate, unemployment rate, poverty ratio. Such well-recognised indicators in the housing and urban sector have not yet been developed and the indicators programme is an attempt towards this goal. Indicators at present are highly aggregated and have to be disaggregated as per the requirements to contribute significantly to the policy and project formulation process. The decision to disaggregate, the extent of disaggregation and the methodology to do it will, again, depend on the capacity of the users as well as producers of the indicators.[8]

Under different baseline assessments the infrastructure and socio-economic conditions across different sections of potential beneficiaries may be studied in order to gain meaningful insights into the deep text of the problems to be addressed.

Such problems may occasionally assume gender-specific orientations [as already mentioned earlier]. Local women inhabitants belonging to low-income categories may perceive issues of community-level infrastructural development in a different manner from the men.

Critical areas related to water supply and sanitation services, safe drinking water, bathing spaces and abru walls [for women], toilet units with proper security and water arrangements, provisions for security lighting, solid waste disposal litterbins/ vats/containers, efficient sewerage and drainage systems, wide enough pathways, plantation of trees, a community hall [for women to meet and undergo vocational training if feasible], safe electricity connections, access to telephone booths and post offices and police stations and transport networks may be highlighted during discussions with women focused on infrastructural improvements in their locality.

Women [as well as women-headed households] happen to primarily nurture the infrastructure-related impacts of development. So it is imperative to involve them as much as possible during the course of developmental dialogues in order to mainstream gender and factor in specifics of gender-driven discourse *vis-a-vis* project designs, goals, objectives and deliverables.

The major heads of study that may be covered under IIA programmes may include critical areas of sustainable urban development such as solid waste management, sewerage and drainage, water supply and sanitation and slum improvement. Social action plans of development agencies that provide time frames to IIA plans may also lay down strategies for collection of data and assessment of the infrastructure under each head [mentioned above].

SAP may also take into account and investigate socio-economic conditions of the principal stakeholders and analyze their perceptions with regard to the available urban infrastructure. Data under these heads may be collected using both qualitative and quantitative methods in order to freeze the ground realities and design physical interventions under urban development projects.

IIA programmes are generally participatory underpinned by the stakeholders' consultation process. SCP is central to the methodology of IIA whose central objective is to move away from conventional top-down approaches [to monitoring and evaluation] that involve measurement of project performance against pre-set indicators by using standardized procedures and tools.[9] The strategy to facilitate community mobilization and participation campaigns under IIA programmes may be divided phase-wise as follows:

1. Devising an institutional structure for participation that entails community networks of mutual trust and cooperation in order to cohere a sustainable stock of social capital.
2. Establishing and putting into operation mechanisms for the effective functioning of such an institutional structure so that a communitarian approach to development may be adopted.
3. Defining roles and responsibilities for planning, implementation and monitoring *vis-a-vis* primary and secondary stakeholders.

IIA programmes underpinned by the rationale of participatory development may [i] define statements of measurable objectives in terms of physical interventions, [ii] design a structured set of indicators covering outputs of goods & services and their possible impact on project beneficiaries and [iii] include provisions for data collection/analyses and reporting to the client and project consultants:

1. Participation of the stakeholders creates conditions for consensus and potential conflict resolution.
2. People's participation not only makes programmes and policies more acceptable but also makes them cost-effective and enhances ownership.

3. The stakeholders once brought into a participatory mode undertake significant follow-up activities on their own accord and enhance social mobilization. These are key contributions to sustainable development.[10]

The client's/executing agency's Management of Information System may serve to streamline the project's database to coordinate inflow and outflow of information *vis-a-vis* the Project Management Unit, development agencies and consultants in terms of IIA findings.[11] The executing agency's expanding database will necessitate exploration of information storage and sharing techniques facilitated by local area networking and made secure by firewalls built into the system. The project's performance at a certain stage may critically depend on the rate and precision of information flow available between PMU, development agencies and consultants.

MIS may reorient "good practices" of Information Technology by broadbasing IT applications to the development sector and may be divided into [1] data collection, [2] data examination, [3] data processing, [4] data organizing, [5] data analysis and [6] data utilization in terms of heuristic strategies and [tactical] projections.

PMU may install an internal messaging system that will be cost-effective and provide an instant interface between PMU, development agencies and consultants. This may also be utilized to hold e-meetings with donors and funding agencies. Dedicated project websites may be constantly updated and uploaded in order to learn from comparable case studies around the world. This will facilitate information exchange and drawing of lessons on a global scale and promote transparency of all project-related activities.

Vital information exchange relates to a worldview of interaction between stakeholders. This also underscores the need for e-governance where citizen-government interface and public-private participation may be suitably facilitated to sustain urban development projects.

Any information management exercise happens to be a sharing of data between peer groups in order to revise strategies and reorient good practices of development. Learning from one another in the light of lessons derived from ongoing project interventions may constitute a key component of management information systems.

MIS may be designed in a realistic manner so that the work packages, milestones, parameters, goals, objectives, philosophy and aspirations of projects are suitably captured within its ambit.

Change management constitutes an important component of MIS. Any social change that is to be brought about by project interventions may be incorporated in MIS so as to gauge the amount of effective community-level progress realized under specific projects. Adequate indicators need to be developed in order to monitor and evaluate this process.

Process indicators are benchmarks that are concerned with the dynamics of change *i.e.* how change is to be effected at the grass-roots, how the process of change is to managed with the help of external interventions and internal facilitation, how best change can be reconciled with conventions *vis-a-vis* the primary stakeholders?

For instance: Operation and Maintenance is a difficult area to be implemented under projects that are funded by global donor agencies. There may not be any moral compulsion to explore the Willingness to Pay factor on the part of the primary stakeholders as there are no financial obligations involved on the part of the executing agency to pay back the amount of project assistance along with interest [staggered across a given number of years].

Voices-Choices Model

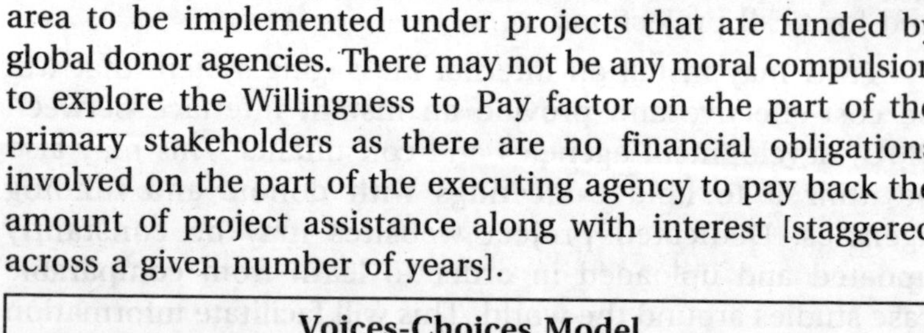

IIA survey reports submitted by development agencies may serve to update PMU, consultants and implementing agencies *vis-a-vis* physical progress of the project. Reassessment and reorientation exercises may be carried out to adjust project priorities in accordance with new demands and perceptions on the part of primary stakeholders.

Urban development projects cannot always follow predetermined approaches. Development more often than not emerges from chaos but subsequently leads to cohesion by resolving the tension between priorities and utilities. MIS may guide PMU, development agencies and consultants to better coordinate project-related activities and avoid overlapping of jurisdictions.

MIS may primarily focus on IIA programmes in order to serve as the consultant-stakeholder interface impacting on crisis management [short-term] and sustainable urban development [long-term]. MIS may also stress on transparency, coordination, accountability and cooperation in order to lend a socially relevant face to information technology.

IIA indicators may be designed keeping in view the fact that development agencies aim to facilitate need-based awareness-generation programmes and the stakeholder's consultation process. Benchmarks may be utilized as indices against which baseline, mid-term and post project surveys may be carried out:

> Henry Taylor and Sam Cole discuss the turning point approach to neighbourhood change as it relates to the barrier and enabler theory. The turning point theory of neighbourhood change challenges existing concepts of urban development, such as the neighbourhood life cycle theory. Taylor and Cole argue that for substantive community revitalization to occur, a city must make a large-scale commitment to removing impediments to societal development by improving housing and education. Then it must create enablers, such as introduction of local commerce and beautification of neighbourhoods, to generate community competence. Community competence, in turn, promotes healthy communities.[12]

IIA sample surveys may be undertaken on a continuous basis throughout the duration of the project in tandem with mid-term and post-project reviews. Consultations with primary beneficiaries as well as project surveys may be scheduled to supply information that may be utilized to plan future project-related activities and reorient ongoing physical interventions. IIA is a continuous process in terms of project-related interventions.

Policy Development Cycle[13]

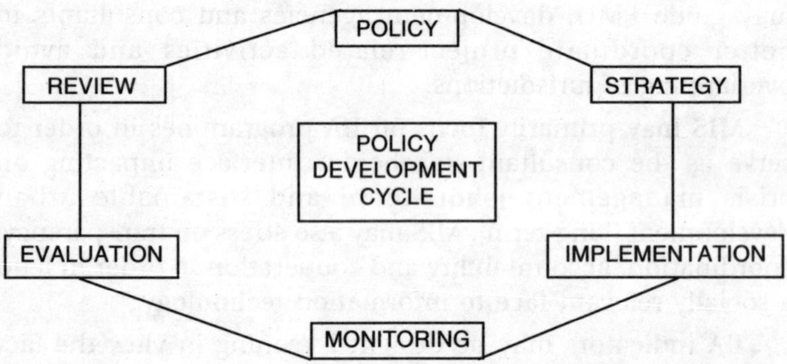

Another critical debate that may be outlined in this context relates to the primary stakeholder versus project beneficiary controversy *i.e.* whether project affected persons as the defining axes of urban development projects may be described as primary stakeholders who define a multiplicity of stakes *vis-a-vis* physical interventions as against the contending role definition of beneficiaries at the center of development predicated by state welfarism and subsidies.

One of the main thrusts of IIA-related initiatives may be the creation of Model Slums on completion of basic infrastructure development works. A slum with a relatively higher level of community cohesiveness and the initiative to assume greater responsibilities may be targeted in this regard.[14]

Intensive community mobilization and participation activities as well as awareness-generation campaigns may be undertaken in such designated slums to ensure maximum role of the community *vis-a-vis* delivery of civic services during implementation of physical works. Formation/facilitation of efficacious community-based institutional arrangements for managing and sustaining project interventions will be the main feature of developmental activities in Model Slums.[15] Water user groups among local women may be formed/ facilitated by development agencies in order to ensure O&M of water supply and sanitation services as well as create employment opportunities at the micro-level of the community. These are imperative measures that may be undertaken to highlight as well as entrench project sustainability measures.

Participation may be defined as an interactive process during the passage of which primary stakeholders gain access to the decision-making process either directly or via institutionalized representation. SCP underscores that community participation is imperative as:

1. It helps identify the needs and perceptions of primary stakeholders.
2. It sustains civic amenities after withdrawal of implementing agencies.
3. It monitors progress of physical works.
4. It streamlines community-level institutional mechanisms.
5. It develops ownership among community members *vis-a-vis* collective assets.

Participatory monitoring and evaluation exercises as a backup to IIA sample surveys are important in order to:

1. Assess the progress of physical works and ensure that maximum benefits accrue to the community in terms of repair/new construction of civic assets and physical infrastructure, and
2. Mobilize the community so that primary stakeholders may undertake Operation and Maintenance of collective assets.[16]

While the first task may be carried out by examining the progress of physical works and interacting with the community in terms of structured as well as unstructured logistics, the second task may be performed by organizing focus group discussions [with community members] related to primary health and hygiene, water supply and sanitation services, safe community practices and poverty alleviation programmes:

Community mobilization and participation activities also seek to build and sustain a stock of social capital at the local-level that may well facilitate monitoring, supervision and evaluation of physical works undertaken during the project cycle. Social capital may also ensure that the community continues to maintain its collective assets after completion of the project and phased withdrawal of interventions.

Community participation strategies operate at two levels: [1] the communitarian level where the community is brought back into developmental focus in order to build and sustain a proprietary sense among primary stakeholders[17] and [2] the neoinstitutional level where "actors and institutions" are transformed into "actors in institutions" *i.e.* end-users of institutionalized civic services are mobilized suitably to identify their personal agenda with community interests. These are in effect utilitarian tools to motivate the community to become proactive and safeguard collective concerns at the level of collectives.

Awareness-generation programmes constitute one of the principal tools utilizing which the community may be made aware of the need for basic services like water supply and sanitation. AGPs may form an integral part of SCP. Based on physical interventions designed by urban planners and policy-makers, development agencies may design awareness-generation campaigns to inform and educate primary stakeholders [intended project beneficiaries] with regard to proposed project interventions, probable outputs of the project [as well as related environmental impacts] and the roles and responsibilities of various project stakeholders as follows:

1. Community mobilization and participation campaigns in order to provide an efficacious/conducive civil

societal backdrop against which the progress of physical works and participatory monitoring & evaluation of such works may be ascertained. CMP exercises may also facilitate formation/institutionalization of formal user groups and representative committees from among the community in order to streamline issues and concerns of a commercially viable Operation & Maintenance system of physical infrastructure [collective civic resources] in the discernible future when "free rider costs/non-merit expenditures" [subsidies] may be discontinued by the concerned municipal authorities.

2. Awareness-generation programmes with regard to primary health & hygiene, sustainable urban development [and best practices associated with such user-friendly type of participatory development], literacy, gender empowerment, community development, civic responsibility and a general sense of urban wealth and well-being sustained by neighbourhood groups/civil societal organizations/ community-based organizations.

Such exercises may primarily focus on areas that have comparatively low educational and literacy levels such as city slums.[18] Community mobilization & participation activities and awareness-generation programmes may be initiated during the inception phase of urban development projects so that such interventions on the part of development agencies continue throughout the project cycle in order to effectively promote sustainable urban development[19] and best practices of good urban governance that is

> characterized by the principles of sustainability, subsidiarity, equity, efficiency, transparency and accountability, civic engagement and citizenship and security, and that these principles are interdependent and mutually reinforcing.[20]

Participation is an interactive process whereby primary stakeholders take part in the decision-making process either in a direct manner or via CBOs/NGOs. Community development events and awareness-generation campaigns are generally strategized to streamline project-related interventions and facilitate dialogues between primary and secondary stakeholders. Such programmes serve to build empathy at the community-level and facilitate dialogic rather than pedagogic terms of discourse at the project implementation, monitoring and evaluation levels. Community mobilization and participation activities are not an end but a means to secure rapport-building that may ensure acceptance of development interventions on the part of project affected persons.[21]

Primary stakeholders may be suitably empowered to sustain developmental impacts of the project *i.e.* their entitlements should be converted into capacities [following Amartya Sen]. This will ensure that project interventions and their benefits sustain over a considerable period of time and motivate future development and further popular initiatives at the grass-roots level where communities have been made capable to make critical decisions affecting the quality of their everyday life.[22]

Axes of civic participation and/or preparedness should be identified in order to plan NGO/CBO/Civil Society Organization interventions in consultation with local-level resource persons and/or key informants. Interventions should be scientifically implemented and underpinned by a definitive plan of action. This is despite the fact that development generally emerges out of flux and can seldom be planned in a rigid manner. Field-level lessons [and insights]—therefore—should be utilized to coordinate between theory and praxes.[23]

Conventional urban development approaches more often than not fail to build the capacities of primary stakeholders to reflect, analyze and act on their own initiative. By contrast, participatory approaches consider primary stakeholders as the agency, rather than the object, of project monitoring & evaluation. Key differences between conventional and participatory M&E are as follows:

Conventional versus Participatory M&E[24]		
Issues & Concerns	Conventional M&E	Participatory M&E
Who plans and manages interventions	Senior managers or outside experts	Local people, project staff, managers and other stakeholders, often helped by a facilitator
Role of Primary Stakeholders (intended beneficiaries)	Provide information only	Design and adapt the methodology, collect and analyze data, share findings and link them to action
How success is measured	Externally defined, mainly quantitative indicators	Internally defined indicators, including more qualitative instruments
Approach	Predetermined	Adaptive

There are different forms of PM&E that are predicated by the type of participants, at what stages such actors are involved and the exact targets of urban development projects. The following principles are generally at the core of PM&E:

1. Participation *i.e.* making the project design flexible to include primary and secondary stakeholders in data analyses and planning and implementation of physical interventions.
2. PM&E inclusiveness requires negotiations to agree on what will be monitored & evaluated and how, what are the implications of data analyses and how survey findings will be shared and action taken to streamline project-related activities.
3. This facilitates learning of lessons that constitute the basis for subsequent project interventions.
4. Flexibility is essential since the number, role and skills of stakeholders, the external environment and related factors change over time.[25]

The advantages of using a participatory approach to IIA [according to United Nations Development Programme guidelines] are as follows:

Advantages of Using a Participatory Approach to IIA[26]

1. Ensures that . . . findings are relevant to local conditions.
2. Gives stakeholders a sense of ownership over . . . results, thus promoting their use to improve decision-making.
3. Helps to "conscientize" stakeholders about the causes of their situation.
4. Increases the understanding of stakeholders of their own programme strategy and processes: what works, what does not work and why.
5. Contributes to improved communication and collaboration between programme actors who are working at different levels of programme implementation.
6. Strengthens accountability to donors.
7. Promotes a more efficient allocation of resources in a time of scarcity.

However, following a participatory approach to IIA can be constrained by low literacy levels in the community, insufficient time, intensity of analytical work to be undertaken during the monitoring/evaluation process and the fact that several issues covered during M&E may not be directly relevant to primary stakeholders. SCP may underpin a participatory approach to IIA. The first step of a participatory IIA programme is to identify key stakeholders whose participation will be sought from a large array of institutions and individuals that could potentially affect—or be affected—by proposed project interventions. The borrowers, donor/funding agencies, beneficiaries, affected groups and other interested groups may be studied in this connection. Participatory evaluations are useful when there are questions about implementation difficulties or programme effects on different stakeholders or when information is wanted on stakeholders' knowledge of programme goals or their view of progress.[27]

Identification of stakes is critical to project designs and will involve assessment of the following items of inquiry:

1. What are the stakeholders' expectations from the project?

2. What benefits are there likely to be for the stakeholders?
3. What resources are the stakeholders able and willing to mobilize?
4. Which interests of the stakeholders are in conflict with project goals?

Once the key stakeholder groups have been identified, their possible interests in the project or economic and sector work may be considered. Certain stakeholder interests are less obvious than others and may be difficult to define, especially if these happen to be covert, multiple or in contradiction with the stated aims/objectives of the organization/individual.

The above questions and answers may guide further inquiries into the interests of each key stakeholder or group. In the case of certain stakeholder institutions/organizations these questions may be answered by reviewing secondary information. For more informal groups, assessment of their interests will probably require consultations either directly with these stakeholders or with persons who are familiar with these groups [resource persons/key informants]. With this background, consideration can be given to how the project might affect these interests: positively or negatively. The process for establishing stakes in a participatory manner is discussed below.

Community mobilization and participation strategies may be divided into the following phases:

1. Formation/facilitation of institutional structure(s) for participation.
2. Establishing and operationalizing mechanisms for the effective functioning of these structure(s).
3. Defining roles and responsibilities for planning as well as implementation and M&E.

This is a comprehensive strategy and may be followed in a flexible manner as per the situation available on the ground. This strategy may be developed keeping slums in mind. The first stage involved in mobilizing the community to participate in project-related activities is to set up an institutional structure whereby participation of primary stakeholders may be solicited in a formal manner. This structure would be the community-project interface, utilizing which secondary stakeholders can hold intervention-related consultations, receive feedback and make decisions with regard to planning, implementation, monitoring & evaluation of project-related activities. This is imperative as it is not always practicable to involve everyone at the community-level during all the stages of project-related interventions. Community-level feedback may inform decision-making in a structured manner on the part of secondary stakeholders to generate tangible outputs.

CMP is not an end but a means to secure rapport-building that—in its turn—may ensure acceptance of consultants at the community level. This acceptance would finally serve the following purposes: [1] needs assessment with regard to civic services/assets and physical works, vocational training programmes and income-generation activities [for poverty reduction purposes], [2] awareness-generation with regard to health & hygiene and safe [*i.e.* eco-friendly] community practices and [3] monitoring & evaluation of physical works carried out for the community by the community itself.

Several formal and informal groups exist within the community. Factors binding the members to a group could be social, economic, cultural or political. Other organizations and institutions, such as NGOs, CBOs and CSOs are also important members of the community exerting influence over group dynamics and community-level interactions.

The first step would be to build rapport with these groups, organizations and institutions. A common way to gain acceptance is to organize creative communication events at the community-level so that primary stakeholders may unite and relate to proposed project interventions. Such events serve as a community-level access while depending all the same on the level of community preparedness in order to assess needs and plan project interventions.

There may already be representative group(s) at the community-level representing different sections of primary stakeholders. Development agencies—in such cases—will have to ensure that all groups [especially the weaker/vulnerable sections or those most impacted by lack of water supply and sanitation facilities] have been adequately represented. The structure created to institutionalize participation should be as representative of the community as possible. The tasks that will be undertaken for this specific objective are as follows:

An initial listing of Resource Persons/Key Informants within slums may be undertaken. This will be achieved through regular interactions with community members, though on a random basis. Assistance of community-based institutions may also be sought in this regard. RPs are community-level spokespersons and opinion-makers who may represent a particular socio-cultural/economic group. They may also have specific political affiliations. RPs may be identified and their profiles prepared for further consultation purposes. Efforts may be made to identify RPs from various geographical locations within slums so that all major settlements are suitably represented. The domain of influence of each RP may also be mapped. Final selection of RPs may be made on the basis of RP profiles and maps.

In order to facilitate participation of women, it may be ideal to identify at least one woman RP per slum. In communities where participation from women would generate overall disapproval, development agencies may ensure that women's views find a place in core committee [user group] consultations.

RPs may prepare a list of formal and informal groups within the community and prioritize these from the perspective of planning and implementing project-related activities. RPs may also select representatives from the prioritized groups (formal or informal). Criteria for selection may be determined by RPs. The objective would be to form a core committee of community-level representatives.

The representative group may comprise individuals as identified and selected by RPs. This representative group will be formed during a joint meeting of RPs and group representatives. Agenda of this meeting may vary. This may depend on the level of preparedness of group representatives to discuss project-related issues, beginning with needs assessment exercises. Advice of RPs may be sought in this connection.

This will involve delegating roles and responsibilities among core committee members and depend on how members want to orient themselves *vis-a-vis* roles and responsibilities. It is important to note that the representative group may decide to function in an informal manner without creating a formal structure. If representative groups already exist [equipped with established procedures and mechanisms] then these will be assessed and developed to ensure community mobilization and participation.

Operational details of functioning, such as frequency of core committee meetings, may also be decided. Similarly, election/nomination of representative group members to responsible positions, criteria for decision-making etc. may also be decided. To what extent these processes/functions can be formalized may be left to core committee members to decide.

Roles and responsibilities of core committee members may define the areas where their capacities need to be enhanced in order to enable them to carry out designated functions. The areas in which capacities of core committee members need to be enhanced will be identified by development agencies in consultation with RPs.

Needs assessment is the first stage of facilitating community mobilization and participation in the project. It will involve undertaking the following set of tasks at the core committee-level. At any stage of these consultations [especially those requiring decisions to be taken], RPs or representatives of formal/informal groups may interact with respective group members for further consultations to facilitate feedback at the core committee-level.

Baseline assessment findings may be discussed with representative groups. A list of identified needs will be accordingly prepared and discussed. The core committee will be requested to comment on identified needs in terms of the severity of problems and urgency of redress. This exercise will generate a list of problems/prioritized needs on the basis of certain criteria that will be suggested by core committee members [who will also rank problems in order of priority]. It is important that problems thus identified and prioritized should be existing and not probable or future ones:

> At the heart of the DISCUS research is the exploration and understanding of the interaction between institutional and social capital. There is naturally a link between these—for example we can assume that existing and well performing local government institutions within the field of sustainable development in the local community can, in fact, create a natural and balanced as well as a supportive environment for different sectors of civil society to further develop those skills necessary to improve their "performance". Putnam [2000] distinguishes between "bonding" and "bridging" forms of social capital. In brief, bonding social capital refers to the networks, links and relationships, which tend to reinforce identities and homogenous groups. In contrast, bridging social capital is more outward looking, often encompassing people from diverse social and geographical backgrounds.[28]

Community-level problems may be identified and cause-effect relationships determined in this process. This may also help to identify benchmarks of solution impacts [facilities proposed to be provided under urban development projects]. The problems identified may be converted into need-based statements. This exercise will require discussions and listing prioritized need statements. Development agencies may next determine areas within slums that need to be upgraded.

A detailed stakeholders analysis may be carried out subsequently, needs and area-wise. Stakes will be established for various settlements in the areas [of slums] that have been identified for upgradation. These settlements may be those that are likely to benefit directly if that need is addressed in that area. This process will be beneficial to determine mechanisms for cooperation from these groups and avoid possible conflicts in the future. Development agencies may share engineering designs [based on community-level feedback] with representative groups. Community meetings may be organized for this purpose.

Representative Groups [or Group Representatives]/ Resource Persons/Key Informants may suggest proposals that will increase income and accordingly increase the effective demand for basic services being provided/strengthened in slums. Skill development needs may be identified accordingly:

> Supporting the development and maintenance of 'bridging social capital' could be through the mechanism of Community Leadership. This term has been applied both to leaders within the community, and to the role that local government plays in encouraging social capital to develop. The literature in this area emphasises the importance of community leaders within civil society organisations [such as social and environmental NGOs]. However, emphasis is also placed on local government providing leadership in terms of 'enabling' communities to develop capacity, but also in the context of municipal entrepreneurship—the role of officers and politicians in promoting and developing a municipality's profile and effectiveness. We need to have some understanding of leadership in order to be able to disentangle charismatic individuals from the processes that might permit both individual and institutional leadership to emerge.[29]

There are different ways to ensure that the community's perspective is taken into account. Early indications of impact may be obtained by surveying beneficiaries' perceptions *vis-a-vis* project progress/services. Such a leading indicator has the twin benefits of consultation with stakeholders and advance warning of problems that may arise.

The achievement of project objectives generally depends on how project beneficiaries respond to the goods or services delivered by the project. Evidence of their response and the benefits they derive requires consultation and data collection that are outside the scope of regular management activities. It is important to identify how beneficiaries are expected to respond to project services because the client and funding/

donor agencies may require evidence of that response if they need to modify activities/strategies. SCP for IIA is relevant in this connection.

Implementing agencies involved need to be responsive to the recommendations that emerge from IIA programmes. Flexibility, a quick response system and beneficiary-orientations are essential characteristics of an implementing agency that will use participatory M&E approaches in an efficacious manner. Consultations with beneficiaries and/or surveys will be scheduled to provide information for use in planning further project activities/rectifying ongoing interventions.

Dissemination of IIA assessment results should include feedback to the stakeholders involved at all the levels of the project, including presentations at the field-level for community representatives, an informal review meeting with project staff and a final workshop with senior project officials:

> Good monitoring is the foundation for good evaluation because it creates a repository of data and other information aimed at assisting evaluators in their work.[30]

For participatory approaches to M&E to be effective, these need to be incorporated into the overall project and undertaken on a continuous basis. The results of an initial self-evaluation exercise, for instance, can provide certain preliminary findings that may constitute the groundwork for follow-up assessments. These results, in turn, can be used to refine the key issues and generate new questions during subsequent M&E. IIA programmes for urban development projects may simultaneously develop new activities and encounter new problems, which may affect the stakeholders' perceptions of project-related activities. Communities may also experience changes from other sources that may have an impact on the progress of the project. All these factors may be built into IIA programmes.[31]

IIA studies in fact act as indices against which project progress in terms of physical work and developmental interventions may be quantified. Such periodic surveys provide insights on the part of both primary as well as secondary stakeholders in the sense that strategies may be revised, goals redefined and praxes reformulated in the light of field-level lessons learnt during implementation of project targets. Such a critical and heuristic manner of learning from past mistakes and making necessary amendments during the project cycle to aim at moving targets more often than not underpin IIA exercises and place such surveys in their proper context from which a panoptic ombudsman role may be played by development agencies *vis-a-vis* project-related interventions.

IIA strategies focus on a central concern of development *i.e.* development for the people, of the people and by the people. IIA strategies lay due importance on the fact that development cannot be like a politics of knowledge discourse that is more often than not imposed from the above without any consideration of ground realities *i.e.* what does the community located at the receiver's end of such development prefer.

Such a superior politics is generally the result of scientific knowledge and an assumption that developmentalist best practices are bound to lead to human wealth and well-being. These are equated with the idea of progress at a material level of the politics of everyday life. But this is just another version of the white man's burden. Although orientalism as a counter philosophy of identity politics was made to suffer considerably by its critics, this much may be asserted that Edward Said's basic challenges and contentions with regard to the claims of superior culture root paradigms and knowledge discourses among civilizations [or constructs and artifacts that we prefer to address as civilizations] still remain largely valid.

IIA studies basically reorient the best practices of community development by bringing back the primary stakeholders into the central focus of interventions. This entails a critical debate between progress versus development and strategy versus interventions:

1. Stage of Exploring: identifying lessons that are of value for redesigning the project or that can be used by others working in the same field.

2. Stage of Explaining: codifying knowledge in such a way that it can easily be identified and used by others.
3. Stage of Exporting: disseminating among other team members, management, or other organizations in the form of lessons learned, the knowledge obtained from the monitoring and evaluation work.[32]

Progress is much more ideational and value-specific *i.e.* community progress indicates changes at the level of value systems, broadbased worldviews, evolution of new managing agencies at the level of the mode of production and dynamic interfaces cohered among the representative collectives who happen to manage community affairs and the agenda of institutionalized civic participation mechanisms.

Development—on the other hand—indicates a compromise between alternative choices, a resolution of policy-level conflicts and exercises in manufactured consent [following Noam Chomsky[33]]. Such discourses may be represented as follows:

Development Discourses Model				
Progress	Culture	Values	Institutions	Policies
Trusteeship	Identity	Planning	Participation	Choices
O&M	Benefits	Sustainability	Interventions	Decisions
Social Capital	Community	Beneficiaries	Stakeholders	Information

The above matrix may be read from any point in a logical sequence that will happen to correlate development with perceived benefits, institutions with social capital that facilitates participation, O&M with trusteeship and identity, culture with values, planning by the community for sustainability, decisions with regard to interventions, choices informed by policies and stakeholders finally emerging as beneficiaries:

> "Sustainable community development is the ability to make development choices which respect the relationship between the three Es—economy, ecology and equity:
>
> 1. Economy—Economic activity should serve the common good, be self-renewing, and build local assets and self-reliance.

2. Ecology—Human beings are part of nature, nature has limits, and communities are responsible for protecting and building natural assets.
3. Equity—The opportunity for full participation in all activities, benefits, and decision-making of a society".[34]

IIA—therefore—emerges as an analytical exercise that may be able to reconcile contending role definitions between stakeholders and beneficiaries[35] as well as resolve the tension of dynamics between the subtle idea of progress and the much more down-to-earth utilitarian notion of sustainable urban participatory development.[36]

NOTES

1. The author is grateful to his colleagues at The Energy and Resources Institute for their field-level insights and theoretical expositions on the subject.
2. http://www.indigodev.com/Sustain.html
3. The Global Urban Observatory [GUO] addresses the urgent need to improve the world-wide base of urban knowledge by helping Governments, local authorities and organizations of the civil society develop and apply policy-oriented urban indicators, statistics and other urban information. The GUO was established by UN-HABITAT [United Nations Human Settlements Programme] in response to a decision of the United Nations Commission on Human Settlements, which called for a mechanism to monitor global progress in implementing the Habitat Agenda and to monitor and evaluate global urban conditions and trends. http://www.unhabitat.org/programmes/guo/
4. See United Nations Development Programme's Millennium Development Goals in this connection. http://www.undp.org/mdg/
5. Adapted from the UNDP Handbook on Monitoring and Evaluating for Results.
6. *Ibid.*
7. Participation of the stakeholders create conditions for consensus and potential conflict resolution; people's participation not only makes programmes and policies more acceptable, they make them cost-effective and enhance ownership; and the stakeholders, once brought into a participatory mode, undertake significant follow-up activities on their own accord and enhance social mobilization. These are key contributions to sustainable development. http://www.ecouncil.ac.cr/rio/national/reports/asia/bangladesh/ban4.htm

8. Stuti Lall (ed), *Economic and Social Indicators for Managing the Growing Economics* [New Delhi: Society for Development Studies, 1996], Chapter III.
9. Participatory Monitoring and Evaluation: Learning from Change. IDS Policy Briefing, Issue 12, 1998. http://www.ids.ac.uk/ids/bookshop/briefs/brief12.html
10. http://www.ecouncil.ac.cr/rio/national/reports/asia/bangladesh/ban4.htm
11. http://solutionportals.com/Components/Overview.htm
12. http://www.utexas.edu/lbj/rhodesprp/01_02/divide/needs.htm
13. Lall [ed], *op. cit.*
14. Networks of community cohesion are sustained by an obtainable level of social capital that facilitates channels of cooperation and trust among primary stakeholders. Enhanced social capital at the grass-roots improves the chances of project success as defined by norms and good practices of participatory development. Any given stock of social capital frozen in socio-temporal contexts is a benchmark of the community's faith in itself as an exemplar of good urban governance.
15. Capacity-building is a dynamic process by which given human entitlements are organically translated into capabilities *vis-a-vis* primary stakeholders. Any given stake is an entitlement that is required to evolve in an enabling environment of sustainable development.
16. Micro-level collectives such as women's water user groups may be established. Self-Help Groups may be formed/facilitated [primarily among women] in order to launch poverty alleviation initiatives and income-generation programmes underpinned by short-term vocational training courses [informed by training needs analyses] and forward/backward linkages. IGPs are required to ensure "affordable access" to basic urban amenities such as water supply and sanitation services.
17. The communitarian approach seeks to reorient the collective in terms of operation & maintenance activities during the project and at the post-project stage.
18. See A. Aoki, B. Bruns, M. Drabble, M. Marope, A. Mingat, P. Moock, P. Murphy, P. Paci, H. Patrinos, Jee-Peng Tan, C. Thomas, C. Winter and H. Yang, "Education". http://www.worldbank.org/poverty/strategies/chapters/education/educat.htm
19. Sustainable development is defined as a pattern of social and structured economic transformations (*i.e.* development), which optimizes the economic and societal benefits available in the present,

without jeopardizing the likely potential for similar benefits in the future. A primary goal of sustainable development is to achieve a reasonable and equitably distributed level of economic well-being that can be perpetuated continually for many human generations. http://sdnp.delhi.nic.in/

20. http://www.un-habitat.org/govern/
21. See Prasenjit Maiti's Introduction to K.R. Gupta [ed], *Urban Development Debates in the New Millennium: Studies in Revisited Theories and Redefined Praxes*, Volumes I-IV [New Delhi: Atlantic, 2004].
22. *Ibid.*
23. *Ibid.*
24. Participatory Monitoring and Evaluation: Learning from Change. *Op. Cit.*
25. *Ibid.*
26. Source: United Nations Development Programme.
27. http://www.unfpa.org/monitoring/toolkit/tool2a.doc
28. http://www.iclei.org/europe/DISCUS/theory.htm
29. *Ibid.*
30. See *Monitoring and Evaluation: Guidelines for Country Gateway Implementation Grants* [Funded by the Development Gateway Foundation], p. 6.
31. "Sustainable communities are defined as towns and cities that have taken steps to remain healthy over the long term. Sustainable communities have a strong sense of place. They have a vision that is embraced and actively promoted by all of the key sectors of society, including businesses, disadvantaged groups, environmentalists, civic associations, government agencies, and religious organizations. They are places that build on their assets and dare to be innovative. These communities value healthy ecosystems, use resources efficiently, and actively seek to retain and enhance a locally based economy. There is a pervasive volunteer spirit that is rewarded by concrete results. Partnerships between and among government, the business sector, and nonprofit organizations are common. Public debate in these communities is engaging, inclusive, and constructive. Unlike traditional community development approaches, sustainability strategies emphasize: the whole community (instead of just disadvantaged neighbourhoods); ecosystem protection; meaningful and broad-based citizen participation; and economic self-reliance." http://www.iscvt.org/FAQscdef.html

32. See *Monitoring and Evaluation: Guidelines for Country Gateway Implementation Grants, op. cit.*, p. 27.
33. The mass media serve as a system for communicating messages and symbols to the general populace. It is their function to amuse, entertain, and inform, and to inculcate individuals with the values, beliefs, and codes of behaviour that will integrate them into the institutional structures of the larger society. In a world of concentrated wealth and major conflicts of class interest, to fulfil this role requires systematic propaganda. http://www.thirdworldtraveler.com/Herman%20/Manufac Consent Prop Model.html
34. *Mountain Association for Community Economic Development (MACED):* Hart Environmental Data. http://www.subjectmatters.com/indicators/Sustainability/DefinitionsCommunity.html
35. *Cf.* Gayatri Chakravorty Spivak, "Can the Subaltern Speak?", in Bill Ashcroft, Gareth Griffiths and Helen Tiffin [eds], *The Post-Colonial Studies Reader* [London/New York: Routledge, 1995]. This essay was originally published in Cary Nelson and Lawrence Grossberg [eds], *Marxism and The Interpretation of Culture* [London: Macmillan, 1988]. Edward W. Said had earlier observed in *Orientalism* [New York: Random House, 1978] that "Orientalism expresses and represents that part culturally and even ideologically as a mode of discourse with supporting institutions, vocabulary, scholarship, imagery, doctrines, even colonial bureaucracies and colonial styles . . . . Taking the late eighteenth century as a very roughly defined starting point Orientalism can be discussed and analysed as the corporate institution for dealing with the Orient—dealing with it by making statements about it, authorising views of it, describing it, by teaching it, settling it: in short, Orientalism as a western style for dominating, restructuring, and having authority over the Orient. I have found it useful here to employ Michel Foucault's notion of a discourse, as described by him in *The Archaeology of Knowledge* and in *Discipline and Punish,* to identify Orientalism. My contention is that without examining Orientalism as a discourse one cannot possibly understand the enormously systematic discipline by which European culture was able to manage—and even produce—the Orient politically, sociologically, and imaginatively during the post-Enlightenment period. Moreover, so authoritative a position did Orientalism have that I believe no one writing, thinking, or acting on the Orient could do so without taking account of the limitations on thought and action imposed by Orientalism. In brief, because of Orientalism the Orient was not (and is not) a free subject of thought or action. This is not to say that Orientalism unilaterally determines what can be said about the Orient, but that it is the whole network of interests inevitably

brought to bear on (and therefore always involved in) any occasion when the peculiar entity 'the Orient' is in question. How this happens is what this book tries to demonstrate. It also tries to show that European culture gained in strength and identity by setting itself off against the Orient as a sort of surrogate and even underground self". Also see—in this connection—Amartya Sen, "Our Culture, Their Culture", *The New Republic* [1 April 1996].

36. Partner Non-Government Organizations to be involved in urban development projects may be selected according to certain pre-set criteria. NGOs so deployed by the Project Management Unit would liaise with Community-Based Organizations in order to jointly work in the area of community mobilization and participation. Such field facilitation exercises involve rapport-building, designing/ implementing vocational training programmes for poverty alleviation and formation as well as facilitation of self-help groups and user groups. Territorial jurisdictions may be earmarked for city-level NGOs in order to streamline their community liaison programmes. Such NGOs may be in an advantageous position to identify local-level Community-Based Organizations that are interested in voluntary social work, understand problems specific to urban slums, gauge the mind set of the community and estimate its level of preparedness so far as actual implementation of training and poverty alleviation programmes is concerned. Personnel strength of partner NGOs may constitute an indicator to assess its human capital. It may be inferred that partner NGOs are adequately equipped to monitor and evaluate CBOs carrying out their community mobilization and participation activities if they employ suitably trained professional staff. Area[s] of activities of NGOs would help identify their expertise in terms of track record and working experience in the field. NGOs specializing in areas such as community development, vocational training and income-generation programmes may be preferred by PMU to liaise with slum-level CBOs in order to carry forward urban projects based on the norms of participatory development. Community-level feedback with regard to the performance of field-level NGOs may constitute a benchmark to assess the perception of primary stakeholders and/or beneficiaries so far project-related socio-economic interventions are concerned. Feedback from CBOs regarding the performance of their partner NGOs is yet another critical indicator that helps assess their acceptance [or otherwise] of professional development agencies/voluntary organizations.

SELECT READINGS

1.1 Civic Infrastructure[1]

Bhide, A.D. "Maintenance of sanitary equipment and organisation of spare parts and inventory system for the solid waste management scheme of Aden in the Peoples Democratic Republic of Yemen" (Nagpur: National Environmental Engineering Research Institute, March 1989).

Coyaud, Daniel P. "Private and public alternatives for providing water supply and sewerage services." Proceedings from *Line Water Sector: Toward Renewed Management*, Baltimore, 12-13 May 1988.

Cristofano, Sam M., and William S. Foster (eds.). *Management of Local Public Works* (Washington, D.C.: The International City Management Association, 1986).

Democratic Socialist Republic of Sri Lanka, *Maintenance Manual for Engineering Services for Municipal and Urban Local Authority* (Bambalapitiya: The Urban Programme Unit, The State Ministry for Provincial Councils, n.d.).

de Saram, S.A. "Maintenance management system for water supply equipment" (Sri Lanka: Institutional Support to the National Water Supply and Drainage Board and World Health Organization, October 1983).

Deschamps, Jean-Dominique. "Privatization of water systems in France," *Journal of the American Water Works Association, February* 1986, pp. 34-40.

Gain, Harvey A. "Financing water supply and sanitation services", paper presented at the Collaborative Council

1. http://www.unchs.org/unchs/english/mainten/biblio.htm

Meeting, Sophia Antipolis, France, 28 November—1 December 1989.

Government of Kenya, Ministry of Local Government and Physical Planning. *Local Authority Development Programme Guidelines,* Manual Six (Nairobi, 1989).

Grigg, Neil S. *Urban Water Infrastructure: Planning, Management and Operations* (New York: John Wiley & Sons, 1986).

Gunnerson, Charles G., and David C. Jones. *Costing and Cost Recovery for Waste Disposal and Recycling* (Washington, D.C., The World Bank, 1984).

Harpharn, Trudy, Tim Lusty and Patrick Vaughan fl (eds.). *In the Shadow of the City.* (New York: Oxford University Press, 1988).

Hatry, Harry P. *Maintaining the Existing Infrastructure: Overview of Current Issues and Practices in Local Government Planning* (Washington, D.C.: The Urban Institute, 1982).

Hatry, Harry P., Sumner N. Clarren, Therese van Houten, Jane P. Woodward, and Pasqual A. Don Vito. *Efficiency Measurement for Local Government Services—Some Initial Suggestions* (Washington, D.C.: The Urban Institute, 1979).

Hébert, Paul A. *Management Information for the Water Supply and Sanitation Sector—A New Initiative for Nepal* (Research Triangle Park: Research Triangle Institute, 1989).

Hébert, Paul A., and IC M. Minnatullah. "Microcomputer water utility billing pilot application in Bangladesh," *American Water Works Association 1989 Annual Conference Proceedings,* Part 1, Sessions 1-23, Los Angeles, California, 18-22 June 1989.

IWSA. "Rehabilitation of mains and pipelines, *IWSA/AIDE Specialised Conference Proceedings* (International Water Supply Agency).

Jones, David C. *Financial Analysis and Cost Recovery: Water Supply Case Study* (Washington, D.C.: The World Bank, 1985).

Marli, John Tepper. *Contracting Municipal Services* (New York: A Ronald Press Publication, 1984).

McCullough, et al. "Urban financial management—Phase 1: case studies and analysis." Final report (Research Triangle Park: Research Triangle Institute, August 1982).

Megeid, L. Abdel, and H.W.E. Davies. *Managing and Financing Urban Services* (Paris: Organisation for Economic Co-operation and Development, 1987).

National Water Supply and Drainage Board, Sri Lanka. "Topographic and Water Distribution Mapping Project—Colombo: requirements for a mapping section in WSDB," prepared by Norplan A/S, Oslo, Norway, July 1983. National Water Supply and Drainage Board, Sri Lanka, "Topographic and Water Distribution Mapping Projcct—Colombo: water distribution and sewerage map report," prepared by Norplan A/S, Oslo, Norway, March 1984.

National Water Supply and Drainage Board, Sri Lanka. "Topographic and Water Distribution Mapping Project—Colombo: field work report: premarking, geodetic work, aerial photography, photo interpretation," prepared by Norplan A/S, Oslo, Norway, October 1982.

National Water Supply and Drainage Board, Sri Lanka. "Topographic and Water Distribution Mapping Project—Colombo: inception report: initial findings, specifications of basic maps, detailed work programmer", prepared by Norplan A/S, Oslo, Norway, December 1981.

OECD. "Municipal street maintenance standards in Sweden," Case study No. 5, Group on Urban Affairs—Project Group on Urban Infrastructure Policies (Paris: Organisation for Economic Cooperation and Development, 1989).

OECD. "Private financing and operating of sewerage works in the State of Niedersachsen (Germany)," Case study No. 6, Group on Urban Affairs—Project Group on Urban Infrastructure Policies (Paris: Organisation for Economic Cooperation and Development, 1989).

OECD. "Private finance for urban road construction (United Kingdom)," Case study No. 7, Group on Urban Affairs—

Project Group on Urban Infrastructure Policies (Paris: Organisation for Economic Cooperation an Development, 1989).

OECD. "Position Paper, United Kingdom." Position Paper No. 6, Group on Urban Affairs Project Group on Urban Infrastructure Policies, (Paris: Organisation for Economic Cooperation and Development, 1989).

OECD. "Strategy for planning infrastructure renewal (Sweden)," Case study No. 4, Group on Urban Affairs—Project Group on Urban Infrastructure Policies (Paris: Organisation of Economic Cooperation and Development, 1989).

OECD. "Upkeep of municipal services—the Toronto system (Canada)," Case study No. 2, Group on Urban Affairs—Project Group on Urban Infrastructure Policies (Paris: Organisation for Economic Cooperation and Development, 1989).

Pasha, Hafiz A., and Michael G. McGarry. *Rural Water Supply and Sanitation in Pakistan: Lessons from Experience.* Technical Paper No. 105 (Washington, D.C.: The World Bank, 1989).

Paterson, Williain D.O. *Road Deterioration and Maintenance Effects: Models for Planning and Management* (Baltimore: The Johns Hopkins University Press, for the World Bank, 1987).

Peterson, George E., Mary John Miller, Stephen R. Godwin, and Carol Shapiro. *Guide to Benchmarks of Urban Capital Condition* (Washington, D.C.: The Urban Institute Press, 1984).

Peterson, George E., Rita Bainberger, Nancy Humphrey, and Kenneth M. Steil. *Guide to Financing the Capital Budget and Maintenance Plan* (Washington, D.C.: The Urban Institute Press, 1984).

Roth, Gabriel. *The Private Provision of Public Services in Developing Countries* (New York: Oxford University Press, 1987).

Wyatt, Alan. *Guidelines for Maintenance, Management in Water and Sanitation Utilities in Developing Countries* (Research Triangle, Par Research Triangle Institute, 1989).

Yepes, G. "Management and operational practice of municipal and regional water and sewer. companies in Latin America and the Caribbean" Internal memorandum (Washington, D.C.: World Bank, 1989).

1.2 UNCHS (Habitat) Publications and Reports[2]

"A focus on financing of building and infrastructure maintenance." (HS/C/12/6/Add.1).

"Case study of urban infrastructure operation maintenance in Chile" (United Nations Centre for Human Settlements [Habitat], Urban Management Programme, draft final report, September 1989).

"Case study of urban infrastructure operations maintenance in Indonesia" (United Nations Centre for Human Settlements [Habitat], Urban Management Programme, October 1989).

"Case study of urban infrastructure operations and maintenance in Southern African Region" (United Nations Centre for Human Settlements [Habitat], Urban Management Programme, final report, March 1990).

Delivery of Basic Infrastructure to Low-Income Settlements: Issues and Options (HS/101/86/E).

Engmann, Eys. "Case study on infrastructure operations and maintenance in Ghana" (United Nations Centre for Human Settlement [Habitat], Urban Management Programme, draft report, February 1990).

Habgood, M.B. "Maintenance of buildings and is financing and cost recovery: a case study for Zimbabwe" (United Nations Centre for Human Settlements, draft report, 1988).

Hansen, Erik. "Diagnostic assessments of operations and maintenance problems—guideline framework" (United Nations Centre for Human Settlement [Habitat], Urban Management Programme, first working draft, May 1989).

2. *Ibid.*

Jucaban, Apolo C. "Case study on operations and maintenance in the Philippines" (United Nations Centre for Human Settlements [Habitat], Office of the Resident Representative in the Philippines, Manila, the Philippines).

Lorentzen, Jens. "Operations and maintenance planning, programming and budgeting" (draft synopsis, United Nations Centre for Human Settlements [Habitat], May 1989).

Lorentzen, Jens. "Overview of issues and strategic options in operations and maintenance" (United Nations Centre for Human Settlements [Habitat], Urban Management Programme, May 1989). "Maintenance of buildings and infrastructure: financing and cost recovery" (HS/C/12/6).

Mlingwa, G. "Maintenance of public buildings in Tanzania" (United Nations Centre for Human Settlements [Habitat], 1988).

Ofori, George. "Maintenance of public buildings and infrastructure in Singapore" (United Nations Centre for Human Settlements [Habitat], Nairobi, August 1988).

Shelter, Infrastructure and Services for the Poor Infrastructure Developing Countries: Some Policy Options (HS/08187-22).

Suchorzewski, Wojciech. "Information on maintenance of infrastructure in Poland" (United Nations Centre for Human Settlements [Habitat], draft report, 1988).

1.3 Community Participation[3]

Dubey, A.K. and Mazumdar, K. "Community Participation—Lessons from Nepal" *Indian Journal of Social Work* 1993, Vol. 54 No. 3, pp. 449-53.

Bamberger, M. "The Importance of Community Participation" *Public Administration and Development* 1991, Vol. 11 No. 3, pp. 281-84.

Moser, Caroline. "Community Participation and Self-help Housing—A Selective Bibliography" *Community Development Journal* 1990, Vol. 25 No. 1, pp. 75-76.

3. http://www.gdrc.org/icm/ref-comparti.html

Yap, Kio Sheng. "Community Participation in Low-income Housing Projects—Problems and Prospects" *Community Development Journal* 1990, Vol. 25 No. 1, pp. 56-64.

Nientied P., Benmhenni S., and Dewit, J. "Community Participation in Low-Income Housing Policies—Potential or Paradox" *Community Development Journal* 1990, Vol. 25 No. 1, pp. 42-55.

Stein, A. "Critical Issues in Community Participation in Self-Help Housing Programs—The Experience of Fundasal" *Community Development Journal* 1990, Vol. 25 No. 1, pp. 21-30.

Fritz, L. "Community Participation and Development—The Saskatchewan Experience" *Canadian Library Journal* 1990, Vol. 47 No. 2, pp. 97-101.

Smithells, J. "The Role of Community Participation in Development-Planning and Project-Management" *Public Administration and Development* 1990, Vol. 10 No. 3, pp. 372-73.

Convers, D. and Hawker, C. "Community Participation in Development-projects—the World Bank Experience" *Public Administration and Development* 1989, Vol. 9 No. 4, pp. 468-69.

Moser, Caroline. "Community Participation in Urban Projects in the Third World" *Progress in Planning* 1989, Vol. 32, p. 2, pp. 73-133.

Stone, L. "Cultural Crossroads of Community Participation in Development—a Case from Nepal" *Human Organization* 1989 Vol. 48 No. 3, pp. 206-13.

Midgley, J., Hall, A., Hardiman, M., Narine, D. and Kleemeier, L. "Community Participation, Social Development, and the State" *Journal of Development Studies* 1988 Vol. 24 No. 2, pp. 264-65.

Christenson, J., Hougland, J., Ilvento T., Shepard, J. "The Organization Man and the Community—The Impact of Organizational Norms and Personal Values on Community Participation and Transfers" *Social Forces* 1988, Vol. 66 No. 3, pp. 808-26.

Yap, Kio-Sheng. "Promoting Community Participation Through Training—The Danida / UNCHS Training Program" *Habitat International* 1987, Vol. 11 No. 4, pp. 77-86.

Yeung, Y.M., Mcgee, Terry. "Community Participation in Delivering Urban Services in Asia" *Third World Planning Review* 1987, Vol. 9 No. 1, p. 91.

Canedo, E.M. and Bienenstein, R. "Community Participation in Brazil: Case Study—Favela Do Gato" *Third World Planning Review* 1987, Vol. 9 No. 1, p. 87.

Midgley, J. and Mylius, B. "Community Participation, Social Development and the State" *Community Health Studies* 1987, Vol. 11 No. 2, pp. 157-58.

Midgley, J., Hall, A., Hardiman, M., Narine, D. and Macpherson, S. "Community Participation, Social Development and the State" *Journal of Social Policy* 1987, Vol. 16, Oct., pp. 593-94.

2.1 Culture Root Paradigms[4]

Anderson, Benedict. *Imagined Communities: Reflections on the Origins and Spread of Nationalism.* London: Verso, 1991.

Bordieu, Pierre.

Clifford, James. *The Predicament of Culture.* Cambridge: Harvard UP, 1988.

DeCerteau, Michel. *The Practice of Everyday Life.* Berkeley: U of California P, 1984.

Fabian, Johannes. *Time and the Other: How Anthropology Makes its Object.* New York: Columbia UP, 1983.

Geertz, Clifford. *The Interpretation of Culture.*

Gramsci, Antonio. *Notes from the Prison Notebooks.*

Habermas, Jürgen. *The Structural Transformation of the Public Sphere.* Cambridge: MIT, 1991 (1962).

Laclau, Ernesto and Chantal Mouffe. *Hegemony and Socialist*

4. http://www.courses.rochester.edu/halle/Germancinema/Bibliography.html

Strategy: Toward a Radical Democratic Politics. London: Verso, 1985.

Layoun, Mary. *Travels of a Genre: The Modern Novel and Ideology*.

Said, Edward. *Culture and Imperialism*.

Taylor, Charles et al. *Multiculturalism: Examining The Politics Of Recognition*. Princeton: Princeton University Press, 1994. (Contains important essays by Habermas, Appiah, etc.)

2.2 Globalization and Transnationalism[5]

Bamyeh, Mohammed. *The Ends of Globalization*. Minneapolis: U of Minnesota P, 2000.

Cheah, Pheng and Bruce Robbins. *Cosmopolitics: Thinking and Feeling Beyond the Nation*. Minneapolis: U of Minnesota P, 1998.

Ham, Peter van. *European Integration And The Postmodern Condition: Governance, Democracy, Identity*. New York: Routledge, 2001.

Hersh, Jacques and Johannes Dragsbaek Schmidt, eds. *Globalization And Social Change*. London: Routledge, 2000.

Huntington, Samuel P. *The Clash of Civilizations and the Remaking of World Order*. New York: 1996.

Weber, Steven. *Globalization and the European Political Economy*. New York: Columbia University Press, 2001.

Waters, Malcolm. *Globalization*. London: Routledge, 2000.

Wallersein, Immanuel. *The Modern World-System*. New York: 1974.

——. *The Politics of the World-Economy*. Cambridge: Cambridge UP, 1984.

Globalization and Culture

Ansell-Pearson, Keith, Benita Parry, Judith Squires, eds. *Cultural Readings of Imperialism: Edward Said and the Gravity of History*. New York: St. Martin's, 1997.

Appadurai, Arjun. *Globalization*. Durham: Duke U P, 2000.

---

5. *Ibid.*

Buell, Frederick. *National Culture and the New Global System.* Baltimore: Johns Hopkins UP, 1994.

Di Leo, Jeffrey R. and Christian Moraru. "Escaping Monstrosity: On Disfiguring and Refiguring Europe." *Symploke: A Journal for the Intermingling of Literary, Cultural and Theoretical Scholarship* 5, no. 1-2 (1999): 95-98.

During, Simon. "Popular Culture on a Global Scale: A Challenge for Cultural Studies?" *Critical Inquiry* 23, no. 4 (1997): 808-33.

Featherstone, Mike, Ed. *Global Culture: Nationalism, Globalization, and Modernity.* London: Sage, 1990.

Grossberg, Lawrence. "Speculations and Articulations of Globalization" *Polygraph* 11 (1999): 11-48. (Special Issue on New Metropolitan Forms)

Hobsbawm, Eric. *Nations and Nationalism Since 1780: Proframme, Myth, Reality.* Cambridge: Cambridge UP, 1990.

King, Anthony D. (ed.). *Culture, Globalization, and the World-System: Contemporary Conditions for the Representation of Identity.* Minneapolis: U of Minnesota P, 1997.

Mattelart, Armand. *The Invention of Communication.* Minneapolis: U of Minnesota P, 1996.

——. *Mapping World Communication: War, Progress, Culture.* Minneapolis: U of Minnesota P, 1994.

Noam, Eli M. and Joel C. Millonzi (eds.). *Globalism and Localism in Telecommunications.* New York: Elsevier, 1997.

Palumbo-Liu, David and Hans Ulrich Gumbrecht, eds. *Streams of Cultural Capital: Transnational Cultural Studies.* Stanford: Stanford UP, 1997.

Surin, Kenneth. "On Producing the Concept of a Global Culture." *South Atlantic Quarterly* 94, no. 4 (1995 Fall): 1179-99.

Wilson, Rob, Wimal Dissanayake, and Paul A. Bove, eds. *Global/Local: Cultural Production and the Transnational Imaginary.* Durham: Duke UP, 1996. (Includes Ella Shohat and Bob Stam)

2.3 Refugees, Migration and Human Rights[6]

Allen, T. and H. Morsink, eds. (1994) *When Refugees Go Home.* London: James Currey.

Amnesty International (1997) *Refugees: Human Rights Have No Borders.* New York: Amnesty International Publications.

Bayefsky, Anne F. and Joan Fitzpatrick, eds. (2000) *Human Rights and Forced Displacement.* The Hague, Boston, and London: Martinus Nijhoff Publishers.

Bertrand, Maurice and Daniel Warner, eds. (1997) *A New Charter for a Worldwide Organization?* Dordrecht: Martinus Nijhoff.

Black, Richard (1998) *Refugees, Environment, and Development.* Essex, United Kingdom: Addison Wesley Longman Ltd.

Cernea, Michael M. "Internal Refugee Flows and Development-Induced Population Displacement." *Journal of Refugee Studies* 3(4): 320-39.

Cernea, Michael M. (1988) "Involuntary Resettlement in Development Projects: Policy Guidelines in World Bank-Financed Projects." World Bank Technical Paper Number 80. Washington, D.C.: World Bank.

Cernea, Michael M. (1991) "Involuntary Resettlement: Social Research, Policy, and Planning." In *Putting People First: Sociological Variables in Rural Development* (Second Edition). Michael M. Cernea, ed., pp. 188-215. New York: Oxford University Press.

Cernea, Michael M. (1995) "Understanding and Preventing Impoverishment from Displacement: Reflections from the State of Knowledge." *Journal of Refugee Studies* 8(3): 245-64.

Cernea, Michael M. (1997) "The Risks and Reconstruction Model for Resettling Displaced Populations." *World Development* 25(10): 1569-87.

Cernea, Michael M., ed. (1999) *The Economics of Involuntary Resettlement: Questions and Challenges.* Washington, D.C.: The World Bank.

6. http://www.aaanet.org/committees/cfhr/bib_hitchcock_refugee.htm

Cernea, Michael M. and Scott E. Guggenheim, eds. (1993) *Anthropological Approaches to Resettlement: Policy, Practice, and Theory*. Boulder, Colorado: Westview Press.

Chambers, Robert (1969) "Settlement Schemes in Tropical Africa." New York: Praeger.

Chambers, Robert, ed. (1970) *The Social Consequences of Resettlement*. London: Pall Mall Press.

Chambers, Robert (1986) "Hidden Losers? The Impact of Rural Refugees and Refugee Programs on Poorer Hosts." *International Migration Review* 20: 245-65.

Clark, Sam, Elizabeth Colson, James Lee, and Thayer Scudder (1995) "Ten Thousand Tonga: A Longitudinal Anthropological Study from Southern Zambia", 1956-1991. *Population Studies* 49(1): 91-109.

Cohen, Roberta and Francis M., eds. (1998) *The Forsaken People: Case Studies of the Internally Displaced*. Washington, D.C.: Brookings Institution Press.

Colson, Elizabeth (1971) *The Social Consequences of Resettlement: The Impact of the Kariba Resettlement Experience Upon the Gwembe Tonga*. New York and Oxford: Oxford University Press.

Cook, Cynthia, ed. (1994) "Involuntary Resettlement in Development Projects: Selected Papers from a Conference on Environment and Settlement Issues in Africa." World Bank Technical Paper No. 237. Washington, D.C.: The World Bank.

Cuny, F., B. Stein, and P. Reed, eds. (1992) *Repatriation During Conflict in Africa and Asia*. Dallas: Centre for the Study of Societies in Crisis.

De Waal, Alex (1997) *Famine Crimes: Politics and the Disaster Relief Industry in Africa*. London: James Currey and International African Institute.

Dorcey, Tony, with Achim Steiner, Michael Acreman, and Brett Orlando, eds. (1997) *Large Dams: Learning from the Past, Looking at the Future*. Gland, Switzerland: IUCN (The World Conservation Union) and Washington, D.C.: The World Bank.

Duffield, M. And J. Prendergast (1994) *Without Troops and Talks: Humanitarian Intervention in Ethiopia and Eritrea.* Lawrenceville, New Jersey: The Red Sea Press.

El-Hinnawi, Essam (1985) *Environmental Refugees.* Nairobi, Kenya: United Nations Environment Program.

Erickson, Laurel (1998) "An Assessment of Adjustment Strategies and Satisfaction with Cultural Orientation of Female Refugees: A Qualitative Comparison Between Refugees from Iraq and the Former Soviet Union in a Midwestern American City (Lincoln, Nebraska)." M.A. Thesis, University of Nebraska-Lincoln, Lincoln, Nebraska.

Farer, Tom J. (1995) "How the International System Copes with Involuntary Migration: Norms, Institutions, and State Practice." *Human Rights Quarterly* 17(1): 72-100.

Ferris, E. (1993) *Beyond Borders: Refugees, Migrants, and Human Rights in the Post-Cold War Era.* Trenton, New Jersey: The Red Sea Press and Geneva: The WCC Press.

Giles, W. and H. Moussa, eds. (1996) *Development and Diaspora: Gender and the Refugee Experience.* Dudas, Ontario, Canada: Artemis Publishers.

Gold, Steven (1992) *Refugee Communities.* Newbury Park, California: Sage Publications.

Gordenker, Leon (1987) *Refugees in International Politics.* London and Sydney: Croom Helm.

Gersony, Robert (1989) "Why Somalis Flee: Synthesis of Accounts of Conflict Experience in Northern Somalia by Somali Refugees, Displaced Persons, and Others." Report to the Bureau for Refugee Programs, Department of State, Washington, D.C.

Gowlland, Vera (1995) *The Problem of Refugees in the Light of Contemporary International Law Issues.* Dordrecht: Martinus Nijhoff.

Hansen, Art and Anthony Oliver-Smith, eds. (1982) *Involuntary Migration and Resettlement: The Problems and Responses of Dislocated People.* Boulder, Colorado: Westview Press.

Hampton, Janie (1998) *Internally Displaced People: A Global Survey.* London: Earthscan Publications.

Hitchcock, Robert K. (2001) *Anthropological Study on the Potential Impact of Refugees in M'Kata, Namibia.* Windhoek, Namibia: United Nations High Commissioner for Refugees.

Hitchcock, Robert K. and Hassan Hussein (1987) "Agricultural and Non-Agricultural Settlements for Drought-Afflicted Pastoralists in Somalia." *Disasters* 11(1): 30-39.

Holtzman, Jon D. (2000) *Nuer Journeys, Nuer Lives: Sudanese Refugees in Minnesota.* Boston: Allyn and Bacon.

Horowitz, Michael M. (1989) "Victims of Development." *Development Anthropology Network* 7(2): 1-8.

Horowitz, Michael M. (1991) "Victims Upstream and Down". *Journal of Refugee Studies* 4(2): 164-81.

Hyndman, Jennifer (2000) *Managing Displacement: Refugees and the Politics of Humanitarianism.* Minneapolis: University of Minnesota Press.

International Organization for Migration (1992) "Migration and the Environment." Background Paper. Washington, D.C.: The Refugee Policy Group.

International Organization for Migration (1996) "Environmentally-Induced Population Displacements and Environmental Impacts Resulting from Mass Migrations." Geneva: United Nations High Commissioner for Refugees, the International Organization for Migration, and the Refugee Policy Group.

Jacobson, J. (1988) "Environmental Refugees: A Yardstick of Habitability." Worldwatch Paper No. 86. Washington, D.C.: Worldwatch Institute.

Jean, Francois, ed. (1992) "Populations in Danger: Medecins San Frontieres." London: John Libbey and Company.

Kane, Hal (1995) "The Hour of Departure; The Forces that Create Refugees and Migrants." Worldwatch Paper 125. Washington, D.C.: Worldwatch Institute.

Kibreab, G. (1996) *Ready and Willing ... But Still Waiting:*

Eritrean Refugees in Sudan and the Dilemma of Return. Uppsala, Sweden: Life and Peace Research Institute.

Kibreab, G. (1997) "Environmental Causes and Impact of Refugee Movements: A Critique of the Current Debate." *Disasters* 21(1): 20-38.

Kleber, Rolf J., Charles R. Figley, and Berthold P.R. Gersons, eds. (1995) *Beyond Trauma: Cultural and Societal Dynamics.* New York and London: Plenum Press.

Koehn, Peter H. (1991) *Refugees from Revolution: U.S. Policy and Third-World Migration.* Boulder, Colorado: Westview Press.

Kourula, Pirkko (1997) *Broadening the Edges: Refugee Definition and International Protection Revisited.* The Hague: Martinus Nijhoff.

Lawson, Michael L. (1994) *Dammed Indians: The Pick Sloan Project and the Missouri River Sioux, 1944-1980.* Second Edition. Norman: University of Oklahoma Press.

Lesotho Highlands Development Authority (1997) Kingdom of Lesotho, Lesotho Highlands Water Project, Compensation Policy. Maseru, Lesotho: Lesotho Highlands Development Authority.

Loescher, Gil (1993) *Beyond Charity: International Cooperation and the Global Refugee Crisis.* Oxford: Oxford University Press.

Macklin, Audrey (1995) "Refugee Women and the Imperative of Categories." *Human Rights Quarterly* 17(2): 213-77.

Mayotte, J.A. (1992) *Disposable People? The Plight of Refugees.* Maryknoll, New York: Orbis Books.

McCully, Patrick (2001) *Silenced Rivers: The Ecology and Politics of Large Dams.* Second Edition. London and Atlantic Highlands, New Jersey: Zed Books.

McMillan, Della E. (1995) *Sahel Visions: Planned Settlement and River Blindness Control in Burkina Faso.* Tucson: University of Arizona Press.

McMillan, Della E., Thomas Painter, and Thayer Scudder (1992) "Settlement and Development in the River Blindness

Control Zone." World Bank Technical Paper No. 192. Washington, D.C.: World Bank.

McSpadden, Lucia Ann (2000) *Negotiating Return: Conflict and Control in the Repatriation of Eritrean Refugees.* Uppsala, Sweden: Life and Peace Research Institute.

Mollica, Richard F. (1988) "The Trauma Story: The Psychiatric Care of Refugee Survivors of Violence and Torture". In *Post-Traumatic Therapy and Victims of Violence,* Frank M. Ochberg, ed., pp. 295-314. New York: Brunner/Mazel.

Nicholson, Frances and Patrick Twomey, eds. (1999) *Refugee Rights and Realities: Evolving International Concepts and Regimes.* Cambridge: Cambridge University Press.

Pipher, Mary (2002) *The Middle of Everywhere: The World's Refugees Come to Our Town.* New York and London: Harcourt, Inc.

Rogers, R. and E. Copeland (1993) *Forced Migration: Policy Issues in the Post-Cold War World.* Medford, Massachusetts: The Fletcher School of Law and Diplomacy, Tufts University.

Scudder, Thayer (1962) *The Ecology of the Gwembe Tonga.* Manchester: Manchester University Press for the Rhodes-Livingstone Institute.

Scudder, Thayer (1973) "The Human Ecology of Big Projects: River Basin Development and Resettlement." *Annual Review of Anthropology* 4: 45-55.

Scudder, Thayer (1980) "River-Basin Development and Local Initiative in African Savanna Environments." In *Human Ecology in Savanna Environments,* David Harris, ed., pp. 383-405. New York: Academic Press.

Scudder, Thayer (1981a) "What It Means to Be Dammed: The Anthropology of Large-Scale Development Projects in the Tropics and Sub-Tropics." *Engineering and Science* 54(4): 9-15.

Scudder, Thayer (1981b) "From Relief to Development: Some Comments on Refugee and Other Settlement in Somalia." Report to the United States Agency for International Development, Mogadishu, Somalia.

Scudder, Thayer (1989) "Conservation Vs. Development: River Basin Projects in Africa." *Environment* 31(2): 4-9, 27-32.

Scudder, Thayer (1990) "Victims of Development Revisited: The Political Costs of River Basin Development." *IDA Development Anthropology Network* 8(1): 1-5.

Scudder, Thayer (1991a) "The Need and Justification for Maintaining Trans-Boundary Flood Regimes: The Africa Case." *Natural Resources Journal* 31(1): 75-107.

Scudder, Thayer (1991b) "A Sociological Framework for the Analysis of New Lands Settlements." In *Putting People First: Sociological Variables in Rural Development* (Second Edition), Michael M. Cernea, ed., pp. 148-87. New York: Oxford University Press.

Scudder, Thayer (1993) "Development-Induced Relocation and Refugee Studies: 37 Years of Change and Continuity among Zambia's Gwembe Tonga." *Journal of Refugee Studies* 6(2): 123-52.

Scudder, Thayer (1997a) "Social Impacts. In Water Resources: Environmental Planning, Management, and Development", Asit K. Biswas, ed., pp. 623-65. London: Macmillan.

Scudder, Thayer (1997b) "Resettlement. In Water Resources: Environmental Planning, Management, and Development", Asit K. Biswas, ed., pp. 667-710. London: Macmillan.

Scudder, Thayer and Elizabeth Colson (1979) "Long-term Research in the Gwembe Valley, Zambia." In *Long-term Field Research in Social Anthropology,* George Forster, Thayer Scudder, Elizabeth Colson, and Robert V. Kemper, eds., pp. 227-54. New York: Academic Press.

Seymour, Frances J. and Vir Singh (1995) *A Preliminary Review of Experience with Resettlement to Achieve Conservation Objectives.* Washington, D.C.: World Wildlife Fund.

Smyser, W.R. (1987) *Refugees: Extended Exile.* New York and Westport, Connecticut: Praeger and Washington, D.C.: The Center for Strategic and International Studies.

Spooner, Bryan (1984) "Refugee Settlement in the Lower Shabelle Region, Somalia." Report to the National Refugee

Commission and Save the Children Federation, (USA), Mogadishu, Somalia.

United Nations High Commissioner for Refugees (1993) *The State of the World's Refugees: The Challenge of Protection.* Oxford: Oxford University Press.

United Nations High Commissioner for Refugees (1995) *The State of the World's Refugees: In Search of Solutions.* Oxford: Oxford University Press.

United Nations High Commissioner for Refugees (1998) *The State of the World's Refugees: A Humanitarian Agenda.* Oxford: Oxford University Press.

United States Committee for Refugees (1995) *World Refugee Survey.* Washington, D.C.: Immigration and Refugee Services of America.

United States Committee for Refugees (1997) *World Refugee Survey.* Washington, D.C.: Immigration and Refugee Services of America.

United Nations Development Program (2000) *Human Rights and Human Development: 2000.* Human Development Program. New York: United Nations.

Van der Veer, Guus (1998) *Counseling and Therapy with Refugees and Victims of Trauma: Psychological Problems of Victims of War, Torture, and Repression.* Second Edition. Chichester and New York: John Wiley and Sons.

Warner, Daniel, ed. (1995) *New Dimensions of Peacekeeping.* Dordrecht: Martinus Nijhoff.

Weiner, Myron (1995) *The Global Migration Crisis: Challenge to States and to Human Rights.* New York: Addison-Wesley Longman Publishers.

Wilks, Alex and Nicholas Hildyard (1994) "Evicted! The World Bank and Forced Resettlement." *The Ecologist* 24(6): 225-29.

Willis, Mary (2002) "The Nuer and the Dinka Take Refuge in Nebraska: The Cattle Are Lowing But It's Not the Sudan." Paper presented at the 62nd annual meetings of the Society for Applied Anthropology, Atlanta, Georgia, March 6-10, 2002.

Wishart, David J. (1990) "Compensation for Dispossession: Payments to the Indians for Their Land on the Central and Northern Great Plains in the 19th Century." *National Geographic Research* 6(1): 94-109.

Wood, William B. (1994) "Forced Migration: Local Conflicts and International Dilemmas." *Annals of the Association of American Geographers* 84(4): 607-34.

World Bank (1990) *Operational Directive 4.30: Involuntary Resettlement.* World Bank Operational Manual. Washington, D.C.: World Bank.

World Bank (1991a) *Environmental Assessment Sourcebook 1991.* Washington, D.C: The World Bank.

World Bank (1991b) *Operational Directive 4.20: Indigenous Peoples.* The World Bank Operational Manual. Washington, D.C.: The World Bank.

World Bank (1992) *World Development Report 1992: Development and the Environment.* Washington, D.C.: The World Bank.

World Bank (1993a) *Early Experience with Involuntary Resettlement: Impact Evaluation on Thailand Khao Laem Hydroelectric (Loan 1770-TH).* Operations Evaluation Department, World Bank, 29 June, 1993.

World Bank (1993b) *Early Experience in Involuntary Resettlement—Overview.* Report No. 12142, June 1993. Washington, D.C.: World Bank.

World Bank (1994a) *Resettlement and Development: The Bankwide Review Projects Involving Involuntary Resettlement, 1986-1993.* Washington, D.C.: World Bank.

World Bank (1995) *World Bank Participation Sourcebook.* Environment Department Papers 019. Washington, D.C: World Bank.

World Bank (1996) *The World Bank's Experience with Large Dams: A Preliminary Review of Impacts.* Washington, D.C.: Operations Evaluation Department, World Bank.

World Health Organization (1996) *Mental Health of Refugees.* Geneva: World Health Organization (WHO).

Young, Lincoln, (1985) "A General Assessment of the Environmental Impact of Refugees in Somalia with Attention to the Refugee Agricultural Program." *Disasters* 9(2): 122-33.

3.0 Social Well-Being Policy[7]

Burawoy, M. 1996. The State and Economic Innovation: Russia Through a China Lens. *World Development,* Vol. 24 No. 66: 1105-17.

Callister 1998 "Some Geographic Dimensions of Being Work-rich and Work-poor: Changes between 1986 and 1996", in *Social Policy Journal of New Zealand,* Issue 11, December.

Canterbury Volunteer Centre. 1999. *Statistical Report—1 April 1998 to 31 March 1999.*

Church, A. 1990. *Community Development: A History of the Involvement of the Department of Internal Affairs in Community Development,* Monograph Series, Research Unit, Department of Internal Affairs, Wellington, New Zealand.

Cox, E. 1995. *A Truly Civil Society,* Sydney: ABC.

Dahrendorf, R. 1996. Economic Opportunity, Civil Society and Political Liberty. *Development and Change,* Vol. 27: 229-49.

Davey, J. 1998 *Tracking Social Change in New Zealand.* Wellington: Institute of Policy Studies.

Evans, P. 1996. Introduction: Development Strategies Across The Public-Private Divide. *World Development.* Vol. 24 No. 6: 1033-37.

Fergusson, D.M. (1998) "The Christchurch Health and Development Study: An Overview and Some Key Findings", in *Social Policy Journal of New Zealand,* Issue 10, June, 158-71.

7. http://www.ccc.govt.nz/Publications/SocialWellbeingPolicy/Bibliography.asp

Fox, J. 1996. How Does Civil Society Thicken? The Political Construction of Social Capital in Rural Mexico. *World Development,* Vol. 24 No. 6: 1089-1103.

Fukuyama, F. 1995a. Trust: The Social Virtues and the Creation of Prosperity. London: Hamish Hamilton.

Fukuyama, F. 1995b. Review of *The Age of Extremes: A History of the World,* 1914-1991 by Eric Hobsbawm. Political and Legal. *Foreign-Affairs,* 74(4), (Jul/Aug): 130-34.

Fukuyama, F. 1995c. Social Capital and Global Economy. *Foreign Affairs,* 75 (Sept/Oct): 89.

Health Funding Authority and Ministry of Health. 1999. *Disability in New Zealand: Overview of the 1996/97* Surveys, Health Funding Authority and Ministry of Health: Wellington.

Heller, P. 1996. Social Capital as a Product of Class Mobilization and State Intervention: Industrial Workers in Kerala, India. *World Development,* Vol. 24 No. 6: 1055-71.

Hernandez, D.J. 1992. *Studies in Household and Family Formation: When Households Continue, Discontinue and Form.* US Bureau of the Census, Current Population Reports, Special Studies. Series P-23, No. 179.

Hirshman, A. 1982. Rival Interpretations of Market Society: Civilizing, Destructive or Feeble. *Journal of Economic Literature,* 20: 1463-84.

Hirst, P. 1994. *Associative Democracy.* USA: University of Massachusetts Press.

Hunter, A. 1993. National Federations: The Role of Voluntary Organizations in Linking Macro and Micro Orders in Civil Society. *Non Profit and Voluntary Sector Quarterly,* Vol. 22 No. 2 (Summer): 121-36.

Inter-agency Workshop on Funding and Purchasing of Social Services from the Community. 1997. Notes of Workshop, Wellington, 11 December. Photocopied.

Jamieson, K. 1998a. “Poverty and Hardship in Christchurch: A Reference Guide” Leisure and Community Services Unit, Christchurch City Council, Christchurch.

Jamieson, K. 1998b. "Poverty and Hardship in Christchurch: Findings from Target Week Survey Data" Leisure and Community Services Unit, Christchurch City Council Christchurch.

Jamieson, K. 1999. "Poverty and Hardship in Christchurch: Findings from In Depth Interview Data Policy Directorate, Christchurch City Council Christchurch.

Johns, K. 1993. *Community Development in Territorial Local Authorities: A Profile*, Department of Internal Affairs.

Kawachi, I. and B.P. Kennedy and R.G. Wilkinson (eds). *The Society and Population Health Reader: Income Inequality and Health*. New York: The New Press.

Kawachi, I. and B.P. Kennedy. 1996. Income Distribution, Social Capital and Mortality. Paper presented to the Conference on Socioeconomic Inequalities in Health, Wellington, 9-10 December. Photocopied.

Kawachi, I. and B.P. Kennedy. 1997. Health and Social Cohesion: Why Care About Income Inequality? *BMJ*, Vol. 314 (5 April): 1037-40.

Kennedy, B.P. and I. Kawachi. 1996. Income Distribution and Mortality Cross Sectional Ecological Study of The Robin Hodd Index in the United States. *BMJ*, 12: 1004-07.

Kirby, S. 2000. Personal communication. (February 2000).

Krieble & Middleton (eds.). *Health Futures*: *2020 Visions*. Institute of Policy Studies, Victoria.

Lemann, N. 1996. Kicking in Groups. *The Atlantic Monthly*. April: 22-26.

Lim, D. 1996. Explaining Economic Growth: A New Analytical Framework. Cheltenham: Edward Edgar.

London, S. 1995. Building Collaborative Communities. Available on the Internet. london@west.net

London, S. 1997. Civic Networks: Building Community on the Net. Available on the Internet london@west.net

Maguire, M. 1995. "Community–Development—The New Zealand Model" unpublished paper.

March, J.G. and J.P. Olsen. 1995. *Democratic Governance*. New York: Free Press.

Ministry of Health. 1998. *Progress on Health Outcome Targets*. Ministry of Health: Wellington.

Ministry of Health. 1999. *Our Health Our Future: The Health of New Zealanders 1999*. Ministry of Health: Wellington.

Ministry of Justice. 1999. *A Summary of the Crime Victims and Women's Safety Surveys*. Available on the internet: www.justice.govt.nz

Narayan, D. and Pritchett, L. 1997. Cents and Sociability: Household Income and Social Capital in Rural Tanzania. Available on the Internet. http//www.worldbank.org.html/dec/publicationsS1700series/wps1796.html

Nugent, J.B. 1993. Between State, Markets and Households: A Neoinstitutional Analysis of Local Organizations and Institutions. *World Development*, Vol. 21 No. 4: 623-32.

Onyx, J. 1996a. Social Cohesion, Justice and Citizenship—The Role of the Voluntary Sector Future Agendas Research and Action. Paper presented to ANZTSR Conference held at Victoria University, Wellington, 3-5 July. Photocopied.

Onyx, J. 1996b. The Measure of Social Capital. Paper presented to ANZTSR Conference held at Victoria University, Wellington, 3-5 July. Photocopied.

Ostrum, E. 1996. Crossing the Great Divide: Coproduction, Synergy and Development. *World Development*, Vol. 24 No. 6: 1073-87.

Portes, A. and Landolt, P. 1996. The Downside of Social Capital. *The American Prospect*, 26 (94) (May-June): 18- 21. Available on the Internet. http://epn.org/prospect26/26-cnt2

Putnam, R. 1993a *Making Democracy Work: Civic Traditions in Modern Italy*. With collaboration of R. Leonardi and R. Nanetti. Princeton: NJ Princeton University Press.

Putnam, R.D. 1995a. Bowling Alone: America's Declining Social Capital. *Journal of Democracy*, 6 (January): 65-78, 24.

Putnam, R.D. 1995b. Ithiel de Sola Lecture: Tuning In, Turing Out: The Strange Disappearance of Social Capital in

America. *PS: Political Science and Politics*, Vol. 28 No. 4 (December): 664-83.

Putnam, R.D. 1996a. The Strange Disappearance of Civic America. *The American Prospect*, 24 (Winter). Available on the Internet. http://epn.org/propect/24/24putn.html.

Putnam, R.D. 1993b. The Prosperous Community: Social Capital and Public Life. T*he American Prospect*, No. 13 (Spring): 35-42. Available on the Internet http://epn.org/propect/13/13putn.html.

Putnam, R.D. 1996b. Robert Putnam Responds: Unsolved Mysteries The Tocqueville Files. *The American Prospect*, No. 25 (March-April): 26-28.

Putnam, R.D. 1996c. Transcript of Presentation at Institute of Policy Studies, Wellington, 20 August. Photocopied.

Randerson, R. 1992. *Hearts and Minds: A Place for People in a Market Economy*. Wellington: Social Responsibility Commission of the Anglican Church in Aotearoa, New Zealand and Polynesia.

Refugee Resettlement Policy in New Zealand. 2000. A *Report for the 1999 Incoming Coalition Government from the NGO Sector* (2000).

Riddell, M. 1997. "Bringing Back the Balance: The Role of Social Capital in Public Policy." Paper prepared for New Zealand Council of Christian Social Services for the Social Capital and Policy Development Workshop, Wellington, 1 July. Photocopied.

Riddell, M. 1997. "Bringing Back Balance: The Role of Social Capital in Public Policy." A Paper prepared for New Zealand Council of Christian Social Services.

Robinson, D. 1986. Voluntary Social Services: A Review of Funding. Planning Paper No. 28 (October). Wellington: New Zealand Planning Council. Photocopied.

Robinson, D. 1992. Innovator or Government Agent: The Changing Role of the Voluntary Sector in New Zealand Social Services. Paper presented to the Third International Conference of Research on Voluntary and Non Profit Organisations, Indianapolis, Indiana, March. Photocopied.

Sandel, M. 1997. Transcript of Panel Discussion with E.J. Dionne, Ellen Goodman, Bill Kristol, Michael Sandel and Phil Sharp: The Electronic Policy Network in *American Prospect,* 2 April.

Short, J.R. 1989. *The Humane City Cities as if People Matter.* New York: Basil Blackwell.

Sirianni, C. and Friedland, L. 1995. Social Capital and Civic Innovation: Learning Capacity Building from the 1960s to the 1990. Paper presented at the Social Capital Session of the American Sociological Annual Meetings, Washington D.C., August. Available on Internet. cpn/sections.new-citizenship/new-citizenship.html.

Sirianni, C. and Friedland, L. 1997. Social Capital: CPN Tools. Available on the Internet. http://www.cpn.org/sections/tools/models/social capital.html.

Skocpol, T. 1996. Unravelling from Above. *The American Prospect,* No. 25 (March April): 20-25. Available on the Internet. http://epn.org/propect/25/25-cnt2.html.

Skopol, T. 1997. American's Voluntary Groups Thrive in a National Network. *The Brookings Review,* Vol. 15 No. 4 (Fall): 16-19. Available on the Internet. http://www.brook.edu/pub/review/fall97/build.htm

Tarrow, S. 1994. *Power in Movement.* Cambridge: Cambridge University Press.

The Treasury. 1993. *Briefing Papers for the Incoming Government.* Wellington: The Treasury. Photocopied.

The Treasury. 1996. *Briefing Papers for the Incoming Government.* Wellington: The Treasury. Photocopied.

The Treasury. 1997. OECD Forum for the Future: Key Points from the Conference, 16 December 1996. Wellington. Photocopied.

Transcript of Panel Discussion with E.J. Dionne, Ellen Goodman, Bill Kristol, Michael Sandel and Phil Sharp. 1997. The Electronic Policy Network in *American Prospect,* 2 April.

Walzer, M. ed. 1995. *Toward a Global Society.* Providence: Berghan Books.

Wilkes, C. 1982. "Development as Practices" in *Development Tracks*, Shirley, I. (eds).

World Bank. 1996. Lessons from Experience. Available on the Internet. http//www.worldbank.org.

Wylie, C. (1994) What Research on Early Childhood Education/ Care Outcomes Can and Can't Tell Policymakers. New Zealand Council for Educational Research.

4.1 Urban Planning[8]

Our Common Future (The Bruntland Report)—Report of the 1987 World Commission on Environment and Development.

A Better Quality of Life—Strategy for Sustainable Development for the UK. DETR May 1999—CM 4345.

Sustainable Urban Development in the European Union: A Framework for Action. October 1998.

Preparing Community Strategies—Draft Guidance to Local Authorities from the Department of Environment, Transport and the Regions. June 2000.

Planning Policy Guidance Notes 1. DETR.

Planning for Sustainable Development: Towards Better Practice. October 1998.

Monitoring Progress—Indicators for Sustainable Development in the United Kingdom. DETR, May 1999.

Sustainable Local Communities for the 21st Century—Why and how to prepare an effective Local Agenda 21 Strategy—1997.

Local Government Act 2000.

Towards an Urban Renaissance: Report of the Urban Task Force 1999.

8. http://www.planningsummerschool.org/papers/year2000/2000MM03.htm

National Strategy for Neighbourhood Renewal: A Framework for Consultation. Report of the Environment, Transport and Regional Affairs Committee, June 2000—HC 185-1.

Sustainable Development Commission—Press Release. July 2000.

Every Little Bit Helps. DETR, May 1999.

4.2 Urban Poverty and Social Problems[9]

Boston: Not Safe At Home: How America's Housing Crisis Threatens the Health of Its Children. Boston Medical Center and Children's Hospital, 1998.

Brooks-Gunn, Jeanne; Greg J. Duncan, and J. Lawrence Abner, eds. Neighborhood Poverty. New York: Russell Sage Foundation, 1997. (Volume I: Context and Consequences for Children. Volume II: Policy Implications in Studying Neighborhoods.)

Chow, Julian; and Claudia Coulton. Was There a Social Transformation of Urban Neighborhoods in the 1980s? A Decade of Worsening Social Conditions in Cleveland, Ohio, USA. *Urban Studies* 35, 8 (1998): 1359-75.

Duncan, Greg J. and Jeanne Brooks-Gunn, eds. *Consequences of Growing Up Poor*. New York: Russell Sage Foundation, 1997.

Enchautegui, Maria E. Latino Neighborhoods and Latino Neighborhood Poverty. *Journal of Urban Affairs* 19, 4 (1997): 445-67.

Gundersen, Craig George. Ph.D. Direct Measures of Poverty and Well-Being: A Theoretical Framework and an Application to Housing Poverty in the United States. Dissertation, University of California, Riverside, CA, 1996. (Available from UMI.)

Katz, Bruce; and Kate Carnevale. The State of Welfare Caseloads in America's Cities. Washington DC: Center on Urban and Metropolitan Policy, The Brookings Institution, 1998.

Mead, Lawrence M. The Decline of Welfare in Wisconsin.

9. http://chud.tamu.edu/files/bibpoverty.html

Discussion Paper No. 1164-98, Madison, WI: Institute for Research on Poverty, University of Wisconsin-Madison, 1998.

Naifeh, Mary. Dynamics of Economic Well-Being, Poverty 1993-94: Trap Door? Revolving Door? Or Both? Current Population Reports (pp. 70-63), Washington DC: U.S. Buereau of the Census, 1998. (Available from the U.S. Government Printing Office)

Ong, Paul, and Evelyn Blumenburg. Job Access, Commute and Travel Burden among Welfare Recipients. *Urban Studies* 35, 1 (1998): 77-93.

Page, Benjamain I. Trouble for Workers and the Poor: Economic Globalization and the Reshaping of American Politics. Working Paper 97-6. Evanston, IL: Northwestern University, Institute for Policy Research, 1997. (Available from the Joint Center for Poverty Research.)

Plotnick, Robert D., Eugene Smolensky, Eirik Evenhouse, and Siobhan Reilly. The Twentieth Century Record of Inequality and Poverty in the United States. Discussion Paper No. 1166-98, Madison, WI: Institute for Research on Poverty, University of Wisconsin—Madison, 1998.

Sandefur, Gary; Molly Martin, and Thomas Wells. Poverty as a Public Health Issue: Poverty since the Kerner Commission Report of 1968. Discussion Paper No. 1158-98. Madison, WI: Institute for Research on Poverty, 1998.

Sawicki, Dacid S. and Mitch Moody. The Effects of Intermetropolitan Migration on the Labor Force Participation of Disadvantaged Black Men in Atlanta. *Economic Development Quarterly* 11, 1 (February 1997): 45-66.

Seefeldt, Kristin S., Jodi Sandfort and Sandra K. Danziger. Moving Toward a Vision Of Family Independence: Local Managers' Views of Michigan's Welfare Reforms. Ann Arbor, MI: Michigan Program on Poverty and Social Welfare Policy, University of Michigan, 1998.

Schill, Michael H., Samantha Friedman, and Emily Rosenbaum. The Housing Conditions of Immigrants in New York City.

Working Paper, Washington DC: Fannie Mae Foundation, 1998.

Washington DC: America's Children: Key National Indicators of Well-Being. Federal Interagency Forum on Child and Family Statistics, 1998. (Available from the National Maternal and Child Health Clearinghouse.)

Washington DC: Welfare Reform: Child Support on Uncertain Income Supplement for Families Leaving Welfare. U.S. General Accounting Office, 1998.

5.0 Water Supply and Sanitation[10]

5.1 USAID, BASICS II, EHP, Unicef and The World Bank

- ❑ Public-Private Partnerships: Mobilizing Resources to Achieve Public Health Goals the Central American Handwashing Initiative Points the Way.
- ❑ The Story of a Successful Public-Private Partnership in Central America: Handwashing for Diarrheal Disease Prevention.

5.2 EHP Applied Studies/WASH Technical Reports

- ❑ Behavior First: A Minimum Package of Environmental Health Behaviors to Improve Child Health (PDF). 1999.
- ❑ Better Sanitation Programming: A UNICEF Handbook (PDF).
- ❑ Vers une meilleure programmation: Manuel de l'Assainissement. UNICEF. July 1998.
- ❑ Hacia una mejor programación: Manual sobre Saneamiento. UNICEF. July 1998.
- ❑ Beyond Participation: Locally Based Demand for Environmental Health in Peri-Urban Areas. 1996 (PDF).
- ❑ Case Studies on Decentralization of Water Supply and Sanitation Services in Latin America. January 2001.
- ❑ Child Survival and Environmental Health Interventions: A Cost-Effectiveness Analysis (PDF). 1996.

---

10. http://www.worldbank.org/html/fpd/water/pubs online.html

- ❑ Financial Services and Environmental Health: Household Credit for Water and Sanitation (PDF). 1995.
- ❑ Institutional Lessons Learned in Environmental Health Programs (PDF). 1999.
- ❑ Prevention: Environmental Health Interventions to Sustain Child Survival (PDF). Revised February 1997.
- ❑ Prevención: Intervenciones de Salud Ambiental para sostenimiento de Supervivencia Infantil. Revised February 1997.
- ❑ Providing Urban Environmental Services for the Poor: Lessons Learned from Three Pilot Projects (PDF). 1998.
- ❑ The Story of a Successful Public Private Partnership in Central America: Handwashing for Diarrheal Disease Prevention, 2002.
- ❑ WASH TR 32 Facilitator Guide for Conducting a Team Planning Meeting (PDF).
- ❑ WASH TR 37 Guidelines for Institutional Assessment: Water and Wastewater Institutions (PDF).
- ❑ WASH TR 41 Facilitator Guide for Conducting a Project Start-Up Workshop (PDF).
- ❑ WASH TR 88 Guidelines for Improving Wastewater and Solid Waste Management (PDF).
- ❑ WASH Fact Sheet: Water Reuse in Developing Countries (including Guidelines for Wastewater Reuse) (PDF).

5.3 IIED

- ❑ Drawers of Water II.

5.3 IRC

- ❑ Keeping It Working: A Field Manual to Support Community Management of Rural Water Supply, 2001.
- ❑ Paying the Piper: an overview of community financing of water and sanitation, OP 18-E 1992.

5.4 Overseas Development Institute

- ❑ Adopting a sustainable livelihoods approach to water projects: implications for policy and practice, 2000.

5.5 UNICEF WES

- ❑ Hygiene Promotion Manual.
- ❑ Manual on Communication for Water Supply and Environmental Sanitation.
- ❑ Manual On School Sanitation and Hygiene.
- ❑ Sanitation Handbook.
- ❑ Water Handbook.

5.6 USAID

- ❑ Water for the World Technical Notes-USAID, 1982. (Made available online by Lifewater International).

5.7 WEDC

- ❑ A Guide to the Development of On-Site Sanitation.
- ❑ Low-Cost Sanitation: A survey of practical experience.
- ❑ On-Plot Sanitation in Low-income Urban Communities: Guidelines for selection.
- ❑ On-Plot Sanitation in Low-income Urban Communities: A review of literature.
- ❑ Success and sustainability indicators for primary collection of solid waste.
- ❑ Sustainable Sewerage: Guidelines for community schemes.
- ❑ The sweeping business: developing entrepreneurial skills for the collection of solid waste.

5.8 WELL / DFID

- ❑ Chlorinating small water supplies—(Task 511).
- ❑ DFID Guidance Manual on Water Supply and Sanitation Programmes, 1999.
- ❑ Environmental health promotion capacity building: A training guide based on CARE's Hygiene Promotion Manual (Task 515).
- ❑ Guidelines for Wastewater Reuse in Agriculture and Aquaculture: Recommended Revisions Based on New Research Evidence, 2000.

- ❑ Groundwater, latrines & health (PDF) (1999) by Ben Cave and Peter Kolsky.
- ❑ Health aspects of dry sanitation with waste re-use—(Task 324).
- ❑ Healthcare or health risks?—(Task 326).
- ❑ Lessons from community-based solid waste initiatives (PDF)(1999) by Dr. Mansoor Ali and Dr. Marielle Snel.
- ❑ Public-Private Partnership and the poor (PDF) (1999) by Mike Webster and Kevin Sansom.
- ❑ Promoting change in environmental health behaviour (PDF) (1999) by Ben Cave and Dr. Valerie Curtis.
- ❑ Review of policy and standards for wastewater reuse in agriculture: A Latin American perspective—(Task 68—Part 2).
- ❑ Sharing it out: Introducing water demand management—strategies for small towns—(Task 513).
- ❑ Stakeholder analysis in local solid waste management schemes (PDF).
- ❑ Technical Briefs on Water and Sanitation.
- ❑ Working together: The sharing of water and sanitation support services for small towns and villages—(Task 510).

5.9 Water and Sanitation Program

- ❑ Achieving sustained sanitation for the poor: Policy and strategy lessons from participatory assessments in Cambodia, Indonesia and Vietnam.
- ❑ An Anthropological view of sanitation issues in rural Bolivia. A Summary Condominial Water and Sewerage Systems: Costs of Implementation of the Model.
- ❑ El Alto Condominial Pilot Project Impact Assessment. A Summary.
- ❑ Launching Sector Reforms: Supporting the Government of India pilot demand-responsive approaches to rural water supply and sanitation, 2001.

- Linking Sustainability with Demand, Gender and Poverty: A Study of Community Managed Water Supply Projects in 15 Countries—World Bank, 2001.
- Lower Costs with higher benefits. Water and Sewerage Services for low income households. Lessons from EAPP.
- Menor costo con mayor beneficio. Servicios de agua y alcantarillado para familias de bajos ingresos. Lecciones del PPEA.
- Methodology for Participatory Assessment with Communities, Institutions and Policy Makers, 2000.
- Multi-Village Rural Water Supply Schemes: An Emerging Challenge, 2001.
- New Technical Standards for the Design and Construction of Sewerage Systems and Wastewater Treatment Plants.
- Promoting Options for Cleaner, Healthier Lives: Translating Sector Strategy into Better Hygiene Practices in Lao PDR, 2001.
- Regional Conference on The Reform of the Water Supply and Sanitation Sector in Africa "Enhancing Public-Private Partnership in the Context of the Africa Vision for Water (2025)".
- Saneamiento y cultura: Síntesis de un estudio Antropológico sobre saneamiento en el Área Rural de Bolivia.
- Sistemas Condominiales de agua y alcantarillado. Costos de implementación del modelo. Evaluación Económica Financiera, PPEA, 2001.
- Sistemas Condominiales de agua y alcantarillado: Evaluacion de Impacto.
- Tariffs and subsidies/Nagari: Twelfth Meeting of the Urban Think Tank, April 3-4, 2001, Mumbai.
- Water Supply and Sanitation in PRSP Initiatives: A Desk Review of Emerging Experience in Sub-Saharan Africa (SSA).

- Water supply, sanitation and hygiene education: Report of a health impact study in Mirzapur, Bangladesh.

5.10 WHO / WSSCC

- Effect of viruses on public health associated with the use of wastewater and sewage sludge in agriculture and aquaculture, 1995. (available in Word format)
- Guidelines for Drinking Water Quality.
- Guidelines for the safe use of wastewater and excreta in agriculture and aquaculture: executive summary. Geneva, WHO, 1989.
- Operations and Maintenance for Rural Water Supply and Sanitation Systems: A Training Package, 1998.
- The PHAST initiative. Participatory Hygiene and Sanitation Transformation: a new approach to working communities. Geneva, WHO, 1996.
- PHAST Step-by-step guide: a participatory approach for the control of diarrhoeal disease. 1998.
- Safe management of wastes from health-care activities. Geneva, WHO, 1999.
- Sanitation Promotion: WSSCC Working Group on Promotion of Sanitation.
- Teacher's guide: Management of wastes from health-care activities. Geneva, WHO, 1998.
- Tools for Assessing the O&M Status of Water Supply and Sanitation in Developing Countries.
- UN Synthesis Report on Arsenic—United Nations/ WHO, 2001.
- VISION 21: Water for the People.
- Water Supply and Sanitation Assessment 2000 Report-WHO/UNICEF, 2000.
- World Water Day 2001: Water for Health.

6.0 Website Links

http://fssl.man.ac.uk/idpm/ediais/az.asp?index=title&az=p

http://poverty.worldbank.org/webguide/category/8

http://web.mit.edu/urbanupgrading/upgrading/resources/bibliography/Evaluation-Impact.html

http://www.ces.fe.uc.pt/emancipa/research/en/ft/fishworkers.html

http://www.faireconomy.org/econ/globalization/globalization_resources.html

http://www.geocities.com/CapitolHill/6027/Bibliography.html

http://www.umweltprogramme.de/millennium/papers/paper10/

http://www.unescobkk.org/gender/gender/resources/bibliography.htm

AUTHOR BIOGRAPHY

Prasenjit Maiti [1971-] pmaiti@vsnl.com is a political sociologist. He joined the development sector in 2003 after teaching and researching at the MA & MPhil Levels of the University of Burdwan during 1995-2002 as a Lecturer in Political Science. Dr Maiti was associated with the Kolkata Environmental Improvement Project. He earlier worked at the Council for Development Studies and also served as a Consultant to the Shelter Promotion Council. He recently edited a volume commissioned by the West Bengal Pollution Control Board and worked briefly for ActionAid.

Dr Maiti was on secondment as a Doctoral Fellow at the Institute of Federalism, University of Fribourg while teaching at the University of Burdwan. He was promoted to Senior Lectureship in 2001. He taught Tourism Administration at Burdwan University and served as a Resource Person for Distance Education Programmes and Teachers' Training Courses sponsored by the University Grants Commission. He presently serves as an Academic Counsellor for the Netaji Subhas Open University. Prasenjit Maiti also worked briefly as a Senior Sub-Editor for *The Telegraph*. He was the Director of North Africa, Middle East and the Indian Sub-Continent on the inaugural technical committee of Fed-Net, a website hosted by Forum of Federations: An International Network on Federalism [Ottawa, Ontario, Canada].

Dr Maiti's maiden publication based on his doctoral thesis developed from a German Research Council project under the auspices of the Department of Political Science at the South Asia Institute, University of Heidelberg. He was invited to the International Conference on Federalism 2002 organized by the Swiss Government at the University of St Gallen.

Prasenjit Maiti served as a Reviewer [2001] for *Policing: An International Journal of Police Strategies & Management* [College of Education, Division of Criminal Justice, University of Cincinnati]. He is also a Referee for *Environment & Development Economics* [University of York, Heslington, York] published by the Cambridge University Press and *Crime Prevention & Community Safety* [Perpetuity Press, Leicester] as well as a Reviewer for *Globalization and Health*.

Dr Maiti holds First Class Graduate and Postgraduate Degrees in Political Science from Presidency College, University of Calcutta and Jawaharlal Nehru University [Centre for Political Studies, School of Social Sciences] respectively. He received the National Merit Scholarship of the Ministry of Human Resource Development, Government of India. Prasenjit Maiti is a Life Member of the Indian Political Science Association, West Bengal Political Science Association, Council for Political Studies and Indian Institute of Public Administration.

TERMS OF DISCOURSE[1]

Actors
Affordable Access
Authority
Awareness Generation
Baseline Assessment
Benchmarks
Beneficiaries
Benefit
Bio-Medical Waste
Capabilities
Capacity Building
Change Management
Choices
Civic Assets
Civic Engagement
Civil Society
Civil Society Organizations
Communitarianism
Community
Community Meetings
Community-Based Organizations
Consensus
Consumerism
Consumption
Cost Recovery
Debate
Democracy
Development
Development Agencies
Development Strategies
Dialogue
Discourse
Displacement
Effective Demand
Elite
Empowerment
Entitlements
Evaluation
Eviction
Focus Group Discussions
Food Security
Free Rider Costs
Freedom
Gender Empowerment
Globalization
Good Governance
Good Practices
Grand Narratives
Grass-roots Activism
Group Games
Group Dynamics
Hazardous Waste

1. Key words at the beginning of each chapter also serve to highlight the major issues and concerns of this work.

Hegemony
High Culture
Household Sample Surveys
House-to-House Collection
Human Rights
Hunger
Immigration
Impact
Indicators
Indigenous Population
Infrastructure Impact Assessment
Institutional Mechanisms
Interventions
Involuntary Displacement
Key Informants
Knowledge
Labor
Laissez-faire
Local Market Surveys
Logical Framework
Majoritarianism
Malnutrition
Matrix Scoring
Methodology
Microcredit
Micro Planning
MIS
Mobilization
Mode of Production
Monitoring
Needs Assessment
Neo-Institutionalism
Networking
Non-Government Organizations
Operation & Maintenance
Outreach
Participation
Participatory Management
Participatory Poverty Assessment
Participatory Rapid Appraisal
Physical Resources
Policy Choice
Politics of Development
Popular Resistance
Poverty
Poverty Alleviation
Power
Priority Ranking
Progress
Project Affected Persons
Project Management Unit
Public Action
Purchasing Capacity
Rehabilitation and Resettlement
Repression
Resource Mapping
Resource Persons
Revenue Streams
Safe Practices
Sanitation
Segregation at Source
Self-Help Groups
Semiotics
Service Delivery
Social Action Plan
Social Capital
Social Impact Assessment
Solid Waste Management
Stakeholders' Consultative Process
Subaltern
Sustainable Development
SWOT
Trade Barriers
Training Needs Assessment